Hacking
Digital Cameras

Chieh Cheng
Auri Rahimzadeh

WILEY

Wiley Publishing, Inc.

Hacking Digital Cameras

Published by
Wiley Publishing, Inc.
10475 Crosspoint Boulevard
Indianapolis, IN 46256
www.wiley.com

Copyright © 2005 by Wiley Publishing, Inc., Indianapolis, Indiana

Published simultaneously in Canada

ISBN-13: 978-0-7645-9651-3
ISBN-10: 0-7645-9651-9

Manufactured in the United States of America

10 9 8 7 6 5 4 3 2 1

1B/QX/QZ/QV/IN

For general information on our other products and services or to obtain technical support, please contact our Customer Care Department within the U.S. at (800) 762-2974, outside the U.S. at (317) 572-3993 or fax (317) 572-4002.

Wiley also publishes its books in a variety of electronic formats. Some content that appears in print may not be available in electronic books.

Library of Congress Cataloging-in-Publication Data

Cheng, Chieh, 1974–
    Hacking digital cameras/Chieh Cheng, Auri Rahimzadeh.
       p. cm.
Indcludes index.
ISBN-13: 9780764596513 (paper/website)
ISBN-10: 0764596519 (paper/website)
1. Digital cameras—Modification—Amateurs' manuals. 2. Photography—Equipment and supplies—Amateurs' manuals. I. Rahimzadeh, Auri, 1975–II. Title.
TR256.C44 2005
775—dc22

                                                                      2005020485

About the Authors

Chieh Cheng has a Computer Science degree and is currently a Senior Software Engineer developing radiation medicine control systems for cancer treatment. He is an avid photographer who has won photo contests and had pictures published in magazines. Hacking cameras is one of his many long-term hobbies. He created and has maintained the *Camera Hacker* web site (www.CameraHacker.com) since its inception in 1998. The web site includes forums and articles on camera hacking projects, practical photography tips, and photographic equipment reviews.

Auri Rahimzadeh has been tinkering with computers ever since he was six years old and loves all technology. Auri collects computers and has been involved with many computer projects, including teaching computers alongside Steve Wozniak, co-founder of Apple Computer. Auri is the author of the book *Geek My Ride,* also published by Wiley in their ExtremeTech series. He has written hundreds of articles on various computer technologies, and has contributed to many standards, including HDTV, DVD, and interactive television. Auri contributes to computer education for students across the country and has promoted technology awareness through the Indianapolis Computer Society, where he has served as president for three years. Currently, Auri runs his own IT consulting firm, The Auri Group (TAG), and spends his free time programming, chatting in Starbucks, and going to Pacers games (Go Pacers!).

Credits

Executive Editor
Chris Webb

Development Editor
Tom Dinse

Copy Editor
Kathryn Duggan

Editorial Manager
Mary Beth Wakefield

Production Manager
Tim Tate

Vice President and Executive Group Publisher
Richard Swadley

Vice President and Publisher
Joseph B. Wikert

Project Coordinator
Ryan Steffen

Graphics and Production Specialists
Carrie Foster
Lauren Goddard
Denny Hager
Melanee Prendergast

Quality Control Technicians
Amanda Briggs
John Greenough
Brian Walls

Proofreading and Indexing
TECHBOOKS Production Services

Cover Design
Anthony Bunyan

To all my family and friends

Acknowledgments

While writing the proposal for *Hacking Digital Cameras*, I envisioned writing two to three pages of acknowledgments. I wanted to thank all the people in the world who had influenced me in one way or another. But during editing, we discovered that the content of the book had exceeded the page limit! Tom Dinse, the development editor, and I had a hard time deciding what to cut. We wanted to provide a quality manuscript. (By the way, thank you, Tom.) So, to preserve the quality of this book, I'll keep this section short and sweet.

My next thank you goes to Chris Webb, executive editor at Wiley Publishing, for finding me and supporting me throughout the process. It's a great learning experience. You and Tom are extremely enthusiastic and very professional at the same time.

Thanks to Sasha Beloussov and Dan LaFuze for encouraging me with the book. As soon as I told them, they immediately said, "Go for it!" They knew I'd finish the book from day one.

Thanks to Ambroise Confetti for providing the Macintosh screenshots. Ambroise is the author of Cellulo, the award-winning Mac OS X movie player. We became great friends after he traveled from France to work, temporarily, in the United States.

Clark Taylor has been a great mentor. He taught me all my racing skills. Clark doesn't know it yet, but he is going to proofread this acknowledgment section for me. Thank you, Clark.

Thanks to Paul Chang, my fellow childhood dreamer, for constantly writing and encouraging both of us to write fiction. I'm sure we will both write fiction one day.

To my mom, Lucia, and my dad, James, thanks for believing in me. Although our family has gone through some rough times and bitter encounters, it's all in the past. I am sure things will only get better. No matter what happens, I will always love you both with all my heart.

To my brother, Chiao: Thanks for being there for me all my life. Although we bond through our brotherly fights and plays, I know you always cared for me. I am always here for you.

To my wife, Hao Yen: You are the loveliest woman I have ever known. I can't wait to see how our future unfolds before us. I love you.

Contents at a Glance

Contents

· ·

Part II: Hacking Lenses

Part IV: Building Fun Camera Tools

Part V: Flash Memory Hacks

Introduction

The University of Kansas (KU) is a very beautiful college campus. During the cool days of autumn, the Hackberry, Hickory, and Silver Maple trees lose the green pigment in their leaves to reveal the yellow. The leaves of the Sugar Maples, on the other hand, turn red, while the Sweet Gum trees become brilliant mixtures of pink, red, purple, and yellow leaves. Sometimes, the leaves are half-red and half-yellow. On slow-paced weekends, the colorful dry leaves cover entire grass fields like a sea of celebration. The crunch under your feet as you walk over the leaves only intensifies the serenity of the natural environment. Through these combinations, on-campus foliage radiates fantastic ambience as a living art.

I was fortunate enough to attend KU and observe this living art for four years. On graduation day, I realized that I was about to part with this wonderful visual and aural stimulation. As a poor student, I spent all of my money on computer equipment (I was a Computer Science major), but none on cameras or camcorders to capture this natural beauty. I left KU with no records (other than the ones in my memory) of its magnificent atmosphere.

It's been almost 10 years since I left KU. In that time, I have picked up several cameras to capture my life and surroundings visually. I studied photography extensively on my own, because I wanted my photographs to be both artistic and meaningful. I have become proficient as a photographer—won several photo contests and have several photos published in magazines. And I have now written this book. I have to say I owe it all to the existence—and invention—of the camera!

A Picture Is Worth a Thousand Words

Without question, the camera is one of the most exciting and influential inventions in the modern world. We are surrounded by its products—appearing in newspapers and magazines, television programs, and even on many product labels, photographs and video carry much of the wealth of information we are exposed to every day. Your own experience of photography probably includes having your picture taken, maybe for a driver's license or school yearbook, or during a family vacation or significant milestone like a birthday, baptism, or wedding, and you've probably taken pictures of friends and relatives at one time or another. My parents, both journalists, are firm believers in the power of language to overcome the ills of the world. And if a picture really is worth a thousand words, then some might argue that photography is just as powerful as language. To help you express yourself through this powerful visual language, you may need to improve on your camera. Maybe you have seen the 360-degree pan special effects first featured in the movie *The Matrix*. This effect was used at the beginning sequence (when Trinity jumped up in the air for a flying kick) and during the scene where Neo dodges bullets. Have you wondered how they did that? The cinematographers rigged a bunch of Canon EOS A2 film cameras together sequentially to shoot that footage. The entertainment industry has hacked cameras to achieve the effects they wanted for years. Using creative hacks, they presented powerful viewpoints. With the creative thinking in this book, you can hack your own camera and get into this extremely fun, exciting hobby. The concepts are applicable for years to come.

Whom Is This Book For?

Everyone. That might be overstating it a bit, but seriously, I did strive to write this book so that it would be beneficial to you—whoever you are. You may be a home hobbyist who loves to shoot pictures of your kids and pets. You might aspire to be a fine art photographer, or you might want to specialize in wild life photography. Maybe you are a professional photojournalist. No matter what your interests, there's sure to be a lot of information here that will enhance both your skill and your equipment.

You don't have to be an advanced photographer or hacker to benefit from this book. Some chapters require no more skill than the ability to read. And if you know how to use basic tools like screwdrivers and saws (and it's unlikely that you'd pick up this book if you didn't), then you can do quite a bit more. Basic soldering skill is also useful, and this book contains an appendix on soldering. So, even if you don't know how to solder, you soon will. Chapter 14 and Chapter 16 require glass cutting knowledge—an interesting skill to acquire—so there's also an appendix covering that. Basic electronic skills will greatly help you with circuitries in Chapter 1. If you are not familiar with electronics, don't let the first chapter scare you—skip it! The other twenty-six chapters don't touch on electronics at all.

Throughout the book I explain the basic concepts required and provide complete instructions and notes. So no matter what your skill level and experience is, you will quickly find that you're equal to the task at hand.

How This Book Is Organized

This book is organized into five parts, and includes four appendixes. Each major division—"Hacking Cameras," "Hacking Lenses," "Creative Photography Hacks," "Building Fun Camera Tools," and "Flash Memory Hacks"—emphasizes a different part of the camera system, and each contains chapters focusing on a different project. The appendixes present vital skills that complement the book's projects. Each chapter briefly explains why you would consider performing the hack, simple photography concepts to make use of the hack, the parts and tools you need to complete the project, instructions with pictures to show you how to perform the hack, and tips to help you succeed. Because the chapters don't necessarily depend on information or skills covered in previous chapters, you can jump to any part or any chapter in the book. Useful cross-references between chapters and sections will help you find related information within the book.

"Is My Camera Compatible with This Book?"

Yes! Over the years, camera technology has gone from pinhole to lens and from film to digital sensor. However, the basic concepts stay the same, such as light's being exposed onto a photosensitive material, the need for remote triggers, the need for tripods, and so on. And many hacks that were useful 20 years (or even a century) ago are still valid today, no matter how the specific equipment has changed.

To walk you through each project, I provide very specific instructions and details. To provide this level of detail, I had to use a specific brand and model of camera for each project. My selection of camera model doesn't mean that the particular hack is applicable only to that camera model, however. The underlying principle for the hack can be applied to almost any camera of the same type (SLR, disposable, digital, and so on) and I emphasize that throughout the book.

So, even if your camera is not mentioned, you can use the concepts provided to experiment with it—and that is part of the fun of hacking your camera.

A Word of Caution

As I mentioned in the previous section, you might have a different camera than those used in this book. Even if you have the same model, manufacturing tolerances could have changed. When you apply the hacking concept to your camera, keep your eyes open and *be careful!* Some of the hacks presented here could void your camera's warranty. Therefore, those hacks might be better applied to your secondary camera, rather than the one you use daily.

About Hacking

To many people, the word *hack* has come to signify doing something illegal. Often it brings to mind the work of hackers who use the Internet to break into others' computers. However, *hack* and *hacker* didn't start with this connotation. Back in the early 1960s, *hackers* were those programmers so proficient with computers that they could quickly *hack* a program to make it do something *useful*—something that wasn't intended by the software's original design. So while today the word can call to mind both good and bad, I like to think of a *hack* as positive, an unconventional solution or enhancement.

For our purposes, a *hack* is a modification to a device that produces something useful that was unintended in the original design.

Before there were thousands of camera equipment manufacturers, distributors, retailers, and mail-order houses, photographers performed hacks all the time. When they wanted a soft portrait effect, they wrapped women's stockings over their camera lens. They built monopods when film became fast enough to shoot sport action. They ignited gunpowder to illuminate the scene (what we now call *flash*). None of these techniques used the equipment or material as it was originally intended.

Today, cameras are more sophisticated than they were in the days of the gunpowder flash. But as photographers, we continue to exercise our creativity to devise ways to improve our gear. We might reprogram the firmware on our new digital camera, glue additional tripod sockets to our cameras, or wire up additional trigger functions. These modifications each benefit our photographs in some way.

Inspired by my definition of *hack*, I started calling all of my camera gear modifications *hacks*. And this inspiration motivated me to come up with even more camera hacks. This book is filled with constructive, helpful, and useful hacks. None are destructive to the camera or to you. These hacks make your camera gear even more fun, exciting, and capable than ever. So break out your toolbox, hack your camera, and capture the photographs that your camera could never shoot before!

Contacting Me

Before I started writing this book, I put many camera hacking ideas, concepts, and instructions on my *Camera Hacker* web site. Many visitors have contacted me to offer praise about the information presented there, and they've corrected some information or given me a piece of their mind—to help me improve the web site.

I would love to hear from you as well—tell me what you think of this book. I would especially like to hear any cool camera hacking ideas you have and what you would like to see in a revision of this book.

Some people have contacted me for help with questions about camera use and troubleshooting, and I try to help as much as I can, but many times I am too busy or don't know enough about your particular gear to help. I suggest you post to and participate in the forums located at my *Camera Hacker* web site. There are many people who may know the answer you are seeking, or have the same question that you do. I also read and write on these forums. By the time this books goes to press, there will be a forum there to discuss this book.

Web site: www.CameraHacker.com/

E-Mail: Chieh@CameraHacker.com

Hacking Digital Cameras

Hacking Cameras

Building Triggers

O ne of the first camera hacks I ever performed was the extension of the remote trigger release on my Canon EOS SLR: I extended it to shoot pictures of myself on roller skates from a distance. The hack was so easy I soon learned to make trigger switches as well. Trigger switches and extensions can serve purposes other than self-portraiture. You might want to set up your camera gear in a remote location to photograph birds and other animals in action. Sometimes I would set my camera in my hamsters' cages to capture their daily activities. Another popular remote trigger application is shooting sporting events. Photographers have been known to rig their gear inside hockey rinks and even in goalie boxes, generally using wireless triggers. But nothing is stopping you from running wired camera equipment to the basketball hoop in your yard. Mounting your camera there can render some awesome pictures of your kids playing basketball.

This chapter helps you make trigger switches and extend their ranges. If you have trigger switches from older generation cameras, you may be able to adapt them for use on your new state-of-the-art cameras. This chapter shows you how to make those adapters. Most single-lens reflex (SLR) cameras have a built-in shutter trigger port, and you connect to this port directly. But most point-and-shoot (P&S) cameras lack this nifty feature. On these cameras, you hack the camera itself and wire a trigger port directly to the shutter switch. This trigger port will use the same interface as the one available on SLRs, so if you have both types of camera systems, you can use the same remote trigger switch and extender for all your gear.

Making a Wired Remote Trigger

Most SLRs, even entry-level ones, have a remote shutter release socket so you can shoot pictures without actually touching the camera body. The remote trigger is used often in long-exposure photography, where even a small amount of vibration can introduce blurriness into the image. As steady as your hands are, they are not machines, and, therefore, they are prone to tiny movements that you may not be aware of until you view your picture. With a wired remote trigger release, the camera body can be mounted on a tripod, and you operate the camera through the wired remote trigger.

In astrophotography, exposure can take several minutes. If you had to operate the camera shutter with your hands on your camera's shutter button, they would probably be shaking like mad after five minutes. Holding the shutter button down for a long time is extremely tiring. Fortunately, many remote shutter triggers can be locked in the down position. An older mechanical trigger without the locking feature can be taped instead.

Remote shutter triggers are usually optional accessories for SLRs. They can cost anywhere from five dollars for a mechanical version to several hundred dollars for a super fancy electronic version. In the following sections, you build your own simple remote trigger so you understand how a remote trigger works. This knowledge will help you to build fancier timing triggers and multiple-camera triggers in the later sections of this chapter.

FIGURE 1-1: This picture of the moon was shot with a telescope and a camera. Both the telescope and camera were mounted on their own tripods. Vibration was still a major issue, so a wired remote and mirror lock-up were used.

How Does a Remote Trigger Work?

On most of today's cameras, a remote trigger works simply by closing an electrical circuit to trigger the shutter. This simple concept is shown in Figure 1-2. The wired remote is simply a switch extended from the camera body.

Note This chapter makes extensive use of circuit diagrams. See Appendix B for a list of circuit symbols.

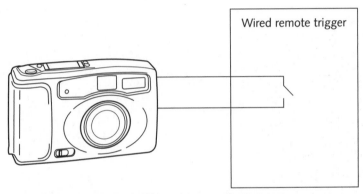

Wired remote trigger

FIGURE 1-2: A schematic of the wired remote shutter trigger

A camera that has auto-focus (AF) capability generally has a two-position shutter trigger. The first position—reached when you press the trigger halfway down—closes the circuit for the auto-focus function. The second position—reached when you press the trigger all the way down—closes the shutter circuit. A wired remote trigger moves these two functions off the camera, as shown in Figure 1-3. Most Canon SLRs use this simple circuit for remote triggering.

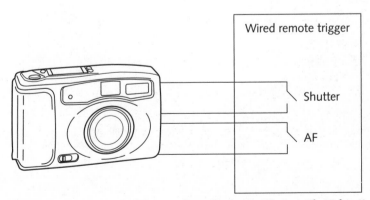

Wired remote trigger

Shutter

AF

FIGURE 1-3: A schematic of the wired remote shutter trigger with AF function

Nikon SLRs use a slightly more complex circuit. The shutter circuit is simply an open/close circuit, like that shown previously in Figure 1-2. But the AF circuit is an open/close switch along with three 1N4148 diodes wired in series. The Nikon wired remote trigger circuit is shown in Figure 1-4.

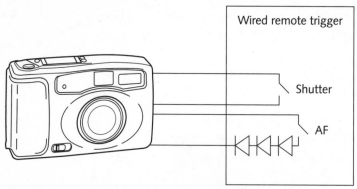

FIGURE 1-4: A Nikon wired remote shutter trigger with AF function

Parts You Need

Your local electronic store carries all of these parts. I prefer Radio Shack because the stores are everywhere. You can also order the parts online from RadioShack.com. I have listed the Radio Shack part numbers for your convenience.

- Mini SPST Momentary Switch (275-1547)
- SPDT Submini Slide Switch (275-409)
- $^3/_{32}$" Submini Phone Jack (274-245)
- 20-gauge wire (278-1388)
- Mini Project Enclosure (270-288)

Note   A 2.5mm jack is the same size as a $^3/_{32}$" jack.

There are many different types of switches (see the "Switch Terminology" sidebar). Each one serves a slightly different purpose. Sometimes, two types of switches can be used for the same purpose. For this project, I chose to use two momentary switches and a slide switch. The normally open momentary switch (see Figure 1-6) is similar to the on-camera shutter button. A normally open momentary switch requires that you hold down the switch to close the circuit. As soon as you let go of the switch, it opens the circuit again.

Canon E3 Connector

The Canon RS60-E3 remote control, used on Canon EOS cameras, is a two-position switch just like the shutter release on the Canon EOS series. Pushing the button down halfway causes the camera to focus, while pushing the button down all the way causes the camera to release its shutter. The wired remote control transmits the signal though a standard 2.5mm (sub-mini) audio head. The contacts on the head are numbered in Figure1-5.

FIGURE 1-5: The E3 connector pins

When the button on the remote control is pushed halfway, contact sections 1 and 2 are shorted together, causing the camera to focus. When the button on the remote control is pushed all the way, all three contact sections are shorted together, causing the camera shutter to be released. Pin 1 is actually the ground connector. Therefore, pin 1 and pin 3 cause the camera to trigger.

When you build your own camera interface, you can split the auto-focus and shutter release functions by using two switches (using two independent circuits).

FIGURE **1-6: Momentary pushbutton switches**

Although this switch is appropriate as a shutter release for high-shutter-speed pictures, it would be tiring to hold down a momentary switch for a long time (minutes or hours), such as during a bulb exposure. To relieve you from having to hold the button down, most remote triggers have a locking feature that holds the button down for you. I have chosen a slide switch (see Figure 1-7) to simulate that feature in this project. When you begin the exposure, slide the switch to on. When you are done with the exposure, slide it to off.

Note | *Bulb exposure* is the term that describes what happens when you control the shutter's opening and closing without using the camera's shutter speed timer. It's generally used for a long exposure in astrophotography and night photography.

FIGURE 1-7: Slide switches

In this project, I chose a mini–project enclosure (see Figure 1-8) and a bunch of sub-mini parts to fit into it. These small parts help create a small remote trigger. A smaller remote trigger is easy to carry around and doesn't take up too much space in your camera bag. I also chose a plastic case because they are generally easier to work with than metal cases. It's easier to drill and shape plastic than metal.

Most photographers like to have a small, wired remote. I've noticed that there seems to be a general consensus that smaller is better, and there's nothing wrong with that. In fact, I picked a very small project case and a lot of sub-mini parts for this project. But you might consider a bigger box to fit bigger switches for action events. If you have rigged a camera in a hockey arena by the goal box, you probably don't want to miss a shot because you are fiddling for a button on your tiny remote. You might want to rig up a table-size remote where the button is the size of your hand, so that you can pound on the buttons during the excitement of the game.

FIGURE 1-8: A small project box

For interfacing, I chose a $^3/_{32}$" (2.5mm) stereo phone jack (refer to the "Canon E3 Connector" sidebar), shown in Figure 1-9. This is the same interface that is used on entry-level Canon EOS SLRs, so you can easily attach this wired remote trigger to them. This interface is common on cellular phone earpieces and other electronic components as well. Both female and male versions are common and easy to source. This is the preferred interface method compared to the proprietary interface found on higher-end Canon EOS SLRs, Nikon SLRs, and others. Later in this chapter I show you how to adapt this simple interface to the proprietary interfaces so that you can use the same remote trigger with the more advanced cameras.

You need some electrical wires to make the connections between the switches and the interface jack. You might already have some leftover wires at home. You can even strip them from your old stereo headphones (3.5mm) or your cell phone earpiece (2.5mm). You won't need very much of it, just about a foot or so of wire. I have listed 20-gauge wire in the part list. But any wire between 18 and 22 gauge will work just fine.

FIGURE 1-9: 2.5mm stereo phone jacks

Tools You Need

Here are the tools you will need to complete this project:

- Drill
- Drill bit
- Small c-clamps
- #1 Phillips precision screwdriver
- Digital multimeter
- Wire stripper
- Solder iron
- 0.032" diameter 60/40 Standard Rosin-Core Solder (64-009E)

 See Appendix A for information on buying and using soldering irons.

Switch Terminology

Switches come in many different physical forms and types. But common to most physical switches are four types of function. Figure 1-10 shows the schematic of each type of switch.

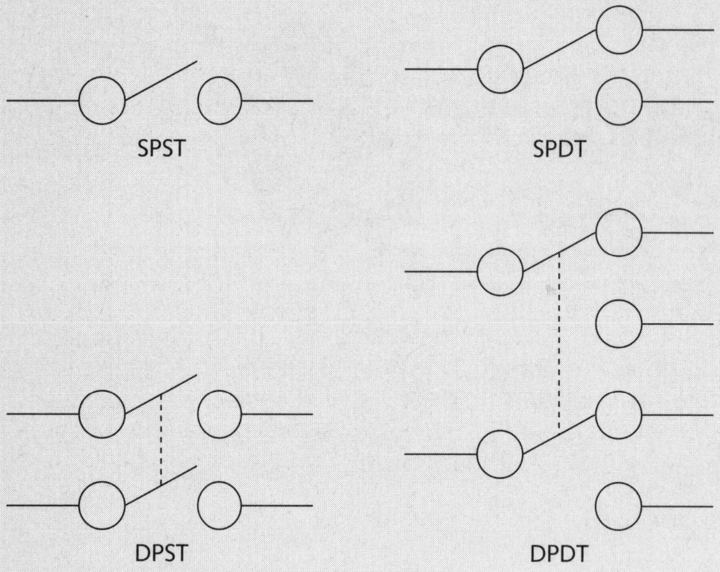

SPST

SPDT

DPST

DPDT

FIGURE 1-10: Different types of switch circuitry

Single Pole Single Throw (SPST)

Single pole single throw switches are the simplest form of switches. This type of switch is either open or closed. There can be no other position. These switches have two contact pins. Most SPST momentary switches are normally open, meaning that the circuit is open unless you activate it. Some SPST momentary switches are normally closed, meaning that the circuit is closed unless you activate it.

Single Pole Double Throw (SPDT)

A single pole double throw switch has two possible positions. In either position, different circuits are connected. Think of it as a railroad switch, where the train would travel over one railroad track versus another, depending on the position of the switch. In physical form, an SPDT switch has three pins. It is possible to wire up an SPDT switch to act like an SPST switch by simply leaving one of the pins unconnected. Most SPDT switches are toggle or slide switches. SPDT momentary pushbutton switches are more rare.

Double Pole Single Throw (DPST)

A double pole single throw switch is basically a pair of SPST switches. The switch position is connected, so when one circuit is closed, the other is closed as well. When one is open, the other circuit is open too. A DPST switch has four physical pins. It is possible to wire up a DPST switch to function like an SPST switch or an SPDT switch.

Double Pole Double Throw (DPDT)

Double pole double throw switches are two SPDT switches. The positions of the two switches are physically connected; when one physical switch is thrown, both circuit switches change position. A DPDT switch has six pins. It is possible to wire up a DPDT switch into any of the previous less sophisticated switches.

For this project, you need a drill to makes holes in the project enclosures for the switches. A low-power electrical version will work fine. The size of the drill bit depends on the switch size. It's easy to measure with a drill gauge, as shown in Figure 1-11 (see Chapter 18 for information about how to make your own drill gauge). Buy a set of drill bits so that you have many sizes on hand. Buying a set is generally cheaper than buying bits individually. Make sure you have a small c-clamp on hand to secure the enclosure on the workbench—you don't want to hold the enclosure with your hand. The drill bit could bite into the enclosure and the drill will have much more torque than your hand can control, which could lead to serious injury. A precision screwdriver is needed for fastening the enclosure together.

FIGURE 1-11: Drill gauge for measuring the switch diameter

When you are ready to put all the electrical connections together, you need a wire stripper to strip the insulation from the end of the wires. A wire stripper costs a few bucks at the local home improvement store. The soldering iron and solder help you create good electrical contacts between the switch contacts and the wires (see Appendix A for a quick guide to the basics of soldering). You can find soldering irons and solder at Radio Shack.

Drilling the Case

The first step in making your own remote trigger is to drill the project enclosure. Before you do so, use the drill gauge to measure the hole required by the switch. Poke the switch through the holes in the gauge until you find the right size. Then mount the right sized drill bit onto the drill.

Before actually starting to drill, use the c-clamp to secure the project box onto the workbench (see Figure 1-12). My workbench has several holes over the surface for drill bits to drill through. If your workbench doesn't have the same facility and you don't want accidentally to drill into it, I suggest you place a block of wood between the project box and the workbench. With a wood block in between, when you drill through the project box, you'll drill into the wood block instead of your workbench.

FIGURE 1-12: The project box is secured onto the workbench

After drilling all of the holes for your enclosure, test fit each jack and switch in the enclosure. This step is your chance to make sure the project box is drilled to your satisfaction, so you can make any additional modification as needed.

Soldering the Wires

When you are done drilling the enclosure, you can start soldering the parts together. Wire up the switches based on the conceptual circuit diagrams presented in the "How Does a Remote Trigger Work?" section. When you are ready to solder the interface jack, refer to the "Canon E3 Connector" sidebar for an overview and solder the connection to match the pin-out. Follow the instructions in Appendix A if your soldering skills are rusty.

After you have soldered all of the wires and contacts, you should test out your trigger before actually fitting everything together. No matter how confident you are about your result, you may find that the trigger is defective. I don't know how many times I put something together, whether it's an electrical project or an internal computer component upgrade, thinking it's perfect, but after tightening the last screw, it fails to work. So, before all the switches and wires and the jack are in the project box, plug it into your camera. Verify that all the switches are working as expected. If everything works properly, you can move to the next step. Otherwise, pull out your digital multimeter (see Figure 1-13) and test all of the connections.

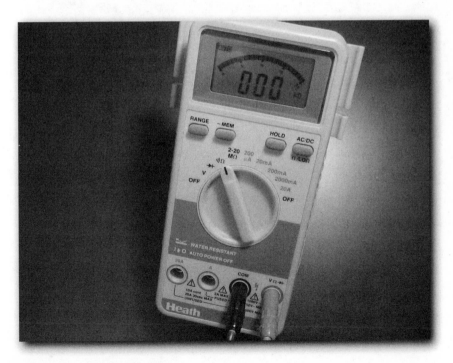

FIGURE 1-13: A digital multimeter

Canon N3 Connector

The Canon N3 shutter release trigger connector, found on higher-end Canon EOS cameras, has three connector pins. The male connector is designed onto the camera body, while the female connector is designed for shutter release trigger accessories. Unlike the E3 connector (refer to the "Canon E3 Connector" sidebar), which is a standard 2.5mm sub-mini connector used in the audio world, the N3 connector, shown in Figure 1-14, is proprietary, made by Canon. Neither the male nor the female connector can be sourced from anywhere. Your best bet is to buy an accessory or cable adapter (such as the T3 to N3 adapter), and then cut the N3 heads off for your project.

FIGURE 1-14: The N3 connector is the circular port on the right. The circular port on the left is a PC terminal for triggering flashes and strobes.

The pin-out for the Canon N3 connector (looking at the N3 connector on the camera) is listed as follows:

- Top - ground
- Left - shutter
- Right - focus

What this pin-out means is that if you short the right pin and the top pin, the camera focuses (in AF mode). If you short the left pin and top pin, the shutter releases.

 Note A digital multimeter is a multi-purpose electronic measurement tool. The digital multimeter can measure voltage, resistance, and current. Using the resistance mode, you can check for bad connections in your circuit.

Fitting the Pieces Together

After you've successfully tested the circuits, you can carefully fit everything into your project box. You may have to bend the circuit wires to fit the box. Try to bend them at sleeved unsoldered locations to prevent breaking the soldered contact points. Once everything is fitted into the project case, use a #1 Phillips precision screwdriver to fasten the screw and the case covers together. At this point, you need to test your finished trigger once again. As careful as you were putting the case together, it is possible for a fragile soldering contact to break loose. You don't want to wait and find out that your remote trigger is not working when you are out in the field.

Making a Delay Trigger

You are probably already familiar with a delay trigger. You use one whenever you place your digital camera in front of a group of people, set the 10-second timer, and run into the scene yourself. Or whenever you want to shoot a self-portrait, such as that shown in Figure 1-15. Most decent cameras on the market have pretty good built-in self-timers. It's practically an industry standard to set them to 10 seconds. There are two reasons you might want to make a delay trigger yourself: First, you can make one in case your camera doesn't come with a self-timer; second, the built-in 10-second timer is either too short or too long for your needs.

I learned to build a delay trigger because I found through experience that the 10-second delay timer is simply not long enough for me to set up a perfect shot. As my photographic experience increases over time, my taste for the "perfect" shot also increases. I found myself taking from several minutes to several hours just to perfectly set up a scene and all the models. When I have to join the scene myself, the setup time for each shot far exceeds the 10 second allowance.

Just recently, I visited the Villa Riviera building in Long Beach, California, and I had a chance to shoot some wonderful environmental portraits of my girlfriend and me. I had to set up my Canon EOS D30 digital SLR on the other side of the courtyard. For each shot, I set the 10-second timer, ran to the other side of the courtyard, and tried to pose before the timer went off. Each time I failed. After taking five unsuccessful frames, I finally gave up.

Without my further rambling, let's start making a delay trigger.

FIGURE 1-15: A self-portrait using the 10-second timer delay

Parts You Need

Here are the parts you will need to complete this project:

- 555CN Timer IC (276-1723) or TLC555 Low-Power CMOS Timer (276-1718)
- SPDT Micromini 5VDC Relay (275-240)
- Pushbutton normally closed Momentary Switch (275-1548)
- 4.7K ohm 1/2W 5% Carbon Film Resistor (271-1124)
- 2200µF Electrolytic Capacitor
- 0.01µF Polyester Film Capacitor (272-1065)
- Heavy-duty 9V Battery Snap Connector (270-324)
- SPST Submini Slide Switch (275-409)
- Stereo $^3/_{32}$" Submini Phone Jack (274-245)
- 6" Matching Solderless PC Board (276-170)
- Project case
- 9-volt battery

Tip These are all fairly basic electronics parts, so they can be found easily at your favorite electronics store. I bought them all at Radio Shack, either locally or online. For your convenience, I have listed their Radio Shack part numbers.

The 555 timer chip has been a popular integrated circuit (IC) ever since its invention (see the "555 Timer Chip" sidebar later in the chapter). All circuits that require some kind of timing have this chip. Because of their popularity, there are tons of supplies from multiple manufacturers, which drives the cost down. Currently, they cost about a buck fifty each. Pick up a few spares for circuit testing purposes. When you put your prototype together, it's likely not going to work correctly the first time. The extra chips can help you determine if it's a bad chip or if it's your circuit at fault.

The SPDT Micromini Relay looks like a black block, which is not very elegant. Its operation is also not elegant—it emits loud clicking noises. The noise is good for testing, but in normal operation, it can get annoying. I had originally wanted to use the SPST Reed Relay (275-233), which has a fast response, a compact size, and a lower cost. And best of all, no loud clicks! Unfortunately, the reed relay is simply an open/close circuit switch, whereas the Micromini Relay is a two-position switch. Because the 555 timer defaults to a signal high during countdown, a simple open/close switch wouldn't have worked without a more complex circuit. For the purpose of learning, you wire up the two-position relay in reverse, or negative, logic to work as a delay trigger.

Note A relay was chosen as the trigger mechanism because it enables circuit independence. Thus, the switch is on the camera's circuit, independent of the timer circuit you create. This independence ensures that the circuit works with most, if not all, cameras. Using an independent circuit also means that you won't ever fry your camera's circuitry with your timer circuit.

The 555 timer circuit changes state on a circuit open rather than a circuit closed signal. Therefore, you use an interesting normally closed pushbutton switch in this project, because the normally closed pushbutton keeps the circuit energized all the time, preventing the 555 timer from changing states. When you push the button, it breaks the circuit, causing the chip to change state and the timer to start.

The resistor and the first capacitor in the list are the components that will control the time delay. See the "Circuit Diagram" section later in the chapter for a more detailed description.

Note Resistors are available in limited values. The resistor value you need may not be available off the shelf. Instead, you can make different resistor values by combining multiple resistors in series and in parallel. When resistors are connected in series, add up the resistor values to obtain the total resistor value. For parallel resistors, add up the reciprocals of the resistance values, and then take the reciprocal of the total to calculate the total resistor value.

The heavy-duty 9-volt battery connector is very useful for connecting a battery source to your project. It can be used with a 9-volt battery or with a battery holder from Radio Shack. The Radio Shack AA battery holders are available in a variety of configurations that can hold from one AA battery to eight AA batteries. Each battery holder has a 9-volt battery connector so that it can be connected to your project.

The slide switch is used to turn the circuit on and off. The sub-mini phone jack is used to connect to your camera. Your finalized circuit is transferred to the solderless PC board. Although it is described as solderless, you actually solder parts onto this circuit board. A 9-volt battery powers the timing circuit.

The following list includes additional parts you'll want to pick up. Although they will not make it into your finalized circuit, they are necessary for prototyping and testing. Without them, you might spend a lot of time putting a circuit together that doesn't work.

- 5mm yellow LED (276-021)
- 100 ohm 1/4W 5% Carbon Film Resistor 5-pack (271-1311)
- AA Battery Holder (270-383)
- 4 AA batteries

The yellow LED is a visual indicator for you to see if your circuit works. In this project it simulates the camera trigger visually. Without this indicator, you would be in the dark about whether the timing circuit works or not. The resistors work with the LED and provide the necessary current-limit to prevent the LED from burning out. See the "Make Your Own Infrared Emitter" sidebar in Chapter 16 for more information on the lack of LED resistance. The AA battery holder and the four AA batteries power the LED.

555 Timer Chip

The 555 timer chip is one of the most useful integrated circuits (IC) in existence. Introduced in the 1970s as the IC Time Machine, it provided circuit designers and hobbyists with an inexpensive commercial electronic timer. Today, 555 timer chips are available from many manufacturers and are readily available at your local electronic store. Information about the 555 timer chip is also widely available on the Internet. My favorite is the National Semiconductor LM555 Timer specification sheet that is downloadable at `www.national.com/ds/LM/LM555.pdf`.

555 timer chips are available in a bipolar and a CMOS version (see Figure 1-16). The CMOS version is typically rated to operate from 3 to 18 volts. The bipolar version operates from 4.5 to 16 volts. The bipolar version also requires more current than the CMOS version, which makes the CMOS timer chips the perfect candidate for low power to very low power applications. On the other hand, the bipolar chip can handle considerably greater current for high-power applications.

FIGURE 1-16: A bipolar timer chip and a CMOS timer chip look identical. The only way you can tell a difference is by reading their packaging and specification sheet.

Continued

Continued

The 555 timer chip has limitations on the values that can be used for R1, R2, and C (see circuit diagrams). The resistor values cannot be less than about 1 kilo-ohm and should not be greater than about 1 mega-ohm. A resistor with resistance less than 1 kilo-ohm results in excessive currents in the circuit, while a resistor greater than 1 mega-ohm does not pass enough current through the circuit. Capacitor values should be between 100 pF and about 10μF. If you follow these rules, the slowest pulses that can be accurately produced have a frequency of around 1 pulse every 10 seconds (0.1 Hz).

The packaging of the 555CN Timer IC (276-1723) mentions "Times microseconds through hours." I suspect that the newer 555 IC design has done away with resistor and capacitor value restrictions.

Tools You Need

Here are the tools you will need to complete this project:

- Breadboard (276-174)
- Solderless Breadboard Jumper Wire Kit (276-173)
- Digital multimeter
- Needle-nose pliers
- Soldering iron
- 0.032" diameter 60/40 Standard Rosin-Core Solder (64-009E)

The breadboard is a piece of white plastic with a lot of tiny square holes (see Figure 1-17). These holes allow you to insert electrical wire and component leads. The holes are connected via different patterns of rows and columns. Figure 1-18 shows the connection pattern. The breadboard is an essential part for prototyping and testing your design.

When working with breadboards, a pair of needle-nose pliers is a must. You really want to use the small type with a long nose. This tool helps you insert wire leads and component leads into the breadboard sockets.

Circuit Diagram

The delay timer circuit is shown in Figure 1-19. It is a fairly simple circuit that is based entirely on the monostable operation shown in the LM555 specification sheet (refer to the "555 Timer Chip" sidebar). The circuit is unchanged, but a few minor components have been added. A battery was added to the circuit to power the timer chip. A switch was added to turn the circuit on and off. A normally closed pushbutton switch was added to start the timer. A relay was added to provide independent triggering of the camera through the timer circuit. And a camera was added to show how to interface the circuit to the camera.

FIGURE 1-17: A breadboard

FIGURE 1-18: The bottom of the breadboard shows the electrical connections. When you buy a breadboard, a label covers the bottom to insulate the metal contacts from other potential electrical contacts. I pulled the label off my breadboard to show you the pattern underneath.

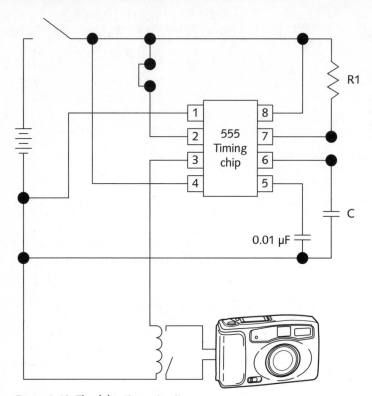

FIGURE **1-19: The delay timer circuit**

Tip Some resources have mentioned that the 0.01μF capacitor may not be needed with a CMOS timer chip. Based on my experience, the capacitor is required for both the bipolar and CMOS timer chips. Without it, the bipolar chip does not work at all, and the CMOS chip becomes extremely speedy. I have noticed a ten-fold speed-up in frequency.

By changing R1 and C, you can vary the trigger timing. The delay time is calculated by the following formula:

$$T = 1.1 \times R1 \times C$$

T is in seconds, R1 is in ohms, and C is in farads. With the 4700 ohms resistor and the 2200μF capacitor picked for this project, the timer delays 11.37 seconds before triggering the camera.

Resistor Color Code

Resistor values are color coded onto the resistor bodies. There are generally three to four bands on each resistor. From the resistor end where the band is closer to the lead, the first color band signifies the first digit in the resistor value. The second color band represents the second digit in the resistor value. The third color band indicates a multiplier for the two digits. The fourth band (if it exists) determines the tolerance defined by the manufacturer for that particular resistor. The possible values for each band are shown in Table 1-1.

Note If you read the "555 Timer Circuit" sidebar, you are probably wondering how I got away with using a 2200µF capacitor. My experience has shown that although timing isn't truly accurate by violating the rules, the 555 timer chip still works. And it still produces a frequency on par with the calculation. For camera triggering, I wouldn't worry so much about accuracy or precision. But if you really need an extremely accurate and precise timer, you need to design a more complicated circuit with all the right parts.

I picked the SPDT Micromini 5VDC Relay because of its double throw characteristic (refer to the "Switch Terminology" sidebar). The 555 timer chip outputs high during the delay and outputs low when the delay elapses. That is exactly the opposite of what you want. You want the circuit to output high after the delay elapses. A simple single throw relay would not work. Fortunately you can emulate that characteristic by wiring up a double throw relay, as shown in Figure 1-20.

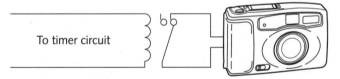

To timer circuit

FIGURE 1-20: The SPDT Micromini 5VDC Relay circuit

This delay timer is a very basic circuit that gets the job done, but it doesn't do it particularly well, especially considering that the trigger is on until the normally closed button is pressed. But the knowledge you gained by building this circuit can start you thinking, and later you can build more advanced and elegant timing circuits.

Table 1-1: Resistor Band Color Chart

First and Second Color Band		Third Color Band		Fourth Color Band	
Band Color	Value	Band Color	Multiplier or Divisor Value	Band Color	Tolerance
Black	0	Black	×1	Gold 5%	5%
Brown	1	Brown	×10	Silver 10%	10%
Red	2	Red	×100	None 20%	20%
Orange	3	Orange	×1,000		
Yellow	4	Yellow	×10,000		
Green	5	Green	×100,000		
Blue	6	Blue	×1,000,000		
Violet	7	Silver	÷100		
Gray	8	Gold	÷10		
White	9				

Prototyping the Circuit

With the circuit worked out, your first task is to prototype the circuit on a breadboard. Typically, I like to use the top row as the positive power source and use the bottom row as the negative ground. These two rows are linked across the entire breadboard, making them easy to access for the rest of the circuits.

The first thing you should do is find a nice spot in the middle of the breadboard for your timer chip. It needs to be inserted horizontally with the pins above and below the trench (see Figure 1-21). This gives each pin its own contact strip and keeps the pins from shorting each other.

Caution Use a chip puller to remove ICs from the breadboard or chip sockets, or use a screwdriver to pry them off. Pulling them off with your fingers forcefully could be dangerous. I've had their tiny legs embedded in my flesh before.

Now wire up the rest of the circuit using jump wires, and attach electronic components as needed. The needle-nose pliers will do wonders on the breadboard compared to your fingers. When working with tiny electronic components, your fingers are big columns from a Greek temple. Use the needle-nose pliers to thread the jumper wires and leads on the prototype circuit. When you are done wiring everything, you'll see a circuit that looks like Figure 1-22.

FIGURE 1-21: The timer chip inserted in the breadboard

FIGURE 1-22: The delay timer prototyped on a breadboard

At this point, you are probably pretty excited about the circuit you just put together. It's time to insert the testing circuit. In place of the camera, wire up the AA battery holder, the resistor, and the LED in series (see Figure 1-23). This series of electrical components will give you a visual indicator of the trigger mechanism. Plug in a 9-volt battery to power the timing circuit and insert four AA batteries to power the LED.

FIGURE 1-23: The breadboard with the testing circuit installed

Once wired, the LED stays on. This is normal because you have wired the relay in reverse. This is also the non-elegant portion of the design that I mentioned earlier. When you push the button, the LED should turn off. You'll hear the relay click. The LED will stay off for 11.37 seconds. Then it will turn back on again. The turning on is what causes the camera to trigger when you finally wire it to your camera.

Because this circuit is not elegant, you will have to set your camera to one-shot mode. Otherwise, when the light turns on and stays on, the camera will continue to fire off pictures.

Soldering the Wires

A breadboard circuit is perfect for prototyping and testing. But it's easy for the circuit to get screwed-up because a lead comes loose. After you have tested the prototype circuit, you can memorialize your design by soldering everything to a PC board. I have found that Radio Shack has made a 6" Matching Solderless PC Board (276-170) that is perfect for this purpose. This PC board matches the breadboard exactly so that you don't even have to rewire your circuit for

Resistor Characteristics

Metal Foil: Low tolerance. Very low temperature coefficients. Long stability.

Metal film: Low tolerance (nominally 0.1 to 1 percent). Low temperature coefficients. Long stability. Thin film is more stable from temperature changes than thick film.

Carbon film: High temperature coefficient. Tolerance nominally 2 to 10 percent.

Carbon: Very high temperature coefficient.

Composition: Tolerance nominally 5 to 20 percent. Tolerance becomes higher over time through aging and humidity.

Because resistors can change characteristics over time, you can place a variable resistor in series with a fixed resistor for precise timing applications. The variable resistor can be adjusted and calibrated for different conditions.

the PC board. Simply transfer all of the wires and components from the breadboard to this PC board and you're done.

Just make sure you test your finalized circuit again with the visual indicator. It's easy to make mistakes even if you are just transferring the circuit from one medium to another. And there could be bad solder connections.

Putting It Together

Once you are happy that the circuit is working correctly on the new PC board, mount it into a project case. The project case helps prevent damage to the components on the circuit board. (And if you drop it, parts won't scatter all over the floor.)

Making an Interval Trigger

In this section you use the 555 timer chip to make an interval trigger. The interval trigger is far more interesting than the delay trigger because it can help you document the changing environment around you. You can take sequential pictures of flowers that bloom in one night. You can shoot a sequence of changing cloud formations. Or you can shoot the motion of the stars.

Most camera manufacturers make interval triggers for their high-end SLRs. For example, Canon makes a TC80N3 Timer Remote Control for EOS cameras that has an N3 connector (refer to the "Canon N3 Connector" sidebar). Because the lower-end EOS Rebel-series of cameras uses the E3 connector (refer to the "Canon E3 Connector" sidebar), the Rebel-series cameras can't connect to the TC80N3 Timer Remote Control. But you can make an interval timer yourself.

The delay trigger in the previous section is the cornerstone to understanding the capability of the 555 timer chip. Therefore, a lot of tips and notes in the previous section apply to the interval trigger as well. For the interval trigger, I will present only pertinent information that differs from the previous section. Unless you are already extremely familiar with the 555 timer chip, I suggest that you thoroughly review the previous section.

Parts You Need

Here are the parts you will need to complete this project:

- 555CN Timer IC (276-1723) or TLC555 Low-Power CMOS Timer (276-1718)
- SPDT Micromini 5VDC Relay (275-240)
- 4.7K ohm 1/2W 5% Carbon Film Resistor (271-1124)
- 100 ohm 1/4W 5% Carbon Film Resistor 5-pack (271-1311)
- 0.01μF Polyester Film Capacitor (272-1065)
- 4700μF Electrolytic Capacitor (272-1022)
- SPST Submini Slide Switch (275-409)
- Stereo $^3/_{32}$" Submini Phone Jack (274-245)
- Heavy-duty 9V Battery Snap Connector (270-324)
- 9-volt battery

Capacitor Characteristics

Capacitors come in different types. Each type has different characteristics appropriate for different applications. Some capacitors have a lower tolerance and are good for accurate and precise timing applications. Others are more tolerant and thus less accurate and precise. In most cases, timing doesn't need to be overly accurate and precise for general-purpose camera triggering. Of course, if you are building a mission-critical camera trigger, stick with the best parts.

Metal film: Film capacitors include polycarbonate, polystyrene, polyester, and polypropylene. All of these film types are excellent for timing applications.

Tantalum: Tantalum capacitors have high dielectric absorption characteristics and high leakage. Therefore they are not suitable for timing applications. Use them only for non-critical situations.

Electrolytic: Electrolytic capacitors suffer from loose tolerances, poor stability, and high leakage. They are also not suitable for critical timing applications.

Ceramic: Ceramic capacitors are highly unstable and should also be avoided for timing applications.

Note Refer to the section "Making a Delay Trigger" for information on these parts.

The following parts are used for testing the prototype:

- 5mm yellow LED (276-021)
- AA Battery Holder (270-383)
- 4 AA batteries

Tools You Need

Here are the tools you will need to complete this project:

- Breadboard (276-175)
- Solderless Breadboard Jumper Wire Kit (276-173)
- Needle-nose pliers
- Digital multimeter
- Soldering iron
- 0.032" diameter 60/40 Standard Rosin-Core Solder (64-009E)

The tools listed basically mirror the tool list from the "Making a Delay Trigger" section, so I won't go into further detail here.

Circuit Diagram

The interval timer circuit is shown in Figure 1-24. It is a fairly simple circuit based entirely on the astable operation shown in the LM555 specification sheet (refer to the "555 Timer Chip" sidebar). The circuit was unchanged, but a few minor components were added. A battery was added to the circuit to power the timer chip, a switch was added to turn the circuit on and off, a relay was added to provide independent triggering of the camera through the timer circuit, and a camera was added to show how to connect the circuit to the camera.

By changing R1, R2, and C, you can vary the interval and trigger timing. The interval timing is the delay between each trigger. For overnight exposure, depending on how many images you want to capture, you can set it from seconds to minutes to hours. The interval time is calculated by the following formula:

$$T1 = 0.693 \times (R1 + R2) \times C$$

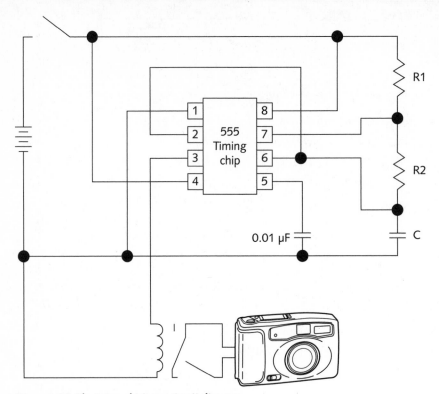

FIGURE 1-24: The interval trigger circuit diagram

The triggering timing determines how long to hold the camera button down. This could range from a few milliseconds to a second or two, depending on the camera. I usually set it to 1 second just to be safe. The trigger timing is calculated by the following formula:

$$T2 = 0.693 \times R2 \times C$$

T1 and T2 are in seconds, R1 and R2 are in ohms, and C is in farads. For my project, I set R1 to 18800 ohms (four 4700 ohms resistors wired in series), R2 to 300 ohms (three 100 ohms resistors wired in series), and C to 4700µF. With these values, the interval of the timer is 62.210 seconds and the trigger time is 0.977 seconds. These values are close enough to 1-minute intervals and holding the camera trigger down for 1 second.

To put the interval trigger together, follow the steps from the sections "Prototyping the Circuit," "Soldering the Wires," and "Putting It Together."

You'll need to refer to the "Making a Delay Trigger" section when you wire up the interval trigger (see Figure 1-25). Remember to test your circuit with the LED, as shown in Figure 1-26.

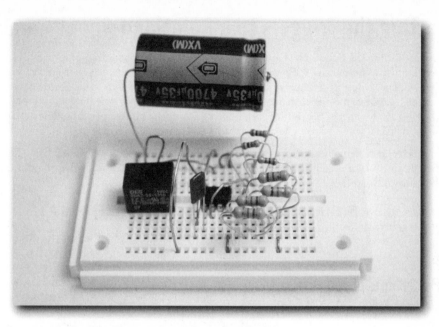

FIGURE 1-25: The delay timer prototyped on a breadboard

FIGURE 1-26: The breadboard with the testing circuit installed

Connecting the Triggers to a Point-and-Shoot Camera

As you learn in the rest of this chapter, it's fairly easy to connect your trigger to an SLR because SLRs already have trigger ports—you just have to build adapters to make the connection work. But most P&S cameras do not come with any trigger ports at all. Fortunately, it is possible to modify most P&S cameras so that you can connect any wired triggers you build. On most P&S cameras, the shutter button is simply a circuit closure switch, so it is a straightforward task to wire a trigger interface to the button circuit.

In this section I demonstrate how to interface to the shutter button on my Sony DSC-P92 digital camera. The modification will be presented on a conceptual level so that you can apply it to any P&S camera.

Cross-Reference Chapter 16 covers in detail how to take the Sony DSC-P92 case apart, so refer to that chapter before getting started.

Parts You Need

Here are the parts you will need to complete this project:

- $^3/_{32}$" Submini Phone Jack (274-245)
- Wires

The $^3/_{32}$" (2.5mm) sub-mini phone jack is the standard trigger port on the entry-level Canon EOS SLRs. The earlier projects in this chapter use this interface because it is common and easy to find the parts. In this project you again use this connector.

Tools You Need

Here are the tools you will need to complete this project:

- #1 Phillips precision screwdriver
- Digital multimeter
- Soldering iron
- 0.032" diameter 60/40 Standard Rosin-Core Solder (64-009E)
- Drill
- Drill bit
- Drill gauge

The Sony DSC-P92 case has four tiny machine screws that must be unfastened with your #1 Phillips precision screwdriver. After getting inside the camera and finding the shutter button's wire and connector, you use the digital multimeter to determine the pin-out. Then you use the soldering iron and solder to add your own trigger port.

Taking the Camera Apart

Follow the instructions presented in Chapter 16 to take apart the Sony DSC-P92. If you are working with another camera, take care to find all the screws you need to remove. When you take the case apart, make sure you do so slowly and avoid breaking any ribbon cables. Surface mount ribbon cables in today's digital camera are nearly impossible to fix at home.

1. After taking the back cover off, remove the ribbon cable connector that links the back cover and the circuit board (see Figure 1-27).

FIGURE 1-27: The ribbon cable connectors on the bottom of the Sony DSC-P92

2. Notice that there is another smaller ribbon cable connector. Remove that as well, using either a small flat blade screwdriver or your fingernails.

3. Next, look at the top of the digital camera, where the power button and the shutter button are located (see Figure 1-28). Note that two tabs are securing the circuit board in the picture—one tab is above the shutter button and the other to the left.

FIGURE 1-28: Two tabs are around the shutter button.

4. Pull those tabs slightly, and the circuit board will come loose.

5. With the circuit board freed from the tabs, separate the circuit board and camera internals from the front cover as shown in Figure 1-29.

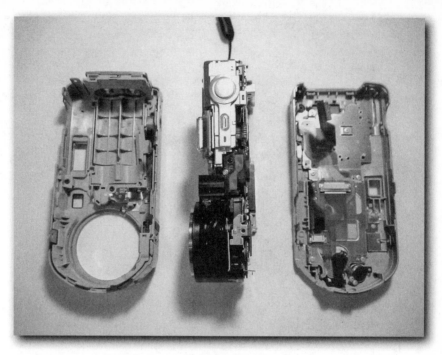

FIGURE 1-29: The camera internals separated from the front and back cover

Looking for the Shutter Switch

With the camera internals separated from the front and back cover, look for the shutter button and examine how it is attached to the camera. On the Sony DSC-P92 digital camera, the shutter button is attached to the camera's internal frame by a tab, as shown in Figure 1-30. Another tab is on the other side, but after you free the tab you see in the Figure 1-31, the whole shutter button panel comes loose.

FIGURE 1-30: The shutter button panel is held to the camera internal by two tabs. One tab is shown in this picture; the second tab is on the other side.

Free the tab to remove the shutter button panel, as shown in Figure 1-31. Don't pull it off just yet because the panel is attached to the circuit board by an orange ribbon cable to the left. If you pull the panel off hastily, you might break that cable, and it is nearly impossible to repair.

Note also in Figure 1-31 that the flash capacitor is beneath the shutter button panel. It is still charged with very high voltage. Notice that the capacitor leads are on the right, protruding from the circuit board. Don't touch them or you might get a nasty surprise. I did accidentally touch both pins with my right thumb once. It gave my thumb a little shock that felt like a numbing vibration.

Tip Use electrical tape to cover the two leads while you are working on the camera to prevent accidental electrical shock.

FIGURE 1-31: The shutter button panel freed to reveal the flash capacitor

Shown from the other side, the ribbon cable connector looks like Figure 1-32. Use a small flat-head screwdriver or your fingernails to pry the ribbon cable connector loose and detach the shutter button panel.

Determining the Shutter Button Pins

Figure 1-33 shows the shutter button panel detached from the camera. The ribbon cable is sticking out on the bottom left. The orange portion of the ribbon cable is the insulated section, while the silver leads are actually electrical contacts. The power button has one position, and the shutter button has two positions. So altogether there are three switches on this button panel, which matches the number of electrical contacts as well—considering that each switch requires two wires.

FIGURE 1-32: The shutter button panel and its ribbon cable connector

You need to use a digital multimeter to determine which electrical contacts are associated with each button. You need a friend for this task—one of you probes the electrical contacts, while the other person pushes down one of the buttons. Turn the digital multimeter on and set it up to measure resistance (ohms). Press and hold one of the buttons. Make sure you test each of the two positions on the shutter button separately.

Place the positive and negative test leads on two different electrical contacts. Try different combinations of electrical contacts until you see zero resistance (a closed circuit). The two contacts that showed the zero resistance are the right contacts for the button that was pressed. On the Sony DSC-P92 digital camera, the shutter button is associated with the third and fifth contacts (counting from the left in Figure 1-33).

Soldering the Trigger Interface

After you have determined the pins for different button functions, you need to solder the 2.5mm ($^3/_{32}$") stereo jack to the pins. The best way is to first solder thin wires onto the pins, and then solder the wires to the stereo jack. Because the contact pins are extremely small and thin, soldering wires to it is a multi-step process. Start by heating the contact pin. Then flow a tiny bulb of solder onto the contact pin. Be careful that you don't heat the adjacent pins or short them out by flowing solder onto them.

FIGURE **1-33: The button panel is detached from the camera.**

Next, tin the thin wire (see the instructions in Appendix A). Heat the thin wire and use it to transfer heat to the tiny bulb of solder. When both the soldering bulb and wire are heated, the solder melts, flowing onto the thin wire. Remove the soldering iron. When the solder cools to a solid form, an electrical contact is made.

Tip Use wires that are long enough for you to locate the stereo jack wherever you want on the camera body. The following section discusses wire length in more detail.

Strip the other end of the wire. Insert the un-insulated wire end through the contact pin on the 2.5mm stereo jack. Make sure the wire is connected to the correct pin (refer to the "Canon E3 Connector" sidebar for the correct connection). Wrap the wire around so that it is temporarily secured on the pin, as shown in Figure 1-34. While the wire is still secure on the pin, use the soldering iron to apply heat to the wire and the contact pin at the same time. Place the end of the solder wire on the wire and the contact. When they get hot enough, the solder melts and flows onto both the wire and the contact. Remove the soldering iron. When the solder cools down, the connection is complete.

FIGURE 1-34: The exposed wire wrapped on the contact pin

Perform this step for each of the Canon E3 connector functions: shutter trigger and auto-focus. If the camera doesn't have auto-focus capability, you can ignore this step.

Modifying the Camera Case

In this step, you want to mount the 2.5mm stereo jack on the camera itself, if possible. The advantages of mounting the trigger jack securely are, first, that it is convenient to access and, second, that there are no loose wires that could break as a result of wear and tear. But it's not always possible to mount the stereo jack on the camera. With today's miniaturization of digital cameras, the internal electronics are already crammed in a very small package. In this situation, where your camera is already crammed with parts, all you can do is drill a tiny hole for the wires to pass through and dangle the trigger port outside. Tie the wires into a knot on both side of the hole to prevent excess wear and tear on the camera internals (see Figure 1-35).

Tip   You can also twist the wires together into a braid, as shown in Figure 1-36. When two wires are braided together, the result is called a twisted-pair. The advantage is that when the wires are braided together, they become more durable.

FIGURE 1-35: Wires tied into a knot

However, if you manage to find space to mount the stereo jack on your camera, make sure the jack still fits when a stereo plug is inserted into it. Once you're satisfied that your plan will work, use a drill gauge to determine the diameter of the stereo jack. Drill a hole in the camera case just slightly bigger than the stereo jack. The stereo jack is secured from the outside with a bolt. Make sure you don't drill a hole that is bigger than the bolt. After drilling the hole, insert the stereo jack through the hole from inside the camera body. Secure it with the bolt from the outside, as shown in Figure 1-36.

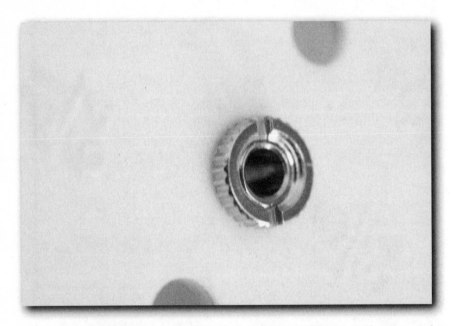

FIGURE 1-36: Secure the stereo jack with the bolt supplied. In this picture, the stereo jack was secured to the drill gauge. But the idea applies to the camera body as well.

Reassembling the Camera

When you reassemble the camera, route the wires around so they won't be crushed. Crushed wires have the potential to deteriorate and short out over time. Route them so they won't get caught and interfere with the camera's operation. Put the camera back together in the reverse order used to take it apart. Don't forget to plug in all the ribbon cables that you unplugged.

Extending the Remote Switch

The wired remote trigger switches you can buy from the manufacturers have a fairly short wire. It might be anywhere from three feet to, at most, six feet long. And unless you had a particular need in mind when you built your own trigger switch, you probably built one with a fairly short cable as well.

Sometimes you'll wish the trigger switch had a longer cable. You might want a longer cable because you want to shoot some self-portraits. Figure 1-37 is a self-portrait that I shot years ago using a homemade extended cable. Running back and forth between the scene and the camera can be extremely inconvenient, especially if the scene is far away. You might want to shoot wildlife. Some wild animals are very sensitive to the presence of humans. By setting up the camera in a remote location, you won't scare them away. Or you might want to take pictures of a hazardous environment, where your physical presence could be a danger to your life. It's better to wire up a remotely triggered camera than to put your life in danger.

FIGURE 1-37: A self-portrait shot with an extended cable. Did you spot the cable? If I hadn't pointed it out, you probably would have never noticed it.

If you have followed the instructions in this chapter and built a remote trigger and interface based on the simple 2.5mm or 3.5mm stereo phone jack, you are in good shape. You can easily buy 3.5mm stereo extension cables at Radio Shack or even build them yourself. Converters for 2.5mm and 3.5mm stereo jacks are also readily available so you can easily convert them back and forth. Figure 1-38 shows these parts.

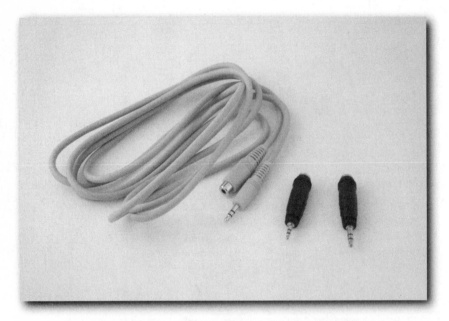

FIGURE 1-38: An extension cable, a 2.5mm to 3.5mm adapter, and a 3.5mm adapter to 2.5mm adapter

If you build your triggers using proprietary interfaces rather than a popular interface, I suggest you build stereo adapter cables for your proprietary trigger. That way you will be able to build your extension from over-the-counter parts. Otherwise, you will always have to build custom cables.

Adding a
Tripod Socket to
Your Camera

A camera mounted on a tripod is a great way to shoot pictures that you normally can't otherwise. With a tripod, you can steady the camera for long exposures, take group shots with yourself included, and shoot self-portraits. Many of today's cameras have a built-in tripod socket. The tripod socket is basically a screw thread on the bottom of the camera that attaches to tripod heads. Figure 2-1 shows an example of a tripod socket.

Every once in a while, you'll find a camera that does not have a tripod socket. Maybe the manufacturer wanted to keep design costs down, maybe the targeted demographic rarely uses tripods, or maybe the camera is too small to include a tripod socket. Generally, the ultra simple and the ultra small cameras lack a tripod socket.

My wife has a Sony Cyber-shot DSC-U30. It's an extremely small digital camera that fits in her purse, and she carries it everywhere. It even has a convex mirror in front of its shell to aid her in taking self-portraits. Sometimes, I want to attach a tabletop tripod to it. Unfortunately, as you can see in Figure 2-2, this small digital camera doesn't have a tripod socket.

FIGURE 2-1: The tripod socket is just a screw thread.

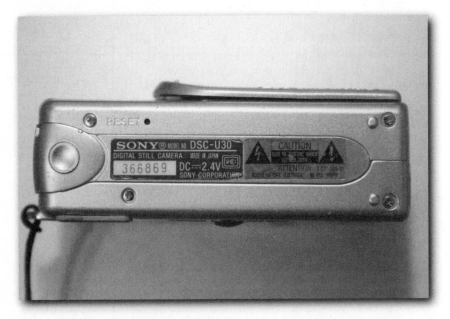

FIGURE 2-2: The Sony DSC-U30 has the tripod socket location marked on its shell
(the circle on the left is sized perfectly for a tripod socket). But for some reason, Sony
decided not to implement it.

In this chapter, you learn how to attach a tripod socket to your camera. This project uses the Sony DSC-U30 digital camera, but the same concept is applicable to any camera.

Parts You Need

Here are the parts you will need to complete this project:

- ¼"-20 nuts (2)
- A scrap wooden board

Reading Bolt Size

There are two standards for specifying bolts size: SAE and metric. These two standards cannot be interchanged. In both standards, the bolts size is based on diameter, thread pitch, and length. The SAE standard specifies these bolt properties in inches. The thread pitch is specified as number of threads per inch. The metric standard, on the other hand, specifies bolt properties in millimeters. The thread pitch is specified as distance between threads in millimeters. Figure 2-3 illustrates the differences in these standards.

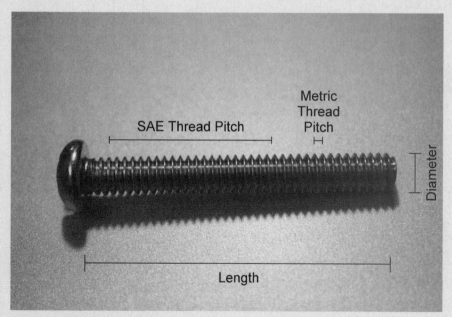

FIGURE 2-3: Bolt measurements

Continued

Continued

An SAE ¼-20 × 2 bolt is ¼" in diameter, has 20 threads per inch, and is 2" long. A metric M8 - 1.25 × 16 bolt is 8mm in diameter, has a thread pitch of 1.25mm, and is 16mm long.

Generally, the SAE standard is used in the United States, while the metric standard is used everywhere else. Because camera technology has advanced all around the world, and de facto standards have been set using both standards, you will encounter both standards in your hacks.

These are basic home improvement parts that you probably have lying around at home, or you can find them at your local home improvement store. The tripod socket is a standard ¼"-20 screw thread. Any ¼"-20 nut can be screwed into a tripod head. A bag of these nuts costs no more than a dollar or two.

The size of the wood piece you need depends on the size of your camera base. A scrap of wood is most likely enough for this project. Find a piece of wood that is slightly bigger than the base of your camera. Your camera is not extremely heavy, so a heavy, sturdy piece of wood is not necessary. Heavy wood is a little harder to work with and overkill for this project. General-purpose wood that is fairly light is a good choice because it's cheap and abundant. Avoid extremely soft wood, such as balsa.

Tools You Need

Here are the tools you will need to complete this project

- Drill
- ¹/₂" drill bit
- Ruler
- Saw
- Sandpaper
- ¹/₄"-20 machine screw
- C-clamps
- Alligator clamp
- 5-minute general-purpose epoxy
- Cardboard
- Toothpick

Manual hand drills, which used to be popular and inexpensive 10 to 20 years ago, are hard to find today. Fortunately, electric drills are now extremely inexpensive and make drilling a lot faster. A ¹/₂" drill bit is needed to drill the hole for the tripod socket nuts (see Figure 2-4).

Generally, a drill bit set doesn't include the ½" drill bit, and a ½" drill bit by itself can cost as much as one of those drill bit sets. An alternative is to use a ½" speed bore, which costs only a few dollars.

FIGURE 2-4: The ¼"-20 nut has an external dimension of ½" as shown in this measurement tool.

For this project, you need some basic home improvement tools. A simple wood saw works just fine. Choose a saw with small teeth. Because of the small size of your wood piece, even a hacksaw works.

Sandpaper is not necessary, but it makes the wood feel nice and smooth. Sanding the wood helps prevent splinters in the fingers.

Assembly

The following sections guide you through the steps required to make your tripod socket.

Making the Tripod Socket

Before you start working on the tripod socket base, start making the tripod socket. It takes some time to dry, during which time you can make the base. Screw two ¼"-20 nuts onto a

$\frac{1}{4}$"-20 machine screw. Keep the two nuts firmly touching each other but not so tight that they are locked (see Figure 2-5). Adjust the two nuts so that they are still touching, but rotate them freely as a unit.

FIGURE 2-5: Screw the two nuts onto the machine screw. Keep the two nuts firmly touching each other but not so tight that they are locked.

Follow the instructions on the adhesive label. For epoxy, squeeze the two chemicals from the plastic syringe onto a disposable piece of cardboard. Mix the two chemicals together with the toothpick. Dab the epoxy on the seam between the two nuts, but don't glue the nuts to the machine screw. (The machine screw is used only to keep the threads aligned.) Set the nuts and machine screw aside to dry.

Measuring the Base of the Camera

While the tripod socket is drying, you can move on to measure the base of the camera. The camera base will determine the dimensions of the wood base you need to cut to support the weight of the camera when it is attached to the tripod head. The measurement need not be exact. As you can see in Figure 2-6, a basic ruler is all you need for this measurement. The Sony DSC-U30 has an 8cm × 2.5cm base.

Your tripod socket is going to be a pair of $\frac{1}{4}$"-20 nuts stacked on top of each other. The pair of nuts stacked together has a height of $\frac{3}{8}$". The wood piece should be at least $\frac{1}{2}$" in height because it should be taller than the pair of nuts.

FIGURE 2-6: A basic ruler will be sufficient for measuring the camera's base. Note that this camera has a reset button on the bottom.

Cutting the New Base

Mark the dimensions of the camera base on the wood board. Start the cut by pulling the saw toward you a few times. When a notch has been started, use both backward and forward motions to saw the wood. When you are working with a small scrap of wood, alligator clamps and C-clamps can help you hold the wood in position, as shown in Figure 2-7.

A Simpler Method of Adding a Tripod Socket

If you don't need a flat base on the bottom of your camera, you can glue the ¼"-20 nuts directly to the base of your camera (see Figure 2-8). This simpler method allows you to add a tripod socket to your small camera quickly. You can even arrange multiple nuts on the base of your camera so that the camera can sit flat on the table without tipping over.

Don't perform this simple hack if you have a large, heavy camera—there is not enough surface area on the nut to support your larger camera. You may risk the camera and tripod socket's breaking apart, resulting in a long drop for your gear. Take the time to build the proper wooden base instead.

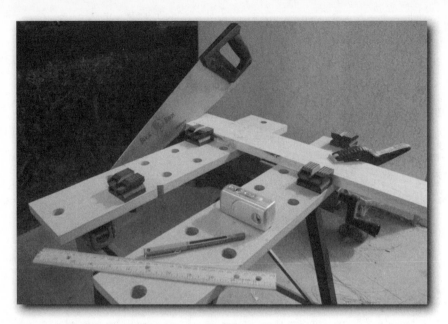

FIGURE 2-7: Cutting the base for the new tripod socket

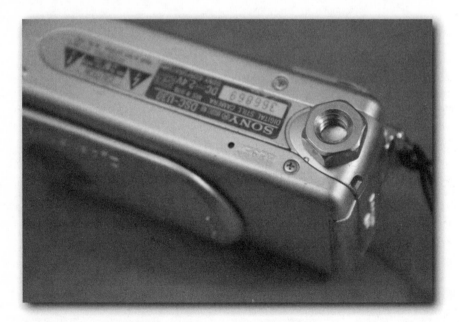

FIGURE 2-8: A nut glued directly to the base of the Sony DSC-U30

Placing the Socket Directly Under the Lens

The intersection of the lens axis and the sensor plane (see Figure 2-9) is the preferred location for the center of the tripod socket. By placing the center of the tripod socket at this location, the lens axis and sensor plane lie on the center of rotation. You can use the camera to shoot very precise panoramic shots by simply rotating the camera on the tripod. But it is not necessary to place the tripod socket at this preferred location if you rarely shoot panorama pictures or if you don't mind a little warping in your panorama shots.

It is easy to tell where the lens axis is located, because you can see the lens. If you draw an imaginary line down the center of the lens vertically, the imaginary line is the lens axis (see Figure 2-9). Unfortunately, it is not easy to determine the film/sensor plane. To determine the plane, you'll have to take the camera apart and make some measurements. But it's a lot of work. Unless you are an avid panorama photographer, there is not a whole lot of value in getting the exact measurement of the sensor plane. So make some guesses to where it is located. The center of the camera is a fairly good guess.

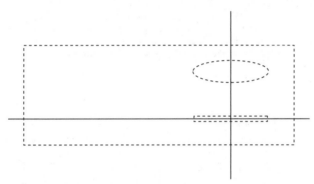

FIGURE 2-9: The preferred tripod socket location is at the intersection of the lens axis and the film/sensor plane.

Drilling the Hole for the Socket Screw

Once you have determined where to place the tripod socket, make measurements on the wood base and mark the center. Use the $1/2$" drill bit to drill a hole deep enough for the tripod socket you made earlier. The two nuts glued together are about $3/8$" in height. Use the $1/2$" drill bit to drill a hole that is just deep enough for the socket. I didn't have a $1/2$" drill bit, so I used a $1/2$" speed bore, as shown in Figure 2-10.

Tip   If you drilled too deep, add flat washers to compensate.

FIGURE 2-10: Drill the hole just deep enough for the pair of nuts.

Caution

When you drill, be sure to drill on a disposable surface. Even though you are not drilling through the wood base entirely, things can go wrong. Be sure to clamp the wood piece down with C-clamps. Don't try to hold it with your hand —you don't want to take the chance of mangling your hands around the fast-spinning drill bit.

Remember the camera reset location while you were measuring the camera base? This is a good time to drill an access hole for the reset. A smaller $1/16$" drill bit is a good candidate for this particular camera.

Gluing the Tripod Socket into the Wood Base

By the time you get to this step, the glue on your tripod socket should be set. Figure 2-11 shows the finished socket. Test the fit of the tripod socket in the wood base. Make sure the socket is flush with the wood when placed in the hole. If the tripod socket doesn't fit because there is too much glue around the seam of the nuts, use sandpaper to sand away the glue.

When you are satisfied with the test fit, glue the socket to the wood base with the Epoxy that you used earlier. You'll want to fill as much of the space between the socket and the wood as you can, but be careful that you do not get any glue on the screw thread. If you do, you may have to start from scratch. Figure 2-12 shows the base with the tripod socket glued in.

FIGURE 2-11: Two nuts glued on top of each other. I also added a flat washer to make up the difference in space.

FIGURE 2-12: The wooden tripod socket base is now formed.

Gluing the Wood Base to the Camera

This is the last step in the process. Use the same epoxy as you've been using to glue the wood base to the bottom of the camera. Make sure that the tripod socket surface is not the side glued to the camera. And make sure that when glued, the tripod socket is at the preferred location or another location that you have chosen.

Manufacturers generally affix product labels to the bottom of the cameras. The product label may include the model name, serial number, and other technical information. Before gluing the wood base onto your camera, make a copy of this label.

When the glue has dried, generally within 15 minutes to half-an-hour with the 5 minute epoxy, you are ready to use your camera with a tripod, as shown in Figure 2-13.

FIGURE 2-13: The Sony DSC-U30 and wooden tripod socket base mounted on a tabletop tripod

Detachable Tripod Socket

Don't want to modify your camera permanently? You can attach the wood base to the bottom of the camera with Velcro (see Figure 2-14). Velcro tape can be found easily in many local stores. Apply the Velcro to the camera and the wood base to create a detachable tripod socket. When you don't need to use the tripod, you can quickly remove the tripod socket to return your camera to its original size. The Velcro can even serve as tripod quick release. I suggest applying Velcro to the entire wood base surface, as it would serve to hold the camera securely on the tripod.

FIGURE 2-14: The tripod socket base secured with Velcro is also useful as a tripod quick release.

Accessing Raw Sensor Data

JPEG is the most popular image file format today, and nearly all of today's digital cameras support it. Although JPEG is sufficient for most purposes and does its job well for home use, it's not the most optimal format. When the JPEG standard was defined, the Joint Photographic Experts Group (JPEG) committee concentrated on specifying a format small enough for efficient network transmission. To keep the image size small and still reproduce the original image as well as possible, the JPEG encoder design utilizes a *lossy* compression algorithm that throws away image data that are nearly too subtle to be noticed. This algorithm is very good—you generally can't tell the difference between the original image and the JPEG encoded image. But this data loss is irreversible. The more you load and save a JPEG image, the more deterioration you may see in the image. Eventually, the JPEG image becomes lousy.

Tip When you modify a JPEG image, save your modified image using a lossless file format, such as TIFF, to preserve all data.

Figure 3-1 shows an example of a highly compressed JPEG image. The high compression used this picture shows clearly that the image data is manipulated and lost permanently during JPEG encoding. In normal JPEG compression setting, you won't see corruption to this level but only because the loss is subtle enough that your eyes won't register it. However, this picture demonstrates that data are lost when you use JPEG compression. Figure 3-2 shows the original lossless picture for comparison.

Note The specification for the JPEG format actually included lossy and lossless algorithms. However, the lossless algorithm performed poorly at compressing images, so the lossless algorithm is rarely implemented or talked about. No digital cameras today implement the lossless JPEG algorithm.

This chapter explains why you should consider using a lossless image format or the raw format (if your camera supports it) for your precious originals. On some digital cameras, the manufacturers do not provide raw images to end-users. This chapter shows you how to enable raw mode on some of those digital cameras, and it also points out free software for processing raw files and how to use it.

FIGURE 3-1: A highly compressed JPEG image

FIGURE 3-2: A lossless image

Understanding Unconverted Real Sensor Data

Some digital cameras, especially professional ones, support a file format called *raw*. The raw file format is lossless and actually contains the data generated by the digital sensor in its native form. Because the data is native to a digital sensor, every raw data file is unique to a specific sensor model in a specific digital camera model. Thus, to see the data as an image on your computer screen, special software is needed to convert raw images to a universally viewable format. The software is specifically designed to convert raw data from one or more distinct sensors to a universal image format such as JPEG or TIFF. Generally, the manufacturer that produced the raw-supporting digital camera will provide the conversion software.

Tip   Raw data is coupled tightly with the imager sensor. It's possible that in the future the conversion software could become obsolete. It's better to convert the raw file into a popular lossless file format such as TIFF and then archive both files.

There are some disadvantages to using the raw format, such as having to go through conversion software prior to working with the actual digital picture. Converting the raw file to a universal image format could take some time. In fact, it could take several minutes on some computers. JPEG is a good compressor because it eliminates subtle data. Using a lossless image format means you can't throw away any data, which translates to bigger file sizes. Plus, you now have two files to deal with: a raw file and a universal image format file.

The disadvantages of using raw format make the workflow time consuming and troublesome compared to workflows where the camera generates JPEGs or TIFFs directly. But there are actually a lot of benefits to using raw data files:

1. The data is directly generated from the digital sensor and is not manipulated.

2. You might want to process the raw data one way today, and then process it another way tomorrow. For example, you can re-process the raw data to change the white balance.

3. Years down the road, someone may invent a better raw processing algorithm that makes your original image even better.

4. Data in raw files are read-only; you can't accidentally save different sets of image data in raw files.

All digital cameras support the raw data internally. After all, the digital sensor has to capture the raw data before the digital camera can process it to generate the final format.

Unfortunately, many consumer digital cameras do not provide the raw data to the user. On some consumer-level digital cameras, raw mode can be enabled through diagnostic software or through hidden menus.

Digital Sensors

The sensor in your digital camera is made up of many tiny photosites. A 2 megapixel digital sensor has 2 million photosites. Each photosite is capable of gathering light to form a pixel of the final image. However, each photosite only has the capacity to gather the intensity of light, not its color.

In order to reproduce color images, a RGB (red, green, and blue) color filter is laid on top of the digital sensor. This RGB filter turns each photosite into a specific color pixel. For example, a blue photosite will only be able to capture light in the blue spectrum. When a picture has been taken on this color sensor, the digital camera uses an interpolation algorithm on the special arrangement of RGB pixels to derive a full color image.

There are currently two popular types of digital sensors: CCD and CMOS. The CCD sensor has had a long successful history. Because of its performance and reliability, it's been the heavyweight of the industry for the past thirty years. In recent years, the popularity of the CMOS sensor has increased. This trend is due to increases in performance, reduction in cost, and reduction in power consumption. Canon has been the sole driver in making CMOS sensor a viable solution through the amount of research and development they put into their professional digital cameras.

The division of CCD and CMOS sensors has separated the digital camera industry into two segments. Currently, the CCD sensor is used in the higher-performance, higher-cost, and lower-volume segment. The CMOS sensor is used in the lower-performance, lower-cost, and higher-volume segment.

CCD and CMOS digital sensors are both manufactured in silicon foundries. Multiple sensors are formed on a silicon wafer through etching of tiny circuits and devices. Then the silicon wafer is cut apart into individual digital sensors. But that's where the similarity ends. The main difference between CCD and CMOS involves their manufacturing process.

CCD Sensor

Bell Labs invented the Charge-Coupled Device (CCD) in late 1969. Its original intent was to use CCD technology as a new type of computer memory. At the same time, Bell Labs was designing a video telephone. CCD turned out to be the perfect technology for imaging applications. In 1970, Bell Labs produced the world's first solid-stat video camera using CCD technology. Five years later, Bell Lab's CCD sensor was powerful enough for broadcast television.

In a CCD camera sensor, the photosite is arranged into rows and columns in a rectangular area. Each photosite is composed of a photodiode and an electron charge holder. The photodiode converts light into charge. The amount of electron charge generated is proportional to the intensity of light.

After data is captured on the sensor as electrical charges, the camera reads the image data out one row at a time. The first row on the sensor is possibly designated as the readout register, meaning it is the row for the camera to obtain data. Once the camera obtains the data in the readout register, the data in every row moves down one row. After the data has shifted down a row, the camera reads the next row of data off the readout register. The process repeats until all data has been extracted from the sensor. The charge-coupled device (CCD) terminology is based on the concept that each row of data is coupled to the next row. When one row shifts down, the charges in next row shift down as well.

When the charge packets for each row are extracted, the packets are sensed by a charge-to-voltage conversion and passed to an amplifier circuit. The image produced through this optimized architecture contains little noise.

To manufacture CCD sensors, camera manufacturers have to build a foundry that uses a specialized and expensive process. This process can be used only to make CCDs and no other electronic component. Therefore, the cost of building the foundry can't be shared with other developments. In turn, the manufacturing process forces CCD imaging sensors to be costly.

Technically it is possible to use the CCD manufacturing process to integrate other camera functions on the same chip as the photosites. These functions may be clock drivers, timing logic, and signal processing circuits. However, because of the low-noise optimization architecture, it is not economical to perform such integration. Instead, to lower the cost of manufacturing, these functions are located on separate chips. Therefore, CCD cameras often contain three to eight integrated circuit chips.

The number of integrated circuit chips required to operate a CCD camera translates into higher energy consumption and increases the overall system size. Increasing the number of photosites, or the surface area of the sensor, to increase resolution means the CCD sensor would require much larger power supplies and make it even more expensive to produce.

CMOS Sensor

Complementary Metal Oxide Semiconductor (CMOS) is the most common chip-producing process in the world. Chip manufacturers make millions of CMOS chips for computer processors and memory. Because manufacturers can use the same process and the same equipment to manufacturer microprocessors, memory, and sensors, this process cuts costs dramatically; the cost of building the foundry is spread over a large number of possible devices. As a result, the production of a CMOS wafer costs three times less than the production of a CCD wafer.

In a CMOS camera sensor, the photosite is arranged into rows and columns in a rectangular area. Each photosite is composed of a photodiode, an electron charge holder, a charge-to-voltage converter, and an amplifier circuit. The photodiode converts light into charge. The amount of electron charge generated is proportional to the intensity of light. A grid of circuits is laid under the photosites, connecting to each photosite for direct access. In contrast to a CCD sensor, the CMOS sensor's architecture is arranged more like a random access memory cell.

Continued

Continued

Unlike a CCD sensor, it is practical to incorporate other circuits on the same CMOS sensor chip, eliminating the requirement for separate processing chips. This allows additional on-chip features, such as image stabilization and image compression, to be included at little extra cost. Overall, the camera can be made smaller, lighter, and cheaper. The CMOS sensor also requires less power to operate, so batteries can be smaller.

While CMOS sensors are fully capable of capturing sunny outdoor pictures, they suffer in low-light conditions. Their sensitivity to light is low because a large part of each photosite is used up by circuitry that performs other functions, rather than gathering light. The area of a photosite devoted to collecting light versus the area devoted to other tasks is called the fill factor. CCD sensors have a 100% fill factor (because processing circuits are in separate chips) but CMOS sensors have a lower fill factor. Because of this lower fill factor, the sensor is less suitable for low-light photography.

Obviously, one method to overcome this deficiency in the CMOS sensor is simply reducing the amount of features added to each photosite. However, this would eliminate the benefits of using a CMOS sensor. To retain the advantages of these features, a micro-lens can be added to each photosite. The micro-lens could cover the entire photosite area to gather light. The light can than be redirected through the lens to the actual photodiode of the photosite.

Data generated by CMOS sensors have more noise than data generated by CCD sensors. Therefore, CMOS sensors are aided by digital signal processing (DSP) to reduce or eliminate the noise. Because of the additional time necessary to perform this signal processing, the processing time for each picture could be much longer than the time necessary to process a picture generated by a CCD sensor.

Canon developed the architecture of the EOS D30 with a CMOS sensor instead of a CCD sensor. The CMOS sensor technology is attractive for its low-power requirements, as well as its ability to integrate with image-processing circuits. However, during development, a few engineering obstacles remained, including problems with the precision of internal transistors. In the end, Canon overcame these obstacles and succeeded with their development of a CMOS sensor-based digital SLR.

Enabling Raw Mode on Nikon COOLPIX

Nikon COOLPIX 950, shown in Figure 3-3, was one of the first digital cameras capable of serious digital photography. Features that allowed this include a swivel body so that pictures can be shot even from inconvenient angles, full manual mode for adjusting aperture and shutter speed, and a macro mode with a very small minimum focus distance at the telephoto setting. Since its inception, COOLPIX 950 has become a classic and Nikon is very successful with its entire line of COOLPIX digital cameras.

FIGURE 3-3: Nikon COOLPIX 950

Despite these powerful capabilities, the earlier COOLPIX digital cameras could not provide users with raw data files. Instead, these early COOLPIX digital cameras stored images in lossless TIFF or lossy JPEG format. Even so, these early COOLPIX digital cameras have the capability to store raw files through a hack that is widely spread on the Internet. You can enable the hack by changing the camera ID through Open Source software called PHOTOPC.

Note *Open Source* is free software, and the source code is available to the public. Through the Open Source license, anyone is allowed to make improvements to the software and redistribute it as Open Source. The goal of Open Source is to encourage users to make improvements to the free software for everyone's benefit.

This hack is known to work with Nikon E700, E800, E950, E990, E995, E2500, E4300, and E4500 digital cameras. (The *E* in the model name is interchangeable with the word *COOLPIX*.) This list of models comes from online reports by people who have tried the hack with their digital camera. It's possible that this hack works with other COOLPIX digital cameras that haven't been reported. Some recent COOLPIXs support raw data files natively and may not work with this hack.

Tip To enable raw mode for COOLPIX 2100, 3100, and 3700, you need to download a special firmware on the web. This section might not be applicable to these three cameras.

The instructions in the rest of this section refer to Nikon COOLPIX 950. Although some minor details will be different if your COOLPIX is not a 950, those differences shouldn't stop the hack from working.

Getting the Software

PHOTOPC is available on SourceForge, a service for remote development and distribution of software. The PHOTOPC software is available for DOS, Windows, and Linux. The URL is http://sourceforge.net/projects/photopc.

This section explains how to download, compile, and install PHOTOPC version 3.05. By the time you read this chapter, a newer version may be released, but the steps will most likely be the same. If you have a more recent version, substitute your version number whenever you see 3.05.

DOS and Windows

The PHOTOPC executable is already compiled for DOS and Windows. All you have to do is download the ZIP file. A ZIP file is a compressed archive containing numerous files. If you have Windows XP, you can view the contents of the downloaded ZIP file with Windows Explorer and pull out the photopc.exe file from the win32 directory. You can also download a free UNZIP utility from www.info-zip.org/ to unzip the archive. For DOS, use photopc.exe in the dos directory.

Linux

On Linux systems, you can download either the ZIP file or the TAR/GZ file. The recent Linux operating system comes with built-in utilities to handle both. Use the unzip command to unpack ZIP files. Use the tar command to unpack TAR/GZ files. In the following example (the commands you type are in bold), I downloaded the archive into a directory called home (I used dir to show the contents of the directory). Then I issued the tar command to unpack the archive.

```
[chieh@penguin home]$ dir
total 132
drwxr-xr-x   2     4096 Mar 11 00:28 ./
drwxr-xr-x  20     4096 Mar 11 00:28 ../
-rw-r--r--   1   122687 Mar 10 23:58 photopc-3.05.tar.gz
[chieh@penguin home]$ tar xvzf photopc-3.05.tar.gz
```

Compiling the Software on Linux

The PHOTOPC package does not come with precompiled executables for Linux. Therefore, you will have to compile it yourself. It's actually quite easy, because PHOTOPC comes with automated configuration and compilation scripts to do all the work for you. Once you have unpacked the archive, change into the directory that was created with the cd command:

```
[chieh@penguin home]$ cd photopc-3.05
```

Next, issue the following two commands to configure and compile the source code:

```
[chieh@penguin photopc-3.05]$ configure
[chieh@penguin photopc-3.05]$ make
```

Command Prompt

The command prompt is a text-based interface that enables you to communicate with your computer. As the name implies, the text interface allows you to issue commands to the computer. The computer will perform the command and respond to your requests. Through the command prompt you can also check the status of and get more information about your computer. What you can do through the command prompt depends on the commands you issue. Although most users would rather deal with the graphical user interface (GUI), the command prompt is a powerful tool to get direct access to the core of the operating system.

Mac OS

Starting with Mac OS X, Apple's Macintosh operating system is based on Berkeley Standard Distribution (BSD) UNIX. UNIX is a very powerful operating system and has been around for a long time, dating back to 1969. One reason it is so powerful is its command prompt, called *shell*. Mac OS X inherited many BSD UNIX features, including the command prompt that was lacking in previous Macintosh operating systems. Some computer users considered a Macintosh a toy because of the lack of a command prompt. Now, with the UNIX shell built into Mac OS X, the Macintosh is no longer just a toy.

You can reach the shell on Mac OS X, and many variant UNIX systems, through the Terminal application, shown in Figure 3-4. To find the Terminal application in Mac OS X, open the Application folder, and then open the Utilities folder. Double-click the Terminal icon to start the application.

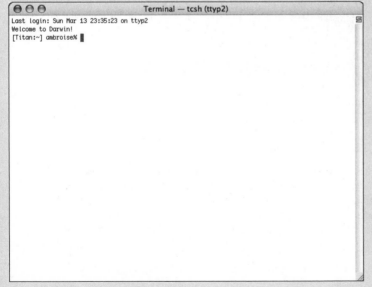

FIGURE 3-4: The Terminal application

Continued

Continued

Windows

Windows is probably best known for its graphical user interface (GUI). Most users are familiar with it and do most of their work in it. Lesser known to most users is the Windows Command Prompt, shown in Figure 3-5, a command-line user interface based on the original DOS. To access the command prompt in Windows, click the Start menu, and then select Programs, Accessories, and Command Prompt. To quit the command prompt, type **exit** at the prompt.

FIGURE 3-5: The Windows XP command prompt. Command prompts for other operating systems are similar.

After the system finishes compiling the PHOTOPC source code, it will have created an executable in the `photopc-3.05` directory called `PHOTOPC`. At this point, you are ready to use it to modify your digital camera.

Setting Raw Diagnostics Mode

During the development of COOLPIX digital cameras, Nikon developers added a raw diagnostics mode. In this mode, COOLPIX stores the raw data file in addition to the regular JPEG or TIFF file whenever the picture is taken. The developers used this raw file for debugging and testing COOLPIX digital cameras.

To enable raw diagnostics mode, connect your Nikon COOLPIX to your computer with the interface cable provided with your camera. My COOLPIX 950 came with a serial cable, shown in Figure 3-6. Your digital camera might also interface with the PC through a serial cable, but if you have a new digital camera, chances are that it interfaces through a USB cable. See your digital camera's instruction manual for more specific details on how to connect it to the computer.

With your digital camera connected to your computer, type the following command at the command prompt:

```
photopc id "DIAG RAW"
```

FIGURE 3-6: The Nikon COOLPIX 950 digital camera connected to the PC through a serial cable

Whenever you want to disable raw diagnostics mode, simply connect your digital camera to the computer again and type the following command:

```
photopc id "NIKON DIGITAL CAMERA"
```

Capturing Raw Files

In raw diagnostics mode, whenever you shoot a picture, the digital camera creates two files sequentially. Both files have the same extension (JPG or TIF, depending on which format you picked). However, the first file is the raw data file and is neither a standard TIF file nor a standard JPG file. Figure 3-7 shows an example of two pictures I shot, one in TIFF mode, the other in JPEG mode. The 2,408KB files are the raw data files. I'll explain more about processing these raw data files in the next section. For now, you should rename the raw data file extension to something more meaningful, such as "RAW."

Name ▲	Size
DSCN0037.TIF	2,408 KB
DSCN0038.TIF	5,633 KB
DSCN0039.JPG	2,408 KB
DSCN0040.JPG	620 KB

FIGURE 3-7: RAW, TIFF, and JPEG files

Watch Out for Side-Effects

Because the raw diagnostics mode is not intended for use by consumers, Nikon developers did not implement protection algorithms for raw mode. Although the side effects are annoying during operation, they are harmless and will not destroy your equipment.

Number of Pictures

In raw diagnostics mode, COOLPIX does not check and make sure that there is enough storage space for raw files before committing a write to the memory card. Therefore, don't use up your memory card completely. Stop on the last image. If you forget, the COOLPIX camera tries to write the RAW file and the image file to the card, which does not have enough space. The camera displays the "System Error" message on the LCD, as shown in Figure 3-8, and displays "Err" on the indicator screen, as shown in Figure 3-9.

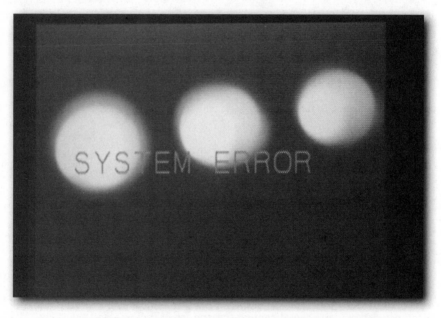

FIGURE 3-8: "System Error" message superimposed on the last picture you shot

If your COOLPIX ever gets into this system error state, the only way to reset the camera is to turn it off and back on. The space on the memory card cannot be reclaimed until you format the memory card either in the digital camera or in your computer's memory card reader. But before you format, remember to download all of the pictures that you shot.

Turning off the Camera during Write

After you shoot a picture, because the raw file is almost 2.5 megabytes in size, it takes awhile for the Nikon COOLPIX 950 to write the two captured image files to memory. If you forget that the camera is still writing and turn it off, the raw file is written, but the second JPG or TIF file is lost.

FIGURE 3-9: "Err" displayed on the indicator screen

FILE CONTAINS NO IMAGE DATA Message

While reviewing the pictures on the LCD, Nikon COOLPIX 950 cannot show the raw files. Instead, it displays the "FILE CONTAINS NO IMAGE DATA" message on the screen.

Nikon COOLPIX 950 Firmware

Before I enabled the raw mode on my COOLPIX 950, I upgraded the firmware from version 1.2 to version 1.3. You can see the firmware version that is installed on your COOLPIX 950 by holding down the MENU button while turning on the camera. I suggest you upgrade to the latest firmware to ensure that your digital camera has the latest features and bug fixes. The latest firmware version is available on Nikon's web site.

Nikon's web site does not allow you to download previous versions (such as 1.0, 1.1, or 1.2), so if you have already downloaded a previous version, you might want to keep it in a safe location. You might have to revert to an older version if there's a bug in the latest version.

I didn't have a copy of the older firmware when I upgraded, so when an obscure problem showed up after I installed the new firmware, I wasn't sure if it was a problem before or after I upgraded. If I had the older firmware, I could have reinstalled it for testing.

Continued

Continued

Once you have downloaded the firmware from Nikon's web site, extract the `firmware.bin` file. This firmware file must be placed in the root directory of a CompactFlash card. I suggest you copy the file to your CompactFlash card through a memory card reader connected to your computer. With the firmware on the CompactFlash card, plug the card into the camera and turn it on. The COOLPIX 950 digital camera asks whether you would like to upgrade the firmware, as shown in Figure 3-10.

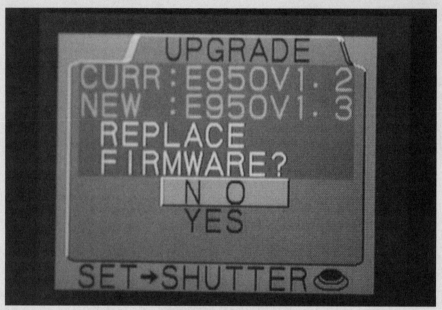

FIGURE 3-10: The firmware upgrade confirmation screen

Move the selection to YES with the up or down arrow, and then press the shutter button to accept. The digital camera will display the screen shown in Figure 3-11 and then attempt to update the firmware. Do not turn off the camera, pull the CompactFlash card out, or push any camera buttons during this firmware re-write process. You could render your camera inoperable if you do, which may require that you send it back to a Nikon Service Center. In fact, I suggest that you leave the camera alone on a table by itself during this process. Writing the firmware to the camera can take a few minutes; be patient.

When the camera completes its firmware upgrade process, it displays the screen shown in Figure 3-12. At this point, you can pick up the camera and press any button to acknowledge the message. I suggest formatting the CompactFlash card at this point, because if you turn the camera off and then on with the firmware still on the memory card, the camera will ask you whether you want to update the firmware again.

FIGURE 3-11: The camera displays this screen while it is writing the firmware to memory.

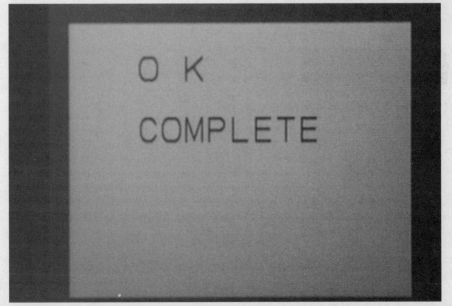

FIGURE 3-12: The camera displays the "OK COMPLETE" message when it finishes updating the firmware.

Continued

Continued

After updating the firmware, you can check the version number again. It should display the new firmware's version number, as shown in Figure 3-13.

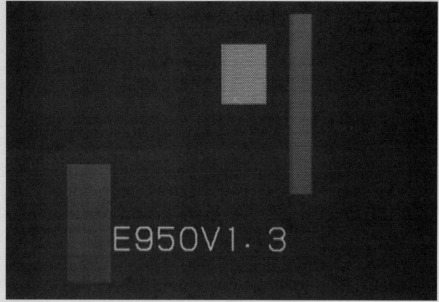

FIGURE 3-13: The firmware version screen showing the updated firmware version number

Enabling Raw Mode on Casio Digital Cameras

The Casio digital cameras have secret diagnostic modes that can be activated through its menu system. Once enabled, these digital cameras generate raw dumps of the CCD sensor data. These data are straight dumps with no compression and no encoding.

The steps outlined in this section are for the following Casio digital camera models: QV-2000UX, QV-3000EX, QV-3500EX, QV-4000, QV-4000EX, QV-5700, Exilim P600, Exilim P700, and Exilim EX-Z55. The procedures and model list are gathered from online reports generated by users who have tried the hack with their cameras. Other Casio camera models might work with one or more of these procedures, but be aware that the procedure may have to be changed slightly for those cameras.

Enabling Raw Mode on QV-2000UX, QV-3000EX, QV-4000, and QV-5700 Digital Cameras

Follow these steps:

1. Turn off your camera.

2. Hold down the MENU and DISP buttons simultaneously, and turn the camera on by switching to REC mode.

3. Release the two buttons you held down during power-up.

4. Quickly press and release the TIMER button two times, and then press the MENU "button to open MENU3. If you can't get to MENU3, try pressing the button sequence faster.

5. MENU3 has three screens. Each screen is designated by 1/3, 2/3, or 3/3. Use the 4-way switch on the back of the camera to navigate to the second screen (2/3).

6. Select BAYER CAPTURE from the menu with the shutter button. This action enables raw mode.

Once you've enabled raw mode, you can take picture as normal. Where the raw file is stored depends on the digital camera model:

- On QV-2000UX, the raw data is written to the NOCOMP.BAY file, overwriting any previous NOCOMP.BAY files in the same directory. This means that you have to retrieve the raw data after every image.

- On QV-3000EX, the raw data is written to the NOCOMP.BAY file, overwriting any previous NOCOMP.BAY files in the same directory. This means that you have to retrieve the raw data after every image. If the picture is the first photo taken, the NOCOMP.BAY file "is stored in the root directory. Otherwise, the file is located in the same directory as the JPEG file.

Caution
Deleting the NOCOMP.BAY file and folder containing the file on the QV-3000EX digital camera will corrupt the memory card. Instead, the file and folder should be deleted only through a memory card reader on your computer.

- On QV-4000, the raw data is stored in KXnnnnnn.RAW, where n is a digit assigned by the camera.

- On QV-5700, the raw data is stored in ddhhmmnn.BAY, where dd is the date, hh is the hour, mm is the minute, and n is a digit assigned by the camera. The files are located in the root directory.

Enabling Raw Mode on QV-3500EX

Follow these steps:

1. Turn off your camera.

2. Hold down the MENU and SHIFT buttons simultaneously, and turn the camera on by switching to REC mode.

3. Release the two buttons you held down during power-up.

4. Quickly press and release the TIMER button two times, and then press the MENU button to open MENU3. If you can't get to MENU3, try pressing the button sequence faster.

5. MENU3 has three screens. Each screen is designated by 1/3, 2/3, or 3/3. Use the 4-way switch on the back of the camera to navigate to the second screen (2/3).

6. Select the BAYER CAPTURE from the menu with the shutter button. This action enables the raw mode.

Once you've enabled the raw mode, you can take pictures as normal. The raw data is written to the NOCOMP.BAY file, overwriting any previous NOCOMP.BAY file in the same directory. This means that you have to retrieve the raw data after every image. If the picture is the first photo taken, the NOCOMP.BAY file is stored in the root directory. Otherwise, the file is located in the same directory as the JPEG file.

 Deleting the NOCOMP.BAY file and folder containing the file on the camera will corrupt the memory card. Instead, the file and folder should be deleted only through a memory card reader on your computer.

Enabling Raw Mode on Exilim P600, Exilim P700, and Exilim EX-Z55

Follow these steps:

1. Turn off your camera.

2. Hold down the MENU and DISP buttons simultaneously, and turn the camera on. It should display a black and white information screen.

3. Release the two buttons you held down during power-up.

4. Push right on the 4-way controller two or more times.

5. Press the MENU button.

6. Navigate to the IMAGE FLAG selection with the 4-way controller.

7. In the IMAGE FLAG menu, turn the BAYER MODE selection to On.

Once you have enabled the raw mode, you can take picture as normal. Where the raw file is stored depends on the digital camera model:

- On Exilim P600, the raw data is stored in CIMGnnnn.RAW, where n is a digit assigned by the camera.
- On Exilim P700 and Exilim EX-Z55, the raw data is stored in nnnnCIMG.RAW, where n is a digit assigned by the camera.

Decoding Raw Files

As mentioned in the introductory section, you have to use special raw conversion software to convert your raw file into another image file format. I call this specialized software the *raw decoding software*. Like all companies manufacturing computer peripherals, digital camera manufacturers tend to produce raw decoding software for the most popular consumer operating systems, such as Windows. Sometimes, they even produce a raw decoder for the second most popular consumer operating system: Mac OS. But if you run any other operating systems, you're out of luck.

When I was working on my Linux server, I found a free universal raw decoder. This raw decoder works with raw files generated by many different digital camera brands. It is also available as source code so that it can be compiled for any operating system (as long as you have the compilation tools and you can understand C code). Compiled versions for Windows and Mac OS also exist. This decoder is called "dcraw" and has been incorporated into many professional graphics applications, such as Adobe Photoshop and BreezeBrowser.

Although this little decoder utility does not have a fancy, friendly, GUI, it does provide an extremely powerful advantage: a command-line interface. The command-line interface allows you to specify raw files to process with masks. But most important of all, the command-line interface allows you to program batch scripts to perform automations that are not possible with a GUI-based decoder.

Getting the Decoder Software

Finding the dcraw decoder software on the Internet is easy. Search for the term *dcraw* with any search engine, such as Google or Yahoo. The search engine will return tons of results. As of this writing, the web page that contains the software from the original author is located at www.cybercom.net/~dcoffin/dcraw/.

Download the dcraw.c file. The .c extension indicates a C source code file. The source code cannot be executed until it has been converted into an executable file (covered in the following section). If you don't feel comfortable with compiling source code, compiled binary executable versions for Windows and Mac OS are available at www.insflug.org/raw/.

Compiled executables are not available for Linux, so you'll have to compile it yourself. The good news is that Linux generally comes preinstalled with the compiler, so it should be a piece of cake to compile dcraw. (See "Compiling the Decoder for Linux," later in this chapter.)

Creating the Decoder Executable for DOS and Windows

After downloading the source code, and if you're feeling adventurous, you can try to compile the source code yourself. If you're already an experienced computer programmer, you can already build the executable without following the instructions provided in this section. This section is written for intermediate computer users who may not be programmers.

Obtaining a Compiler for DOS and Windows

Although DOS and Windows don't come with compilers, there is tons of support for these two popular operating systems. One free C/C++ compiler that you can download from the Internet is DJGPP. DJGPP is a complete C/C++ compiler that is capable of producing executables for DOS and Windows running on Intel 80386 and better personal computers. The programs you write with DJGPP can be distributed without license or royalty to the producer of DJGPP. DJGPP can be downloaded from www.delorie.com/djgpp/.

By answering a few questions on the web site's DJGPP Zip File Picker, you'll be presented with a list of packages to download and directions for installation. In the picker, make sure you select "Build and run programs with DJGPP." Then select the C and C++ checkboxes. Follow the instructions provided by the picker to install the packages. I was able to get DJGPP running by installing just the Basic Development Kit, basic assembler, linker, basic GCC compiler, C++ compiler, and Make packages.

Acquiring the JPEG Library

Before you can compile the dcraw source code, you'll have to download and compile the JPEG library. A library is a package of precompiled source code modules. In the case of the JPEG library, the package contains modules to perform JPEG compression. A free library for JPEG image compression can be downloaded from the Independent JPEG Group at http://www.ijg.org/.

After downloading the JPEG library, extract the content using the unzip utility supplied with DJGPP, the built-in unzip feature in Windows, or your own unzip utility. The unzip utility should have placed all of the contents into a directory called jpeg-6b. Change to this directory (see the "Useful DOS Commands" sidebar later in this chapter) and issue these two commands from the command-line:

```
copy jconfig.dj jconfig.h
copy makefile.dj makefile
```

These two commands configure the JPEG library so that it can be compiled with DJGPP. Each command simply copies a file specifically written for the DJGPP compiler with the correct name recognizable by the compiler. With the JPEG library configured, issue the following three commands to start the build:

```
set PATH=c:\djgpp\bin;%PATH%
set DJGPP=c:\djgpp\djgpp.env
make
```

These three commands set up the DJGPP compiler for a build. The make command reads the two files you copied previously to build the JPEG library. During the build, you'll see quite a few lines of text scroll down the screen. When that's done, the command prompt will return. The result is shown in Figure 3-14.

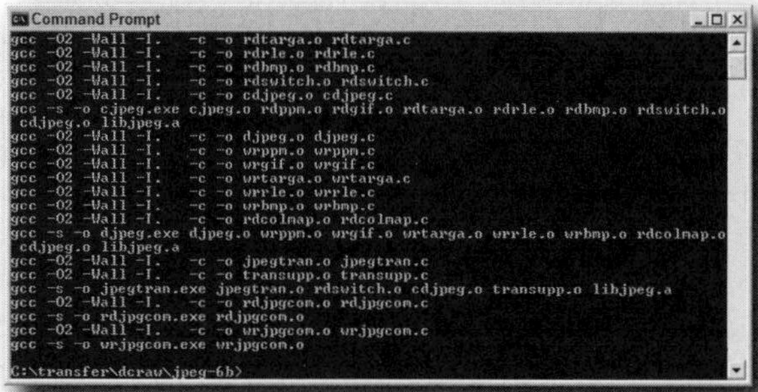

FIGURE 3-14: The command prompt returns after the build is complete.

After building the JPEG library, you'll have to install the necessary include and library files into the DJGPP include and library directories. Issue the following commands to copy the four include files and one library file into the DJGPP installation location:

```
copy jpeglib.h \djgpp\include
copy jerror.h \djgpp\include
copy jconfig.h \djgpp\include
copy jmorecfg.h \djgpp\include
copy libjpeg.a \djgpp\lib
```

After the files are copied, you're ready to compile the dcraw executable.

Compiling the Decoder for DOS and Windows

After all that work, building the dcraw executable is easy. All you have to do is to change into the directory containing the `dcraw.c` file. From that directory, issue the following command to compile the source code into the executable file:

```
gcc -o dcraw -O3 dcraw.c -lm -ljpeg
```

When the prompt returns, the compiler has built the dcraw executable. You should see a `dcraw.exe` file in your current directory. That's it! Now you're ready to give dcraw a try. See "Running the Decoder" later in this chapter to continue your journey.

Useful DOS Commands

The Windows command prompt is based on the original DOS text interface. DOS stands for Disk Operating System and is one of the early operating systems for IBM PCs. The Windows command prompt still recognizes most of the original DOS commands. The command prompt can look quite daunting, but it just takes a little familiarity with frequently used commands to get comfortable with it. This sidebar explains these frequently used commands. The commands are shown in uppercase, but DOS is case-insensitive, which means you can use lowercase as well.

Continued

Continued

Change Directory: CD

Most operating system storage structures are based on directories and files. (Sometimes the term *directory* is used interchangeably with *folder*.) The directories and files are organized in a tree-like structure. Each *parent* directory can contain multiple files and additional directories (child or sub-directories). The single top-most directory is called the *root* directory. To change to a sub-directory, issue the following command:

```
CD "directory name"
```

The double quotes are not mandatory unless the directory name contains one or more spaces. To change to the parent directory, issue the following command:

```
CD ..
```

You can change to the root directory by typing the following command:

```
CD \
```

After issuing the CD command, your current directory will always change to the directory you specify, unless you type the command or directory name incorrectly. Issue the CD command by itself to see the current directory. The command prompt shown in Figure 3-15 shows the execution of this command.

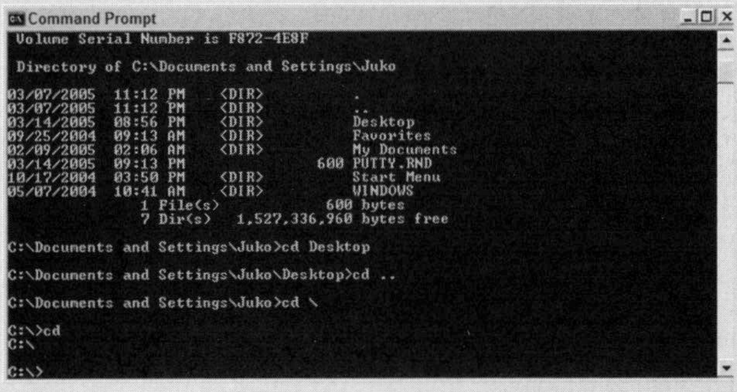

FIGURE 3-15: Executing the CD command

Directory Listing: DIR

The directory listing command will show you all the directories and files in the current directory. In the listing (see Figure 3-16), the single dot is always the current directory. The double dot is always the parent directory. A line with the string <DIR> means that entry is a child directory. A line with a number by the name indicates a file.

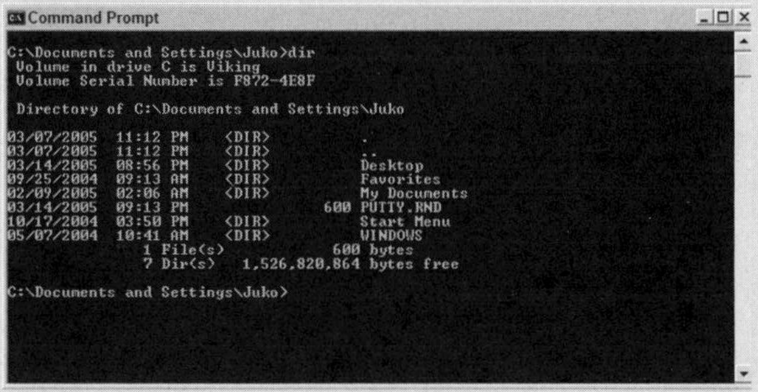

FIGURE 3-16: Executing the DIR command

Delete File: DEL

The delete file command allows you to eliminate one or more files from your system (see Figure 3-17). You can't remove directories with this command (see the Remove Directory command for this). To remove a file, type the following command:

```
DEL "file name"
```

The file name must include the full name and extension (letters after the period). Double quotes are not mandatory unless the file name contains one or more spaces.

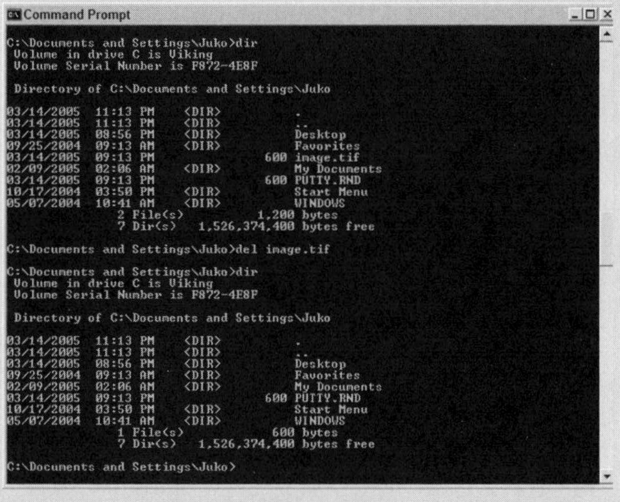

FIGURE 3-17: Executing the DEL command

Continued

Continued

Make Directory: MD

The make directory command helps you create new directories in your system (see Figure 3-18). Change to any directory where you want to create the new directory, and then issue the following command:

```
MD "directory name"
```

Double quotes are not mandatory unless the file name contains one or more spaces. Figure 3-21 shows the MD command being executed.

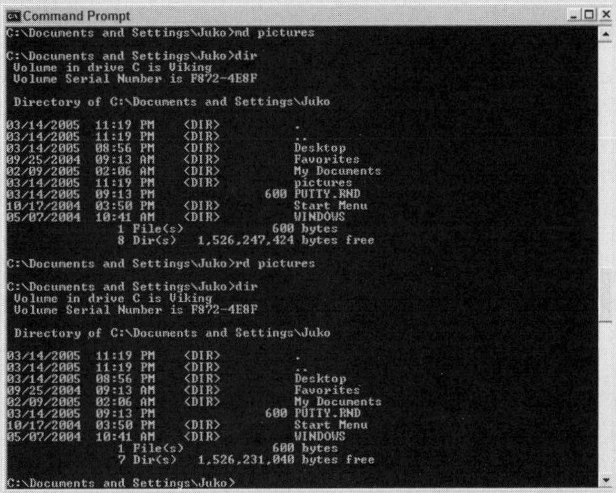

FIGURE 3-18: Executing the MD and RD command

Remove Directory: RD

The remove directory command allows you to eliminate folders from your system. The directory must be empty (no files or child directories). To remove the directory, issue the following command:

```
RD "directory name"
```

The directory name must include the full name and extension (letters after the period). Double quotes surrounding the directory name are not mandatory unless the directory name contains one or more spaces. Refer to Figure 3-18 to see the RD command in action.

Compiling the Decoder for Linux

The Linux operating system is like a Swiss Army knife—it is loaded with built-in tools. All you have to do is choose to install these tools when you install the operating system. If you installed everything from your Linux distribution, then you already have the compiler tool needed to compile the dcraw source code. If not, refer to your Linux documentation to learn how to install the compiler.

With the compiler installed, change to the directory where you have placed the dcraw.c file. Then type the following command to compile dcraw into an executable binary:

```
gcc -o dcraw -O3 dcraw.c -lm -ljpeg
```

This command generates a file called dcraw, which is the binary executable. You can run it by typing **dcraw** on the command-line.

Useful UNIX Shell Commands

The UNIX shell is the command-line interface built into Linux and Mac OS X. The shell is similar to the DOS and Windows command prompt, but it is much more powerful. As a result of its strength, the command-line interface is even more daunting than the DOS and the Windows command prompt. But it just takes a little familiarity with frequently used commands to get comfortable with it. This sidebar explains these frequently used commands. The UNIX shell is case-sensitive. Therefore, cases for file names, directory names, and commands must match exactly. Otherwise, you will get an error.

Change Directory: chdir or cd

Most operating system storage structures are based on directories and files. (Sometimes the term *directory* is used interchangeably with *folder*.) The directories and files are organized in a tree-like structure. Each *parent* directory can contain multiple files and additional directories (child or sub-directories). The single top-most directory is called the *root* directory.

In older UNIX shells, chdir is the command for changing directories. In the new Linux BASH (Bourne-Again SHell), cd is the built-in change directory command. To change to a sub-directory, issue the following command:

```
chdir "directory name"
```

The double quote is not mandatory unless the directory name contains one or more spaces. To change to the parent directory, issue the following command:

```
chdir ..
```

To change to the root directory, issue the following command:

```
chdir /
```

Continued

Continued

After issuing the `chdir` command, your current directory will always change to the directory you specify, unless you type the command or directory name incorrectly. Issuing the `chdir` command by itself changes the current directory to your home directory. The Command Prompt in Figure 3-19 shows the execution of this command.

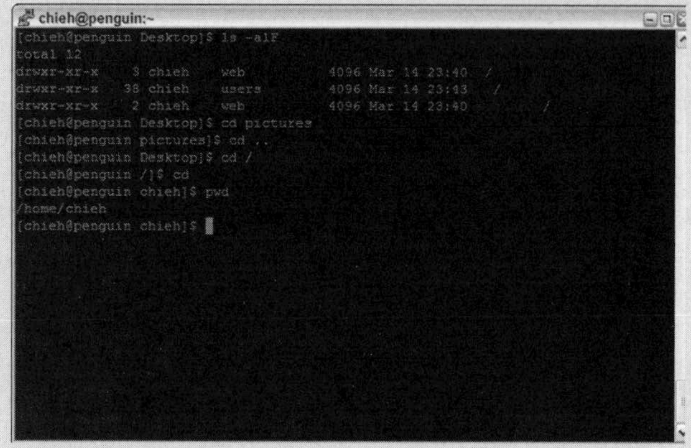

FIGURE 3-19: Executing the chdir, ls, and pwd commands

Current Directory: pwd

The shell command for displaying the current directory is `pwd` (see Figure 3-19). This command does not accept any arguments.

List Directory Contents: ls

The list directory content command shows you all directories and files in the current directory. In the listing (see Figure 3-19), the single dot is always the current directory. The double dot is always the parent directory. A slash behind the file name means that entry is a directory.

The `ls` command has many different options. See the on-line manual command later in this sidebar for details on the `ls` options.

Remove File: rm

The remove file command allows you to eliminate one or more files from your system (see Figure 3-20). You can't remove directories with this command; use the remove directory command instead. To remove a file, type the following command:

```
rm "file name"
```

The file name must include the full name and extension (letters after the period). Double quotes are not mandatory unless the file name contains one or more spaces.

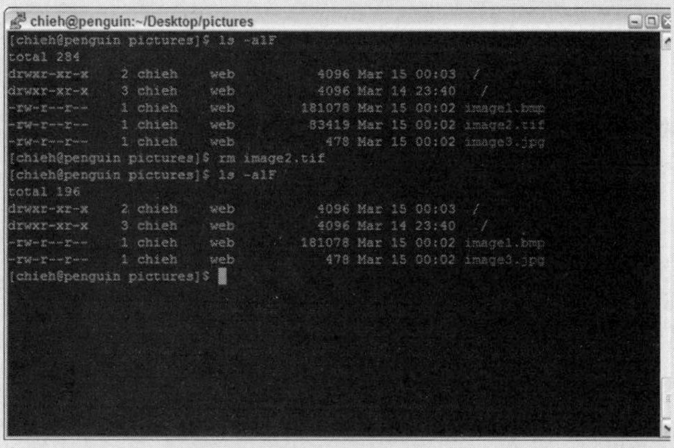

FIGURE 3-20: Executing the rm command

Make Directory: mkdir

The make directory command helps you create new directory in your system (see Figure 3-21). Change into any directory where you want to create the new directory, and then issue the following command:

```
mkdir "directory name"
```

Double quotes are not mandatory unless the file name contains one or more spaces. Figure 3-21 shows the mkdir command being executed.

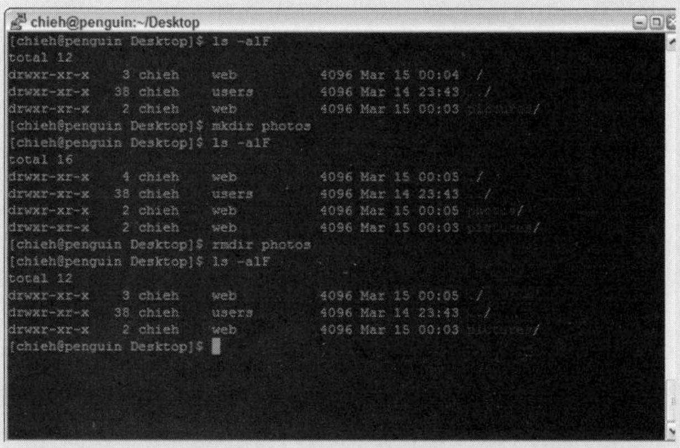

FIGURE 3-21: Executing the mkdir and rmdir commands

Continued

Continued

Remove Directory: rmdir

The remove directory command allows you to eliminate folders from your system. The directory must be empty (no files or child directories). To remove the directory, issue the following command:

```
rmdir "directory name"
```

The directory name must include the full name and extension (letters after the period). Double quotes surrounding the directory name are not mandatory unless the directory name contains one or more spaces. Refer to Figure 3-21 to see the `rmdir` command in action.

On-Line Manual: man

One really neat feature of the UNIX shell is that you can pull up the manual for any command by issuing the `man` command. The syntax is as follows:

```
man command_name
```

Shell commands do not have spaces in them, so there are no double quotes around the name. The underscore signifies that no spaces are allowed. You can even pull up the on-line manual for the `man` command by issuing:

```
man man
```

Running the Decoder

It's easy to run the decoder, especially if you place the decoder software in the path of your operating system, because you can then run it from anywhere. Please refer to your operating system reference manual to find out how to change the path environmental variable or how to place the dcraw file into the path. To decode a raw file, type the following on the command line:

dcraw "file name"

The double quotes are mandatory if any spaces are in the file name. For example, to process one of the raw files generated by my Canon EOS Digital Rebel camera, I would issue the following command:

```
dcraw CRW_8584.CRW
```

In this case, dcraw would quietly produce a file named CRW_8584.ppm. The letters "ppm" stand for Portable Pixel Map, which is a lossless image format like TIFF. Most decent image manipulation software, such as Adobe Photoshop and Paint Shop Pro, can read PPM format.

Wild Cards

You can run dcraw on each raw image. But that sort of defeats the purpose and power of a command-line interface. The true power comes into play when you start using wild cards (or *file masks* to be more technically correct) to specify the files to process. You may have shot 200 pictures at your friend's wedding, so picking each one to process would be tedious and time-consuming.

You may have to do something like that through a GUI, but with dcraw, you can issue a command such as:

```
dcraw *.CRW
```

This simple yet extremely powerful command would activate dcraw to process all of the raw files in the current directory. The * means match zero or more characters. In the *.CRW pattern, it means match any file names with zero or more characters in front of the .CRW extension. With this little command, you can process all 200 pictures at once! Each of the 200 pictures is stored with an associated file name, each having the .ppm extension. Figure 3-22 displays a list of unprocessed raw images. Figure 3-23 shows the same list after all images have been processed.

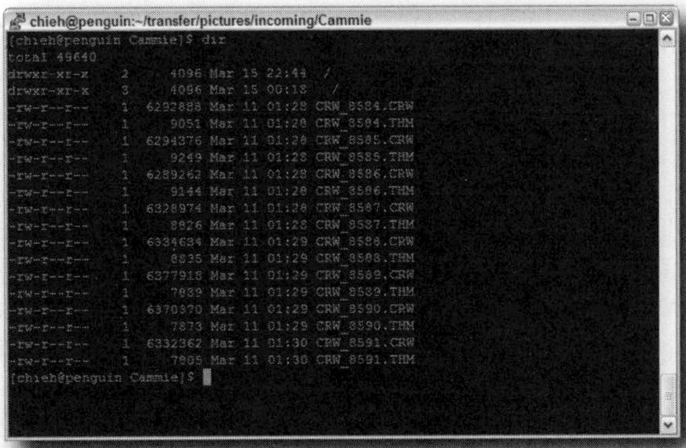

FIGURE 3-22: A list of unprocessed images

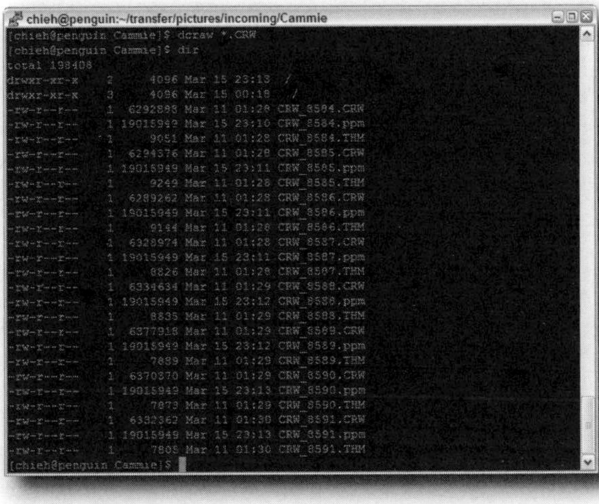

FIGURE 3-23: The new file list after running dcraw on all of the raw images

You might not be impressed just yet. You might say you can do that with your GUI as well. Select the first picture, hold down shift, and select the last picture. Now you can process all two hundred pictures at once as well. Then I'll ask: What if you want to process every picture with the digit 5 in its file name? You'll have to select each file one at a time if you use a GUI. But with command-line interface and dcraw, you can do that by issuing another simple command:

```
dcraw *5*.CRW
```

As an infomercial would say, "But that's not all!" In fact, you can specify with dcraw that you only want to process picture files where the digit 5 is located in the second to last character location prior to the extension. For example, you only want to process CRW_1050.CRW, CRW_1152.CRW, etc. You can do that with a second wild card, the question mark:

```
dcraw CRW_??5?.CRW
```

The preceding command processes every raw file with the digit 5 in the second to last character position prior to the .CRW extension. The ? means "match exactly one character."

Background Process

Now, if you've started processing your 200 wedding pictures with dcraw as I recommended in the previous section, you're probably twiddling your thumbs now, while waiting for dcraw to finish. It takes a long time to process 200 raw pictures with today's technology. But if you are running on Linux, or another UNIX-equivalent platform, you can place the task in the background. When you do, the task is executed, but you can still issue commands on the command prompt. To put tasks in the background, use the & character at the end of your command. For example, the following command will process in the background all of the raw files in the current directory:

```
dcraw *.CRW &
```

Automating the Decoder with Batch Processing

Using wild cards to specify multiple files for processing is very powerful. But there are still limitations. You can only process the files in the current directory. Most of the time, I like to sort my photos into their discrete directories prior to processing them. For example, Figure 3-24 shows a list of my photo folders sorted by event. You won't be able to use your GUI application or dcraw to process all of the raw files in all of the folders without manually selecting all the raw files in each directory. But with a command-line interface, dcraw, and a script (a program) you can easily process all of the raw files in all of the folders.

The following code is a simple shell script named ProcessRaw.sh that would allow you process all of the raw files in all of the subdirectories. It recursively enters each subdirectory and process all of the raw files in them. The script is *recursive* because it calls itself multiple times. When all of the directories have been visited, the recursion terminates. This script is very simple (only 12 lines), yet it demonstrates the power of the shell command-line interface. It's possible to write even more sophisticated scripts to accomplish more complex automation tasks. But I'll leave those up to you.

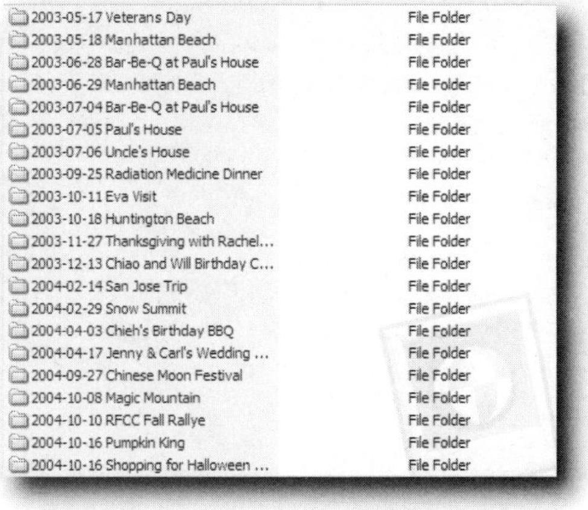

FIGURE 3-24: Directories containing my photos

```
#!/bin/sh

dcraw *.CRW

filelist=`ls -1`
for entry in $filelist
do
  if [ -d $entry ]
  then
    cd $entry
    ProcessRaw.sh
    cd ..
  fi
done
```

Hacking Power

There are several good reasons to hack the power source of your digital camera. First, you might want to photograph in extremely cold weather. In cold environments, batteries don't last as long as they do in warm environments. In extremely cold conditions, the batteries could die after only a few minutes. By hacking the power source interface to your camera, you can install a remote battery pack. With the remote battery pack under your jacket, close to your body, the batteries can last far longer in cold winter conditions.

A second reason for hacking the power source is that interfacing a larger battery pack to your digital camera means you can use it for prolonged periods. You may be able to shoot all day. Or if you are traveling through a tropical jungle with no power outlets, you can rig up a huge battery pack that would last for weeks of shooting.

Another reason for this hack is that by modifying the power source to your camera, you can increase its operational life as well. Over time, battery technology becomes obsolete as new technology replaces it. But whether new or old, batteries still provide a positive and a negative terminal, and batteries will always provide voltage and current. Only the physical form-factor changes. By adding the capability to interface new batteries that might not otherwise fit your old digital camera, you can prolong its life.

This chapter begins by showing you how to interface to your SLR and P&S digital camera. It then shows you how to make a portable battery pack and how to adapt other types of batteries for your camera's use.

Interfacing to SLRs

SLRs today generally use proprietary battery packs instead of standard size batteries, and some of them use proprietary AC adapters that plug into a proprietary battery port. Among cameras with this setup is the Canon EOS series of digital SLRs, and this chapter shows you how to interface to these proprietary types of cameras. I use my Canon EOS D30 as an example throughout.

Parts You Need

The following parts are available at Radio Shack. The numbers in parentheses are Radio Shack part numbers.

- DC power plug, size M, coaxial, male (274-1569)

- DC power plug, size M, coaxial, female (274-1577)

The DC power plugs are widely used on electronic devices and gadgets. Your portable walk-man or notebook computer probably uses these plugs to interface to power. Radio Shack specifies the plug sizes from letters A to Z. I picked size M because Radio Shack seems to have a bundle of these in every form-factor imaginable. But you can really pick any size you like, because they all do the same thing. Size M has an outer dimension of 5.5mm and an inner dimension of 2.1mm.

Tools You Need

Here are the tools you will need to complete this project

- Wire cutter

- Soldering iron

- 0.32" diameter standard 60/40 resin core solder

- Digital multimeter

Cross-Reference   See Appendix A for information on buying and using soldering irons.

This section shows you the pin-out for the Canon DR-400 power adapter cable for Canon EOS digital SLRs, so if you are modifying your Canon DR-400 power adapter cable, you won't need the digital multimeter. But if you are following this section as an example only and are modifying a proprietary power cable for another camera system, then you'll need a digital multimeter to determine which wire is tied to which contact after you cut the wires (see "Cutting the Cable" later in this chapter).

Canon DR-400 Pin-Out Diagram

The Canon DC Coupler DR-400 came with my Canon EOS D30 SLR. It is also the standard accessory cable for the recent EOS D60, 10D, and 20D SLRs. This equipment connects the digital camera body to the Canon Compact Power Adapter CA-PS400 (the dual BP-511 battery charger), which then connects to the AC outlet to power the camera. The DR-400 connects to the camera body via a fake BP-511 battery pack at one end of the cable (see Figure 4-1). Ever since I've had the D30 camera, I thought of hacking this cable to serve as an interface to portable power supplies. To do so, you need to understand the pin-out for all connectors and contacts.

Figure 4-2 shows the connector at the other end of the DR-400 cable. It connects to the Canon Compact Power Adapter CA-PS400. As you can see, it is a proprietary connector, one that I have never seen before. Therefore, it's practically impossible to source the female connector for it.

FIGURE 4-1: A proprietary AC adapter for the Canon EOS D30 that plugs into the battery port

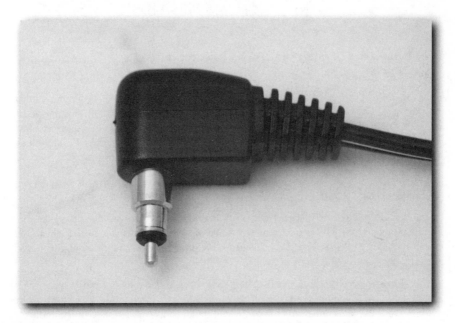

FIGURE 4-2: The connector at the end of the Canon DR-400 adapter cable

The fake BP-511 battery pack contains three contacts (D, -, and +); just one less contact than the real BP-511 battery pack (B, D, -, +). It was fairly easy to determine how the contacts and pins are associated, because Canon imprinted the pinout on the Canon Compact Power Adapter CA-PS400 (see Figure 4-3).

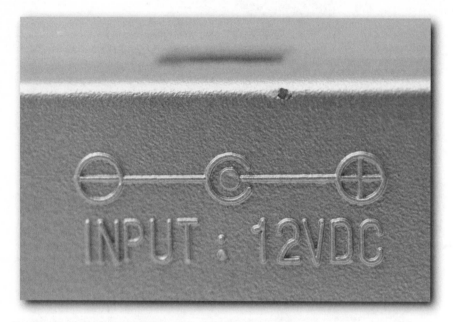

FIGURE 4-3: The polarity indication on a DC electronic device

As you can see from the picture, the middle pin is the positive (+) signal, while the outer contact is the negative (-) ground. However, the fake BP-511 battery pack contains one additional contact D. I used a digital multimeter to determine that this contact is also connected to the negative (-) ground contact. Contacts B and D are actually not used by the D30 digital camera nor the CA-PS400 battery charger. Therefore, I will ignore them for this project.

Cutting the Cable

The Canon DR-400 power adapter has a proprietary connector, so you need to splice the cable with the more common DC power connectors. You will be able to splice both male and female connectors into the cable so that the cable can serve dual functions: its original purpose and its new purpose.

The first thing you need to do is cut the cable so you can splice the connectors onto it. You might be reluctant (I was) to cut the cable, because it looks so well made. But know in comfort that after you splice the connectors onto it, it will look just as well made. Cut the cable close to the plug end so that the cable is still a decent length for remote power.

After cutting the cable, use the digital multimeter to determine which wire belongs to which polarity. I determined that the wire with the white strip belongs to the negative (–) ground polarity (which matches common electronic practice). So the black wire must belong to the positive (+) polarity.

Wiring the Connectors

Once you have determined the polarity on the wires, it's time to strip the wire and solder the DC power connectors to them. Solder the male DC power connector to the fake battery cable and solder the female DC power connector to the plug cable (see Figure 4-4).

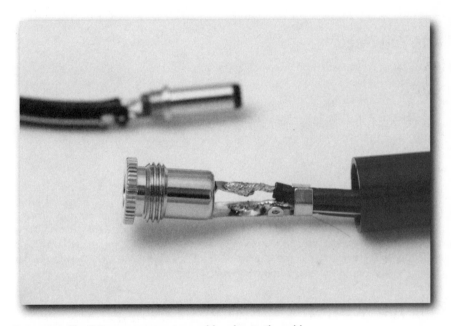

FIGURE 4-4: The DC power connectors soldered onto the cable

 See Appendix A for information about how to tin and solder.

When you solder the DC power connectors, follow the convention used by the original cable. For example, the positive polarity for the Canon DR-400 cable is the middle contact, and the negative polarity is the outer contact. By staying consistent in this manner, you prevent a potential mix-up, reverse-polarity, and frying your device.

Interfacing to Point-and-Shoot Digital Cameras

In this section, I explain how to interface external power sources to digital cameras that use standard AA-size batteries. You make fake AA-size batteries to insert into the battery compartment, drill a small hole in the cover to route the wires, and power the camera via an external power source.

Note   It's also possible to interface to digital cameras that use specialized batteries, though it would take more work on your part because you would have to disassemble the camera to find the power cables.

Parts You Need

Here are the parts you will need to complete this project:

- $^3/_8$" × 10' pex pipe
- $^1/_4$"-20 × 2" flat Phillips screw with nut
- Wires
- Electrical tape
- DC Power Plug, Size M, Coaxial, Male (274-1569)

I managed to find the pex pipe at the local hardware store. It's a white plastic pipe that is about the same diameter as an AA battery. It's sold in ten feet lengths for less than five dollars, so it is extremely affordable. After you cut the pex pipe down to size, threading the screw through it, and tightening it down with the nut, the pipe can act as a fake AA battery. You can solder wires to the screw and/or nut for external power source interfacing.

Tools You Need

Here are the tools you will need to complete this project:

- Wire cutter
- 16-gauge wire
- Soldering iron
- 0.32" diameter standard 60/40 resin core solder
- Hacksaw
- Vise

- Drill
- Drill bit

Making the Fake Battery

An AA battery is about 2" in length. The nut you're using is about $^3/_{16}$" in height, and the screw will stick out by about $^1/_8$", so if you cut the pex pipe to a length of $1^{11}/_{16}$", when you put it all together, the result will be the same length as a regular AA battery. .Stick the screw though the pex pipe and tighten it at the other end with the hex nut. And there you have it: a fake AA battery.

The screw is 2" in length plus the additional length added by the screw-head. You may need to trim off $^1/_8$" from the threaded end. You can do this by gripping the screw on a vise. Then use a hacksaw to cut the end of the screw.

You'll need to make two of these fake batteries for your camera, whether your camera uses two AA batteries or four. The camera cares only about the positive polarity and the negative polarity, which is what your power source has to supply through the fake batteries.

The wire you'll run from each of these fake batteries can be simply tightened down with the hex nut or soldered to the screw. If you solder it, I suggest you cut a small slit at one end of the pex pipe for routing the wire. Solder the wire somewhere in the middle of the screw rather than at an end. The ends will touch the camera's internal battery contacts, and if you solder the wire there, your fake battery will not fit properly. In most cases, you'll want to tape over one end of each battery with insulation tape (electrical tape works well) so that the fake batteries don't short out your power supply when they are installed in the camera.

Insert the two fake batteries into the digital camera and make sure they fit. Try closing the battery cover and make sure it closes. If the batteries don't fit, modify them so that they do.

Building the Connector

After making two fake batteries and adding wiring to them, you'll need to solder the wires to the DC power plug. It doesn't matter which wire is soldered to which contact on the DC power plug, because both fake batteries are exactly the same (unless you used different color wires or colored the fake batteries differently to differentiate the polarity). But after you solder on the DC power plug, mark the wires and the fake batteries so that you can tell which fake battery is which polarity.

Modifying the Camera

Now that the fake batteries are made and wired, it's time to see how you can modify the camera battery cover to route the wire. First insert the two batteries into the digital camera and determine the wiring location relative to the battery cover (see Figure 4-5). Look for non-critical locations (no electrical contact) on the cover. Pick one of the locations to cut a slit for the wiring to pass through.

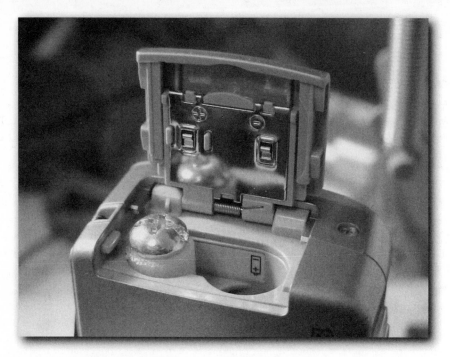

FIGURE 4-5: The fake battery inserted into the battery compartment

Making a Portable Battery Pack

A professional photographer's digital camera must have enough power to run for a full day in the field. Having a ton of battery packs to swap is one option for achieving this, but when you are being paid for your work, you can't take the chance that you'll miss an important shot while you are swapping out battery packs. A wedding photographer will never take the chance of running out of juice during the ring exchange. A portable battery pack that will last all day is the better option.

In this section, you make a simple portable battery pack for your digital camera. This battery pack has a universal interface so that, as you learn later in this chapter, you will be able to interface it to any camera you have. In fact, the idea behind this interface is so popular that you can even extend it to other non-camera electronic gadgets.

Parts You Need

Here are the parts you will need to complete this project:

- Battery pack
- Wires
- DC power plug, size M, coaxial, female (274-1577)

Using Standard-Size Batteries

The portable battery pack idea can be extended for use with standard-size batteries, such as AA alkaline batteries. Radio Shack sells battery holders of all sizes and 9-volt battery snap connectors (270-324). The battery holder and snap connector are shown in Figure 4-6. The snap connector leads will be used to interface to your camera later in this chapter.

FIGURE 4-6: A four AA battery holder and a 9-volt battery snap connector

All you have to do is determine the voltage your digital camera uses and then buy the battery holder that will supply enough voltage. Alkaline batteries provide 1.5 volts. Rechargeable batteries, such as NiCD and NiMH, provide 1.2 volts. Four alkaline batteries, connected in series, provide a total of 6 volts, while four rechargeable batteries provide 4.8 volts. Most digital cameras that can use AA size batteries can generally accept from 4.8 volts to 6 volts of power.

You can also do the same calculation in reverse. A digital camera that uses a specialized 7.2-volt battery can be modified to accept six AA size rechargeable batteries (7.2 divided by 1.2 equals 6).

For this project, you'll need to have a battery pack that can be either single-use or rechargeable, as long as it's small and portable. (If it's rechargeable, you'll need a battery charger for it as well.) You'll probably want to find a battery pack that is small and light enough that you can carry it in a camera pouch for your belt. The battery pack must match the voltage rating of your equipment. See the following sidebar, "Using Standard-Size Batteries," for calculating voltage.

Making an Adapter for a 7.2V RC Car Battery

The 7.2 volt battery used for radio control (RC) cars is perfect for hacking digital camera power because it provides the same voltage used with most digital cameras and camcorders. These battery packs use a special quick release connector, shown in Figure 4-7. Hobby stores and Radio Shack sell these connectors (23-444). Buy a pack to interface with your camera, and you'll be able to use any RC car battery as your portable battery source.

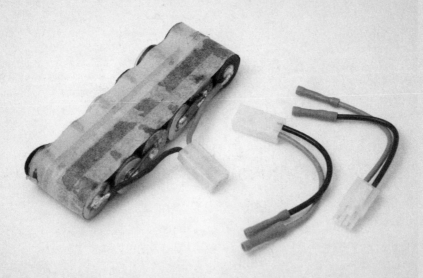

FIGURE 4-7: An RC car battery pack. I made this one myself, so its packaging is not good for photography in the field. But a pre-made battery pack from a hobby store or Radio Shack is packaged perfectly for your purpose. Note the special connector.

I found a Lithonia Lighting ELB06042 6V 4AH Sealed Lead Acid Rechargeable Battery at the local Home Depot. It is small enough to fit in a small camera pouch. It weighs a considerable amount, but is still light enough to carry around on your belt. Rated at 4 amp/hour, the battery pack will power your device for days. It's perfect for digital cameras that use four AA batteries. It costs about $20, and you'll need to find a charger for it.

Tools You Need

Here are the tools you will need to complete this project:

- Wire cutter
- Soldering iron
- 0.32" diameter standard 60/40 resin core solder

Cross-Reference

See Appendix A for information about buying and using soldering irons.

Assembly

After choosing your battery source, you need to wire the female DC power connector onto the battery so you can interface to it with the cable you modified earlier. Solder the wires to the DC power connector contacts. Use the same polarity that you determined for the interface cable earlier in this chapter. Depending on the battery pack you choose, you either have to solder the other end of the wires onto the battery or use some type of detachable connectors.

Hacking the Lenmar Mach 1 Speed Charger Battery Adapter Plates

Lenmar Mach 1 Speed Charger is a super fast battery charger that can charge your battery pack quickly. But that's not all it's good for. It's got an innovative design that allows each manufacturer's rechargeable battery pack to interface to the charger via a different battery adapter plate (see Figure 4-8). My Lenmar Mach 1 Speed Charger came with adapter plates for Canon, JVC, Panasonic, and Sony battery packs. The adapter plate is easily hackable so that you can locate your battery pack remotely.

Even better, you can use other manufacturer's battery packs with your gear. Thus, if you have tons of electronic gadgets at home, you can prolong the use of any one of them with all of the battery packs you collected. For example, use your Sony camcorder battery pack with your Canon digital camera (as long as their voltage ratings are the same or very close).

Parts You Need

Here are the parts you will need to complete this project:

- Lenmar Mach 1 Speed Charger adapter plates
- Coaxial power jack, panel-mount, size M, female (274-1582)
- DPDT submini slide switch (275-407)
- Wires

FIGURE 4-8: The Lenmar Mach 1 Speed Charger comes with a number of adapter plates for batteries made by different manufacturers.

You can get the adapter plates by buying a Lenmar Mach 1 Speed Charger. Lenmar also sells adapter plates individually, because those packaged with the charger may not be right for your camera. If someone you know has a charger and is not using the adapter plate you need, you might be able to snatch it from him or her (with their permission, of course).

The coaxial power jack is the female DC connector that you interface with. Because in the previous section I made the interface cable with the size M connector, I use it for this hack as well. But as I said before, you can use any size convenient to you.

You use the DPDT slide switch to make this modification flexible. With this switch, you modify the battery adapter plate so that it can be used as a remote battery pack and still retain the ability to charge your battery on the Lenmar Mach 1 Speed Charger. It's possible to wire the modification so that you can do without the switch, but that would create an unprotected circuit, so if you're charging the battery and have your camera connected at the time, you could fry your equipment. The switch is a much safer approach.

Tools You Need

Here are the tools you will need to complete this project:

- Phillips-head screwdriver
- X-acto knife

- Drill
- Drill bits
- Sharpie marker

Picking the Right Battery Adapter Plate

Before hacking the Lenmar battery adapter plate, you need to decide which plate to modify. Obviously, you'll want to modify the plate specifically made for your camera's battery. But if you have batteries for other electronic gadgets as well, you can modify the plates for those batteries. Just make sure the voltage rating of the battery is the same as your camera. The Lenmar battery adapter plates show the voltage rating on their surfaces for your convenience.

Disassembling the Adapter Plate

After you have decided which adapter plate to modify, you can disassemble the adapter plate by removing the two screws from the bottom of the adapter plate. The screws require a Phillips-head screwdriver to remove. With the screws removed, the plate can be easily taken apart, as shown in Figure 4-9

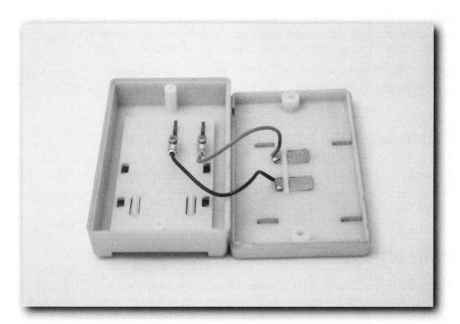

FIGURE 4-9: The battery adapter plate disassembled

Soldering the Wires

As you can see in Figure 4-8, the wiring within the battery adapter plate is extremely simple. There are only two wires (positive and negative) going from the battery terminals to the base of the adapter plate to connect to the charger. You'll need to de-solder the wires from the base of the adapter plate (remember the polarity) and solder them to the common pins on the slide switch. Use a digital multimeter to determine the common pins. The two middle pins on the DPDT switch are generally the common pins.

Now, solder additional wires to connect one side of the slide switch to the contacts on the base of the adapter plate. Then solder additional wires to connect the other side of the slide switch to the power jack. Use the same polarity convention as you have determined in the previous sections of this chapter.

Drilling a Hole and Cutting a Slot

You'll need to drill a hole on the battery adapter plate to mount the coaxial power jack. The power jack listed in the part list at the beginning of this section fits a $^{21}/_{64}$" mounting hole, so use the appropriate sized drill bit to drill the hole. Make sure you don't use a drill bit that makes the hole too big, because the mounting is done with a hex bolt that is not much bigger than the mounting hole.

The second step of this process is to cut a slot for the DPDT sub-mini slide switch. Use a sharp knife to cut a slot. If you are more comfortable with a drill, you can use a round toggle switch in the same manner as the power jack, instead of the slide switch.

I suggest placing the power jack and the slide switch on top of the battery adapter plate. It's more convenient to route the wires from the top when the battery and adapter plate are in your pocket.

Reassembling the Adapter Plate

After mounting all of the components, put the two halves of the adapter plate together and fasten them with the two Phillips screws that you removed. The adapter plate is ready to use on your charger or as your remote battery pack. Remember to mark the switch positions with a Sharpie marker.

Powering on Your Camera

After you have wired up all of the cables and batteries, make sure you check that all the connections and the polarities are correct. Then connect the power source to the camera and power it on. It should power up immediately as if the original battery source is installed.

If it doesn't power up within the time that it used to, turn off your camera immediately. Test your camera with the original power source to make sure it still works and hasn't burnt out. Then double-check your wiring and connections to see if there are any mistakes or bad connections. Try again after you've fixed the problem.

Controlling Your Digital Camera from Afar

chapter

5

One of my favorite hacks is controlling my cameras wirelessly with a universal remote. This hack is easy to perform, requires no special tools or parts, won't void your camera's warranty, and will give you the ability to capture yourself in the picture with a bunch of friends. All you need is a camera that supports an infrared wireless trigger and a home universal remote (see Figure 5-1).

In many instances, a wireless remote is an optional accessory for your digital camera. By using a universal remote, you save the cost of buying another accessory. Even if your camera came with a wireless remote, you might consider programming a universal remote with it and keeping the original remote in a safe location.

in this chapter

☑ Basic Infrared Signal Characteristics

☑ Using a Universal Remote Control with Your Camera

☑ Using Nevo with Your Camera

☑ Using Total Remote with Your Camera

FIGURE 5-1: Universal remote controls

Basic Infrared Signal Characteristics

Infrared is a part of the light spectrum. Although it resides in the same electromagnetic spectrum as visible light, its range is outside what our naked eyes can see. Because infrared light and visible light are in the same spectrum, infrared light exhibits very similar characteristics to visible light:

- Infrared light travels in a straight line.
- Infrared light diffracts around a sharp bend.
- Infrared light can be bounced with mirrors and other reflective surfaces.

Tip Infrared lights are invisible. But if you modify your digital camera to see infrared as described in Chapters 15 and 16, you'll be able to see infrared light with your digital camera. Your modified camera becomes a very useful tool for diagnosing infrared remote problems.

When you use your TV remote control, you will experience these characteristics. For example, you have to aim the TV remote control at the TV in order to turn it on with the remote. If the remote control is behind a wall, you will not be able to command your TV with it. If you put your hand in front of the remote, sometimes the TV will still turn on; the infrared signal diffracted around your hand.

Tip Infrared signals can be redirected by a mirror or other shiny, reflective surfaces. Just make sure the surface is clean of oily substances such as fingerprints. Sometimes even cotton balls or tissue paper will work as reflectors.

How Does IR Transmission Work?

When you press a button on a remote, the remote sends a signal to the device via its IR LED. So how does the remote differentiate the IR signal coming from one button from that coming from another? The answer is that the remote sends IR signals using 0s and 1s like your computer and all digital electronic devices. The buttons are differentiated from each other by using different patterns of 0s and 1s. In fact, signals from different remotes are also differentiated with different patterns. Signals that use 0s and 1s are binary signals. Each digit in the signal is called a bit. The data carried by the IR remote's binary signal can vary in size (number of bits) and can vary in time (how long it takes for each bit to transmit).

Light bulbs and other common light sources at home transmit IR as well, so a remote must modulate the IR signal at the frequency of 40 kHz to differentiate its own signal from other ambient IR light.

There are many ways to transmit 0s and 1s using IR light (or for that matter, any type of light). One common method is to vary the length of the pulse, but keep the length of spaces fixed. In electronics, a pulse is considered a signal high, while a space is considered a signal low. A pulse-coded IR signal is depicted in Figure 5-2. In this figure, 1s have a pulse length twice as long as 0s.

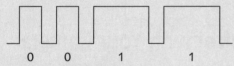

FIGURE 5-2: A pulse-coded signal

Another common IR signal implementation is to vary the length of space, while keeping the pulse length fixed. Figure 5-3 depicts a space-coded signal. In this figure, 1s have a space length twice as long as 0s.

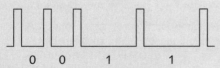

FIGURE 5-3: A space-coded signal

Continued

Continued

A third commonly used implementation, although slightly more complex than the first two, is the shift-coded signal. The 0s and 1s in a shift-coded signal are exactly the same length (see the upper portion of Figure 5-4). The signal is clocked to each bit. However, 0s are defined as a transition from high to low, while 1s are defined as a transition from low to high. An example signal is shown in the lower portion of Figure 5-4.

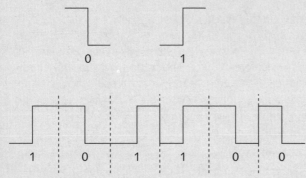

FIGURE 5-4: A shift-coded signal

By now, you are probably wondering, "Is it possible to come up with even more combinations of IR signals, such as 0s being three times as long as 1s?" The answer is yes. It's possible to come up with numerous different combinations to define IR signal patterns. The three implementations shown here are just samples of possible combinations.

Using a Universal Remote Control with Your Camera

I was bored at home one night when I learned that you could control your camera with a universal remote control. (Figure 5-5 shows an IR receiver on a camera grip.) That night, I happened to have a Magnavox REM100 universal remote control for my home theater system in my hand, and I decided to try it on my Canon EOS IX APS film camera. The Canon EOS IX is compatible with the RC-1 wireless remote, which I didn't have. But I figured maybe I'd get lucky and one of the buttons would work. After going through a bunch of different remote control codes, the camera actually released its shutter!

 Note Fluorescent light may interfere with infrared light. I have fluorescent lights at home. Sometimes my wireless PDA keyboard and my camera remotes don't work too well in this environment.

FIGURE 5-5: A wireless infrared receiver on a camera grip

Searching for the Right Remote Code (Automatic Programming)

This section uses the Magnavox REM100 and the Canon EOS IX as examples. Keep in mind that the process introduced here will work with most remote controls and most cameras that support an infrared wireless remote.

1. Turn your camera on and set it to accept remote trigger, if necessary.

2. On your universal remote, hold down the SET button until the LED stays on.

3. Press the equipment button (TV, VCR, or CBL) that you want to associate with your camera.

4. Keep pressing the POWER button at one-second intervals, until the camera triggers (see Figure 5-6). That is the code that works with your camera.

5. Press the ENTER button to set the code.

FIGURE 5-6: This picture was shot when I was searching for the right remote code.

Note While searching for the right remote for my Canon EOS Digital Rebel, the camera hung and stopped responding to any user input. The only way to reset the camera was to remove the battery. After some experimenting, I found that one of the infrared commands would cause the Digital Rebel to hang. If you go through a sequence of searches, check periodically that your camera is still responding.

Tip The Magnavox REM100 instruction sheet mentioned the use of the channel up button to scroll through thee codes. I found that the POWER button works as well.

Note Search through each of the function modes individually. In TV mode, only TV codes will be searched. In VCR mode, only VCR codes will be searched.

What Code Was Set?

When you set a code through the automatic code search mode, you may not know which code was set. Some universal remote controls, such as the Magnavox REM100, allow you to read the equipment code that is set in the remote. Check with your remote control manual to see if your remote has this feature. The following instructions outline the procedure to read the equipment code on the Magnavox REM100 Universal Remote.

1. Hold down the SET button until the LED is lit.

2. Press the mode button (TV, VCR, or CBL) for the function code you want to read.

3. Press the SET button. The LED blinks once.

4. Press the digit buttons from 0 to 9. When you press the digit that represents the first digit of the code, the LED blinks.

5. Find the next two digits of the code by following the instruction in the previous step. When the last digit is found, the LED turns off automatically.

Tip   If you have two or more cameras that are controllable by the same wireless remote, you can trigger them all at the same time with a single remote.

Manually Programming the Universal Remote

Sometimes you can find remote control codes that will work with your camera online. Knowing the code, you can also program your universal remote manually. The following procedure is for the Magnavox REM100 Universal Remote. Your universal remote control probably has a very similar procedure.

1. Press and hold the SET button until the LED stays on.

2. Press the equipment button (TV, VCR, or CBL) that you want to associate with the code.

3. Enter the three-digit code. The LED blinks for each button press.

4. Press the SET button to complete the process. The LED turns off when the code is acceptable.

Note   During the process, the remote allows 15 seconds of inactivity. When the inactivity exceeds 15 seconds, the LED will blink rapidly to show that the remote is exiting the manual-programming mode.

If you see the LED flash for about three seconds, the remote did not recognize the code. You'll have to repeat the procedure with the right code.

Programming a Teachable Universal Remote Controller with a Camera Remote

Some universal remote controls have a learning feature. With the learning feature, you can teach it with any infrared signal. Even if you already have the actual remote control for your camera, it would be a good idea to teach the signal to a universal remote and store the original remote in a safe place. Or, perhaps you have a lot of cameras and several different remotes. You can teach their codes to the universal remote and carry just one remote with you.

Tip Use fresh batteries on both remotes. By using fresh batteries, you can avoid pulling your hair out when you can't get the programmable remote to learn your camera remote functions.

Learning Commands from a Camera Remote

I have a Philips PHDVD5 Universal Digital DVD remote, which has the capability to "learn" functions from other remote controls, so this section will be illustrated with this particular remote (see Figure 5-7). However, the same concept can be applied to your specific model. Consult the instruction manual that came with your programmable remote control.

1. Press and hold the CODE SEARCH button (several seconds) until the red indicator turns on.

2. Press and release the desired mode button (TV, VCR, DVD, CBL, or SAT). Although you are controlling your camera, this mode selection simply picks which mode the remote stores your camera functions in.

3. Press and release the LEARN button.

FIGURE 5-7: The Philips PHDVD5 remote has a learning feature.

4. Press and release the button you want to teach. This is the button that will duplicate the camera remote button.

5. Position both remotes with the infrared LEDs facing each other. Keep the remotes about one inch apart (see Figure 5-8).

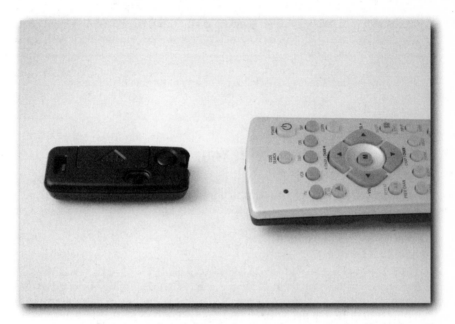

FIGURE 5-8: Place the remotes face-to-face and 1" apart for optimal infrared signal transfer.

6. Press and hold the camera remote button until the red indicator blinks once and stays on.

Repeat the last three steps for any additional camera remote functions that you want to teach the programmable remote. When you are done, press the CODE SEARCH button to complete the process.

If the red indicator blinks for three seconds and stays on at the last step, there is a problem learning the infrared signal. You'll have to repeat the last three steps and try again.

Tip

To cancel the learning process, press the CODE SEARCH button at any time before the last step.

Using Nevo with Your Camera

When HP/Compaq released its line of iPAQ Pocket PCs, it added a really cool application that no other Pocket PC manufacturers included: Nevo. Nevo is a universal remote control application for iPAQ. With Nevo, you can control your TV, cable, satellite, DVD, VCR, PVR, audio receiver, and many other devices. You can also apply the concept of searching for remote control codes that will work with your camera. In this section, I explain how you can program Nevo with your camera's remote control and how you can use pre-made Nevo remote control files from the Internet.

Tip   Using a wireless remote control is an excellent way to capture birds in action.

Programming Nevo with Your Camera's Remote

Nevo allows you to control an unlimited number of wireless devices. This feature is really nifty when you have several cameras all using different infrared remotes. You can program Nevo with all of the remotes so that you can carry a single Pocket PC to control any of your cameras.

Adding a Device

The first step to setting up Nevo to control your camera is to add a new device to Nevo. From the Nevo main page, tap the Add Device icon to start the Device Wizard. Tap the Next button to move to the Device Selection screen. For your camera, I suggest you select the Home device, but any will work. Tap the Next button to move on to the next step.

In the Device Setup Methods screen, choose the Select Brand option and tap Next to move forward. In the next screen, leave the default setting alone and tap the Next button. You'll be modifying all of the pre-set buttons later, so it doesn't matter which device you picked in this step.

Nevo Enhanced Devices

Nevo, shown in Figure 5-9, is currently not available for purchase as in independent consumer product. Instead, the only way you can get Nevo is to purchase a Nevo enhanced device. There is a good reason for this. Universal remote controls use infrared (IR) transmitters and receivers that operate differently from the standard IrDA port on handheld PCs. The IR transmitter has to have a long range to be useful. The IR receiver has to operate at twice the frequency rate to learn from a remote correctly. Most IrDA ports have a short transmission range of a few inches. And the IrDA receiving LED operates too slowly for learning. Thus, most handheld PCs are unsuitable to run Nevo.

FIGURE 5-9: Nevo is built into some HP/Compaq iPAQ Pocket PCs.

Currently Nevo 1.0 is preinstalled on the following iPAQ Pocket PCs: HP/Compaq iPAQ 2200 series, iPAQ 3950 series, iPAQ 3970 series, iPAQ 5400 series, Viewsonic Smart Display 110, and Viewsonic Smart Display 150. And the following devices have Nevo 2.0 preinstalled: HP/Compaq rx3100 series, rx3400 series, and rx3700 series.

In the Device Image Selection screen, pick an image you like to represent your remote control device. I like the Video Accessory and Video Projector images because they remind me of cameras. Tap the Next button to move on. In the Label Device screen, put the name of your camera or remote in the Device Label text box. Tap the Next button to complete the add device process. You should see the device show up on the Nevo screen as shown in Figure 5-10.

Modifying the Device Layout

Tap on the device you just created in Nevo. You will be presented with the layout in Figure 5-11. This layout has 12 buttons, which is probably a little too many for your camera's remote control. By tapping the little wrench icon on the bottom left hand corner of Nevo, you can add, edit, copy, move, and delete buttons. Start by deleting all of the excess buttons until the number of buttons matches your camera's remote. If your camera's remote has more buttons than Nevo's default layout, you can add them. Don't worry about what the buttons look like just yet; you will be changing their looks soon enough.

FIGURE 5-10: A Canon RC-1 device has been added.

FIGURE 5-11: The default layout of a new device

Once you have the right amount of buttons, you can use the move feature to change the layout of the remote to your liking. My Canon RC-1 remote has two functions, so I arranged the layout like the one shown in Figure 5-12.

Learning from Your Camera's Remote

After you've moved the buttons to all of the right places, you can start programming them. Tap on the wrench icon and select Edit Key to start the Key Wizard. Tap the Next button to move forward. In the Key Action Selection screen, select Learn Key from a remote control and tap Next.

FIGURE 5-12: My Canon RC-1 layout

In the Learn IR from a remote screen, Nevo will prompt you to aim the camera's remote control at the iPAQ's infrared sensors. Keep the two remotes about an inch apart from each other (see Figure 5-13). When the two remotes are positioned, tap the Learn button in Nevo. Within five seconds, press and hold the button on the camera's remote that you want to program.

FIGURE 5-13: Keep the infrared remote about an inch away from the iPAQ.

FIGURE 5-14: Nevo is successful at learning the remote command.

The next screen is the Key Button/Symbol Selection. You are presented with images of what your buttons can look like. Your choices are: Blue Silver, Green Power On, Green Silver, Red Power Off, Red Power Toggle, and Red Silver.

All of the button images can be labeled with your earlier entry or with a pre-made label. Select the image you like from the drop-down menu. Then select the label you want to place on the button in the next drop-down menu. When you tap the Next button, Nevo brings you back to the device layout screen, shown in Figure 5-15.

FIGURE 5-15: The finalized device layout screen

If your camera's remote has any additional functions, you can repeat the steps in this section to program the additional buttons.

Using Total Remote with Your Camera

In the previous section, I explained how you can use Nevo to control your camera. Unfortunately, Nevo isn't sold separately from devices that come with it. If you have a Pocket PC that doesn't come with Nevo, then you can't use Nevo. However, Nevo isn't the only combined hardware/software universal remote control for the Pocket PC.

Total Remote, shown in Figure 5-16, is a product developed by Griffin Technology, an innovative supplier of Apple iPod accessories. Total Remote comes with a special IR transmitter that plugs into the stereo headphone port of the Pocket PC and the universal remote control software. The Total Remote combination has the ability to control your camera, learn from camera remotes, and use remote codes downloaded from the Internet. You can get Total Remote directly from Griffin Technology at www.griffintechnology.com/ or from other online and local stores.

Nevo will let you know if it was successful at learning the command from your camera's remote (see Figure 5-14). If so, tap the Next button to move on. Otherwise, repeat the learning step in the last paragraph. On the next screen, Nevo asks for a label to assign to this button. My Canon RC-1 has two functions: trigger immediately or delayed trigger. I use the Now and Delay labels, respectively. When you have made up your mind about the label, tap the Next button to move to the next screen.

FIGURE 5-16: The specialized Total Remote IR transmitter hardware

Total Remote Compatibility

Total Remote software runs on Pocket PC 2000 and above. It is compatible with Intel StrongARM or XScale processors. Your Pocket PC PDA must meet the following general specifications:

- StrongARM or XScale processor
- High fidelity 3.5mm stereo headphone jack
- 1.05MB of storage space
- Pocket PC 2000 or later (including Windows Mobile 2002 and 2003)

Your desktop computer must meet the following specifications:

- 1.09MB of hard drive space
- Windows 98 and above

The following is a list of compatible Pocket PCs. If your Pocket PC is not in the following list, it should still work if it meets the preceding general specifications.

- Acer n20, n20w
- Asus MyPal 620
- Audiovox Maestro ARM, Thera ARM
- Compaq iPAQ 31xx, iPAQ 35xx, iPAQ 36xx, iPAQ 37xx, iPAQ 38xx, iPAQ 39xx
- Dell Axim X5 (range limited to less than 10"), Axim X3 (built-in IrDA only), Axim X3i (-built-in IrDA only)
- Fujitsu/Siemens Pocket LOOX
- HP Jornada 56x, 19xx (works with Griffin IR transmitter only; also requires a 2.5mm to 3.5mm stereo adapter), 22xx, 41xx (built-in IrDA only), 43xx, 51xx, 54xx, 55xx, 56xx
- NEC MobilePRO P300
- Packard Bell PocketGear 2060, PocketGear 2030
- PC-Esolutions MIA-PD600C
- Toshiba e31x, e33x, e35x, e4xx (built-in IrDA only), e5xx, e74x, e75x (built-in IrDA only), e8xx (built-in IrDA only), Genio e550 (GX/GS)
- UR There @migo 600C
- Viewsonic PDV35, V37
- Zayo A600

Programming Total Remote with Your Camera's Remote

Total Remote can help you manage multiple remotes for multiple cameras with ease. If you're going to be carrying your personal data assistant (PDA) anyway, you might as well put all of your remotes on it as well.

New Device

The first step to get Total Remote to work with your camera is to add a new device. In Total Remote, tap the Device menu, and then tap the New menu item. These actions will bring up the New Device screen shown in Figure 5-17. In the Device Name entry box, enter the name for your remote. I used "Canon RC-1" in this example. Select Other for Device Type. For the Skin file, I picked Standard (VCR) because it had the least amount of buttons. You are welcome to use any of the available skins to represent your remote. Tapping Finish and Total Remote brings you back to the layout of the remote you just made (see Figure 5-18).

FIGURE 5-17: The New Device screen

FIGURE 5-18: A Canon RC-1
device has been added.

Learning Your Camera's Remote

Tap the Edit menu and select Start One-Shot Sampling from the menu shown in Figure 5-19. Total Remote will take you to the full-size remote screen shown in Figure 5-20. Tap the button that you would like to program and Total Remote will display the Button Sampling screen.

FIGURE 5-19: The Edit menu

FIGURE 5-20: The full-size
remote screen

In the Button Sampling screen, Total Remote will prompt you to align your remote at the infrared ports. Since the Total Remote IR transmitter does not have a receiver, you can only learn remote commands through the Pocket PC's built-in IrDA port. Therefore, aim your remote at the PDA's IrDA port. Keep the remote about an inch away from the PDA. When the two devices are positioned, press and hold the remote button you want Total Remote to learn.

Tip

Total Remote learns a remote function by sensing repeated IR signals. My Canon RC-1 remote does not repeat its signal. The only way I can get Total Remote to learn it is by pressing the RC-1 remote button repeatedly until Total Remote senses it.

Total Remote will let you know if it was successful at learning the command from your camera's remote (see Figures 5-21 and 5-22). If it wasn't successful, you can try again. Otherwise, tap Finish to complete the process. When you are done, Total Remote returns you to the full-size remote view. Click the button on the lower left of the screen to return to menu view.

FIGURE 5-21: Total Remote
successfully read the remote code.

FIGURE 5-22: Total Remote could
not read the remote code.

CCF

Several years ago, Philips created a programmable universal remote control called Pronto. One of Pronto's versatile features is its ability to connect to a computer. When connected, new remote control codes and cosmetics (called skin), stored in configuration files, can be uploaded into Pronto's memory. Pronto's configuration file is called *CCF*, which stands for Cabernet Configuration File. Cabernet was the codename for Pronto during its development.

Ever since the success of the Philips Pronto remote, many enthusiasts make CCFs for their favorite remotes. Today, CCFs are easily found on the Internet. The CCF format has become an unofficial standard for the universal remote control industry. Now there are many remote controls that are compatible with CCF files, including remote control software for the Palm and Pocket PC. Griffin's Total Remote is one such product. It can read CCFs to control infrared electronic devices.

Remote Central, located at www.remotecentral.com/, is a large Internet repository of CCFs and related utilities. It stores many film and digital camera remote control CCFs that can be downloaded for programming into your CCF compatible universal remote.

If you would like to make CCFs for yourself and others, you can look into Philips ProntoEdit, Marantz Touch Screen Setup, and CHAD Edit. These software packages allow you to design skins, set up remote sequences, add graphics, and program IR codes. These software packages are free for you to download and use; however, they work only in the Microsoft Windows environment. There is another CCF editing software program called Tonto. Tonto is written in Java and will work on Windows, Mac OS, Linux, and many other Java compatible operating systems. Tonto is also free to download and use. Although some programmable universal remote controls, such as the Pronto, allow you to edit functions directly on the remote, the following software allow you to customize the remote with more powerful features.

- ProntoEdit: www.pronto.philips.com/
- Touch Screen Setup: www.marantz.com/
- CHAD Edit: www.chadremote.com/
- Tonto: giantlaser.com/tonto/

If your camera's remote has any additional functions, you can repeat the steps in this section to program the additional buttons.

Using Pre-Made Remote Files from the Internet

Total Remote has a really cool feature. It has a *CCF* (Cabernet Configuration File) mode, which can emulate any remote that has a CCF. CCFs are the standards for defining remote functions. They work on many programmable remote controllers, including Total Remote. So, even if you don't have a remote for your camera, some remote enthusiasts have probably already made one. There are many CCFs available on the Internet to download. I have found remote CCFs for Canon, Nikon, Olympus, and many other digital camera brands.

Installing CCFs

Once you have downloaded some CCFs, you are ready to install them on your Pocket PC. My iPAQ Pocket PC has a SD Card slot, so I use it to transfer files back and forth between the PDA and my computer. If your Pocket PC does not have a memory card slot, or you feel more comfortable connecting it to your computer for file transfer, you can use ActiveSync to move files back and forth. Please refer to your Pocket PC owner's manual for instructions on how to use ActiveSync.

Total Remote is quite smart. You can place the CCFs anywhere in the Pocket PC's storage space or on your memory card. Total Remote will automatically find them.

CCF Mode

To switch to CCF mode in Total Remote, tap the Tools menu. One of the menu items is CCF Mode (see Figure 5-23). Tap that menu item. When Total Remote switches to CCF mode, it displays the screen shown in Figure 5-24.

FIGURE 5-23: CCF Mode is under
the Tools menu.

Tap the Open CCF File button to see a list of CCFs available on your Pocket PC. On my Pocket PC, I have only one CCF on the open file list (see Figure 5-25)—it's a remote for the Canon S70 digital camera. If you have more than one CCF loaded on your Pocket PC, they will all show up on the list. Tap once on the CCF you want to open to bring up the remote, as shown in Figure 5-26. You can tap any of the buttons to use your Pocket PC, just like a real remote. When you are done, tap the Menu button and select Exit CCF Mode (see Figure 5-27).

FIGURE 5-24: CCF Mode
opening screen

FIGURE 5-25: The open CCF list

FIGURE 5-26: The Pocket PC now works
just like a Canon WL-DC100 remote.

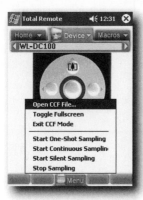

FIGURE 5-27: The CCF Mode menu

Turning Your Digital Music Player into a Universal Remote

Rumor has it that when Griffin invented Total Remote, they intended to market it for the popular Apple iPod, but during discussions with Apple for licensing, Apple turned Griffin down. Whether this rumor is true or not, the idea of turning your MP3 player into a universal remote control is interesting and fun. With the Total Remote, you can do just that.

Basically, Total Remote controls its special IR transmitter through the audio port. It does so by sending stereo signals. It's possible to record the signal transmitted by Total Remote on your computer. All you need is an audio cable with 3.5mm male stereo plugs on both ends. Plug one end in the headphone port on your Pocket PC and plug the other end into the line-in port on your computer.

When you have all the hardware connected, use sound recording software to record the audio signal. (The Sound Recorder software that comes bundled with Microsoft Windows works just fine.) Remember to record the signal in PCM 44.100 kHz, 16 bit, stereo format. Record and save each button signal in a separate file. Name the files something meaningful.

When you are done recording and saving all of the signals, copy or move them onto your MP3 player (see its owner manual). Plug the Total Remote transmitter into the headphone port of your MP3 player. Aim the MP3 player at the device you want to control and play back whichever command you want to send to your electronic device. Viola! Your MP3 player is now a universal remote.

Improving Your Canon EOS Digital Rebel

The Digital Rebel, shown in Figure 6-1, is Canon's entry-level digital SLR. Prior to its release, a typical digital SLR cost more than $1,000. But Canon's Digital Rebel changed that—for less than $1,000, you get a digital SLR and a Canon EF 18–55mm f/3.5–5.6 lens. The release of the Digital Rebel was well received by the public, and it soon out sold all other digital SLRs on the market.

Note Digital Rebel, 300D, and Kiss Digital are identical cameras. Kiss Digital is the marketing name in Japan, 300D in Europe, and Digital Rebel in North America. The firmware hack presented in this chapter will work with any of these Digital Rebel variants.

The Digital Rebel is the entry-level camera in Canon's EOS-series. It features many automated functions and an easy-to-use interface, but it lacks many manually selectable options that are available on its higher-end siblings.

With the Canon EOS Digital Rebel reaching the mass market and falling into some clever people's hands, a new generation of modified firmware began to pop up on the Internet. Of all the Digital Rebel firmware, the most complete and useful version is the Russian modified firmware (by Ravil and Wasia) known as the *Wasia* firmware.

Features of the latest Wasia firmware include ISO 3200, auto-focus mode selection, flash exposure compensation, mirror lockup, the capability to change the SET button function, and many others. These features are so useful that it's almost like having a new, more advanced digital SLR. With this firmware hack, the Digital Rebel far outpaced many competitive entry-level digital SLRs on the market.

FIGURE 6-1: Canon EOS Digital Rebel with Canon EF 18-55mm f/3.5-5.6 lens. The kit sells for less than $1,000.

Note There are currently two versions of the Digital Rebel. The original Digital Rebel had a silver surface. It looks classy and sophisticated, but deviated from the normal black body style in the Canon EOS-series of cameras. A year later, in 2004, Canon released the black version of the Digital Rebel. The entire body is black, but other than the color change, there are no other differences. The onboard firmware is exactly the same and this hack will work with both silver and black versions.

Getting the Hacked Firmware

The best way to find the hacked firmware is through an Internet search. A search of "wasia firmware" on Google renders plenty of results leading to the hack.

Caution Someone not associated with Canon produced the modified firmware. It is possible that this firmware could cause problems with or damage to your Digital Rebel camera. Installing this firmware will void your warranty, so you've been warned: install at your own risk!

Wasia Firmware Releases

There are three major firmware releases: E3kr111M, E3kr111B7, and E3kr111B71.

E3kr111M (Released 2004-04-07)
With this version you could:

- Change Flash Exposure Compensation (FEC) using the SET button
- Change the SET button functionality in shooting mode
- Configure shutter releases without a CompactFlash (CF) card
- Fix the flash sync speed to 1/200 seconds in Av mode

E3kr111B7 (Released 2004-06-01)
This version:

- Moved FEC from the SET to the JUMP button
- Added ISO 3200
- Introduced mirror lockup
- Let you change the parameter set using the SET button.
- Let you change the Auto-Focus mode.
- Provided Review Enhancement (See the *Review Enhancement* section later in the chapter).

E3kr111B71 (Released 2004-06-16)
The features and operation of this latest release are covered in this chapter, so read on.

Note The good news is that this firmware has been installed by a *lot* of people. Many of them (including me) have reported great success, and their Digital Rebel now operates with cool new features.

I recommend downloading the latest version of the hacked firmware, since it will have the most advanced features, the fewest bugs, and the most stable platform. The latest version as of this writing is E3kr111B71.

Getting the Official Digital Rebel Firmware

Before proceeding any further, you should download the official Canon Digital Rebel firmware from Canon's web site (www.canon.com). Keep it in a safe place in case you ever want to reinstall the official firmware on your Digital Rebel.

The latest version of the firmware is, as of this writing, 1.1.1. I recommend that you download the latest version because it generally has the most advanced features and the most recent bug fixes, and it is supported by Canon—if you call Canon's support with a camera problem, it is very likely that they will ask you to upgrade to the latest firmware as the first step toward resolving your problem.

Updating the Camera Firmware

The procedure for updating the camera with either the official Canon firmware or the hacked firmware is the same, at least for firmware versions up to 1.1.1 (the most recent as of this writing). However, be sure to consult the installation instructions for the firmware version you are using. The step-by-step instructions presented in this section are for Canon firmware versions up to 1.1.1 and also apply to the hacked firmware version (up to E3kr111B71). These instructions might also be valid for newer firmware version installations, but you should verify that by checking the instructions provided with the firmware.

Note If your Digital Rebel does not have the Canon Digital Rebel Firmware version 1.1.1 installed (you have version 1.0.2), you should install version 1.1.1 first. This will eliminate many potential conflicts when you install the hacked firmware.

Copy the Firmware to a CompactFlash Card

To install the firmware onto your camera, you will have to copy it to a CF (CompactFlash) card. The CF card you use has to be at least 8MB, but less than 2GB. When you have a CF card that meets this requirement, check to be sure it's blank. If not, copy any data you want to keep off the card. Once you are satisfied that there is nothing important on the card that you don't have a copy of somewhere else, format it. This eliminates any possibility that the card is corrupt.

Canon Firmware Releases

So far, Canon has released only one Digital Rebel firmware upgrade: version 1.1.1. This version includes the following bug fixes:

- Increased reliability of communication between the camera and the RemoteCapture application

- Increased reliability when the camera is connected to a Windows XP or Mac OS X computer while the PTP mode is chosen (in Communication settings)

How Do I Check My Current Firmware Version?

You can find the firmware version in the Digital Rebel menu. Turn the camera on, press the MENU button, and then use the arrow key to move to the last tab (the set-up 2 menu) as shown in Figure 6-2. Firmware Ver. is one of the items on the menu.

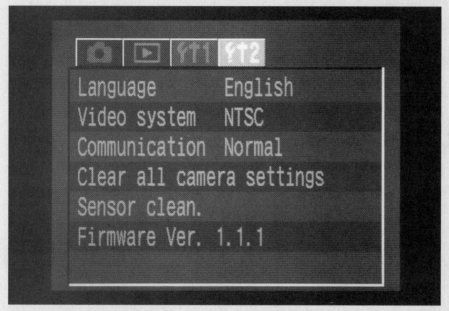

FIGURE 6-2: The set-up 2 menu

Keep in mind that although you will be able to see the firmware version (currently either 1.0.2 or 1.1.1), it will not indicate to you whether the firmware is the official Canon version or the hacked version. You can tell the difference by looking at the next menu item. If there is no other item (Firmware Ver. is the last item), then you have the official Canon version. On the other hand, if you see Custom Functions (C.Fn), you have the Wasia firmware.

There are two ways to copy the firmware to the CF card. You can either use a dedicated CF card reader, or use the Digital Rebel itself as a CF card reader. To do the latter, you will have to use Canon's UploadFirmware utility software that comes with Canon's official firmware (see "Getting the Official Digital Rebel Firmware" earlier in this chapter). The first method, however, is more convenient, and it's superior to the second method because you don't have to deal with the confusion that could be caused with the utility software or your Digital Rebel camera.

Note Using Canon's UploadFirmware utility could be confusing, because you are using the digital camera as a card reader. Afterward, your Digital Rebel reverts back to a digital camera for firmware update. It's too easy to confuse the two roles, which could potentially cause the firmware upgrade process to go wrong.

CompactFlash Card Reader Method

Once you have the freshly formatted CF card, copy the firmware file (it has a .fir extension, so the file will be named something like E3kr111.fir) to the root directory of the CF card. The root directory is the very top directory, above all subdirectories.

UploadFirmware Utility Software Method

If you do not have a dedicated CF card reader, you will have to use the UploadFirmware utility software that came with the Canon's official firmware download.

Insert the CF card into the Digital Rebel. Then connect the Digital Rebel to the computer with the Interface Cable IFC-300PCU. Next, execute the UploadFirmware program. On Windows and Mac OS computers, simply double-clicking the icon will execute the program. Follow the instructions on the screen to proceed with the copy.

Tip Interface Cable IFC-300PCU is really just Canon's fancy name for a USB mini-B cable. This is a standard cable that comes with various USB devices. You may already have one at home, so if you can't find the Canon IFC-300PCU, you might be able to substitute it with another.

During this copy process, do not open the CF card slot cover or turn the camera off. These actions may cause problems with your firmware install.

Installing the Firmware onto the Digital Rebel

With the firmware on the CF, you can now install it onto the Digital Rebel. Turn your Digital Rebel off. Place the CF card into the Digital Rebel CF card slot. Turn your Digital Rebel on. It will recognize that firmware is loaded on the CF card and ask you whether you would like to execute the upgrade, as shown in Figure 6-3. Select OK with the arrow keys and press the SET button to execute the upgrade.

Next, a "Checking Firmware" message is displayed. It takes about six seconds for the camera to check the firmware. Do not press the shutter button during the check—if you do, the upgrade process will be cancelled.

When the checking process succeeds, the camera asks whether you would like to replace the current firmware with the one on the CF card. The screen shows the current firmware version and the new firmware version (see Figure 6-4). Select OK with the arrow keys and press the SET button to approve the upgrade.

FIGURE 6-3: Execute Upgrade screen

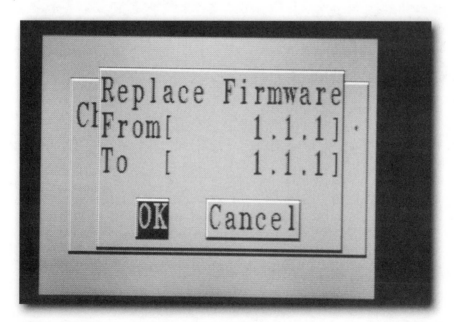

FIGURE 6-4: Replace Firmware screen. Note that the firmware version numbers are the same. The hacked firmware uses the same version number.

Once the upgrade process has started, the Re-writing Firmware screen, shown in Figure 6-5, shows a progress bar. Sometimes the progress will speed up, while at other times it slows to a stop. The rewriting firmware process takes approximately four minutes.

Caution

Do not power off the camera, open the CF card slot cover, or press any camera buttons during this firmware rewrite process. You could render your camera inoperable if you do, which may require that you send it back to a Canon Service Center.

FIGURE 6-5: Re-writing Firmware screen

When the upgrade is complete, the "Firmware Replaced Successfully" message is displayed (see Figure 6-6). OK is selected automatically on this screen. Press the SET button to end the upgrade process. Your camera is now upgraded with the new firmware.

FIGURE 6-6: Firmware Replaced Successfully screen

Using the Hacked Firmware

The firmware covered in this section is the newest E3kr111B71 firmware. There are actually two versions of this firmware: one new and one old. The difference between the old and the new firmware is some cosmetic changes in the menu text. See the "Older E3kr111B71 Firmware" sidebar later in this chapter for more detail.

High Speed Shooting at ISO 3200

The original Canon firmware gave the Digital Rebel sensor five different sensitivity levels. These levels are specified in ISO film speeds: 100, 200, 400, 800, and 1600. With the hacked firmware, the ISO sensitivity has been increased to 3200, the sixth sensitive level.

Tip   A high ISO number means that the film, or sensor, is more sensitive to light than it is with a low ISO number. An ISO 200 film is twice as sensitive to light as an ISO 100 film. Higher sensitivity allows the use of higher shutter speeds and smaller aperture. However, high sensitivity also introduces more grain in film or more noise on a digital sensor.

You can activate ISO 3200 through the normal operation of changing ISO speeds:

1. Press the "ISO" button.

2. While looking at the LCD, rotate the main dial until the desired ISO speed is displayed.

3. Press the shutter button halfway to return to shooting mode.

Note ISO speed can only be adjusted in the Creative Zone. In the Basic Zone, the camera sets the ISO speed automatically. See the Canon EOS Digital Rebel instruction manual for more information about its automatic settings.

The only difference between selecting ISO 3200 and the other ISO speeds is that *3200* is not displayed on the LCD. Instead, you will see the letter *H*. Don't be alarmed. This is the indication that Canon used for ISO 3200 on the Digital Rebel and its big sibling, the 10D. Once set, the selection remains in memory even when the power switch is turned off.

Auto-Focus Modes

On Canon EOS SLRs, three auto-focus (AF) modes are provided: One Shot AF, AI Servo AF, and AI Focus AF. Unlike its higher end siblings, the Digital Rebel provides these modes, but does not allow the user to manually select them. Instead, it automatically picks the mode it thinks is best for the situation.

AF Modes Explained

One Shot AF—In this mode, the camera will achieve focus first. When the focus is achieved, it is locked as well. Thus, if the scene is recomposed, the camera will not refocus. Before focus is locked, or if focus cannot be achieved, the camera will not allow the picture to be taken. In evaluative metering mode (see the instruction manual), the exposure setting is also locked when the focus is locked.

AI Servo AF—In this mode, auto-focus continues to adjust its focus on the subject. If the subject moves, or the camera is recomposed, the auto-focus is adjusted to focus on the subject. The exposure is set when the picture is taken.

AI Focus AF—In this mode, the camera automatically switches between One Shot AF mode and AI Servo AF mode. If the camera senses that the subject starts moving, it will switch over to AI Servo AF mode to continuously focus on the subject. If the subject is static, the camera will switch over to One Shot AF mode to lock focus.

In the Basic Zone, the Digital Rebel will pick an AF mode that best suits the selected situation. It chooses One Shot AF for Portrait, Landscape, Close-Up, and Night Portrait modes. It chooses AI Servo AF for Sports mode. And it chooses AI Focus AF for Fully Automatic Shooting and Flash Off modes. In the Creative Zone, Digital Rebel always chooses AI Focus AF. One exception is when the mode dial is in A-DEP mode, where Digital Rebel will pick the One Shot AF mode.

Note AF mode can be changed only in the Creative Zone. In the Basic Zone, the camera sets the AF mode automatically. See the Canon EOS Digital Rebel instruction manual for more information about its automatic settings.

With the hacked firmware installed, you can set the AF mode in the Creative Zone. To set the AF mode, press the left arrow on the Cross Keys (see Figure 6-7).

FIGURE 6-7: The Cross Keys are composed of the up, down, left, and right arrows.

The LCD will display one of the following modes:

- AF 0S - One Shot AF (default mode)
- AF AI - AI Focus AF
- AF SE - AI Servo AF
- AF OF - Off, when the lens is in MF mode

Use the main dial to choose the AF mode you want. Press any button to set the mode. Once set, the AF mode stays in memory after the power switch is turned off.

Note AF OF is a special mode that you won't normally see when the lens is in AF mode. You will only see AF OF when the lens is in MF mode. —To select an AF mode, you have to move the switch on the lens to AF (see Figure 6-8).

FIGURE 6-8: The AF/MF selector on a lens

Note The current version of the hacked firmware still has a problem with AI Servo AF mode. Currently, when using the AI Servo AF mode, the camera will not let you trigger the shutter, so no picture can be taken. (I did manage to get it to trigger a few times but not many.) However, the AI Servo AF in Sports mode still works just fine.

Flash Exposure Compensation (FEC)

Although Flash Exposure Compensation (FEC) is a wonderful feature on higher end Canon SLRs, FEC is used to change the camera's standard flash exposure setting. With FEC, you can make the image look brighter (overexposed) or darker (underexposed), as shown in Figures 6-9 through 6-13. However, the Digital Rebel did not provide this useful feature, forcing you to use the standard exposure setting.

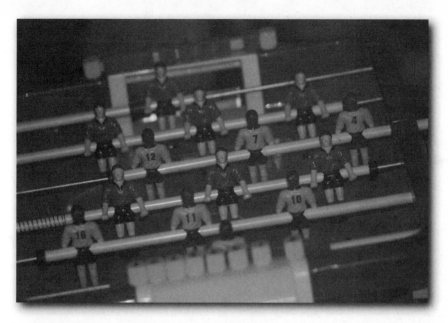

FIGURE 6-9: FEC set to underexpose by -2 stops

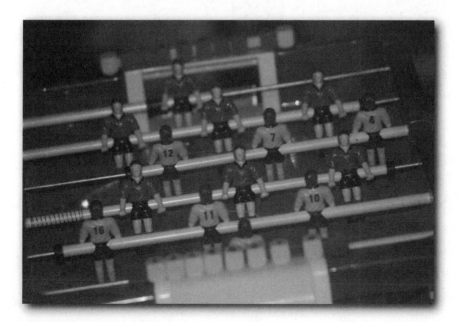

FIGURE 6-10: FEC set to underexpose by -1 stop

FIGURE 6-11: FEC set to normal exposure

FIGURE 6-12: FEC set to overexpose by +1 stop

FIGURE 6-13: FEC set to overexposure by +2 stops

The good news is that the hacked firmware added the FEC feature to the Digital Rebel. Using the hacked firmware, you can adjust the FEC in $^1/_3$-stop increments. To adjust the FEC, press the JUMP button until you see FEC1 on the LCD. Rotate the main dial to underexpose or overexpose the picture with flash. You will see the exposure level indicator change. Press any button for the change to take effect. Once set, the amount of FEC remains in memory after the power switch is turned off.

Tip You can also adjust FEC in ½-stop increments. See "C.Fn 06: Exposure Level Increments" later in the chapter for details.

Note The FEC adjustment only applies to the built-in flash. External flashes, such as the EX-series Speedlite, have their own FEC adjustment.

Note FEC can be adjusted only in the Creative Zone. In the Basic Zone, the camera sets the FEC to the standard exposure setting.

Tip If you are using an older version of the hacked firmware, the button to activate FEC adjustment could be the SET button. In the current version of the hacked firmware, the FEC function has been moved to the JUMP button, because a custom function now uses the SET button.

How Does Automatic Flash Work?

The flash built into your SLR is generally completely automatic. It usually takes advantage of through-the-lens (TTL) metering for good exposure accuracy. Through-the-lens metering means that the camera reads the exposure through the lens and then communicates the required flash exposure to the flash unit.

An external, dedicated flash unit is generally more powerful than the built-in flash. Because it is dedicated to the camera, it is also able to communicate with the camera. The camera measures the exposure of the scene through the lens and then communicates the exposure to the flash unit before it fires.

An external, non-dedicated flash unit is also usually more powerful than the built-in flash. However, being non-dedicated, it does not know what camera it is talking to. Instead, it only knows when the shutter is opened and when it should fire the flash. In order to expose the subject with the proper amount of light, it uses a sensor to detect the amount of light reflecting off the subject. When it senses enough light, it automatically turns off the flash.

Automatic flashes are extremely useful in various flash situations, such as bounce, fill-in, and multiple flashes. When the flash unit is aimed at the ceiling or the wall to provide indirect lighting, the technique is called *bounce flash*. *Fill-in flash* is used during daylight to fill-in shadows on the subject. Because each of these situations could cause more or less light to fall on the subject, an automatic flash will be able to automatically shut itself off when enough light has reflected off the subject.

A-TTL

Some of Canon's external flash units operate in a mode called A-TTL, which stands for Advanced Through-The-Lens. A-TTL is available on the EZ-series of Speedlites. To make an exposure, the A-TTL flash unit first fires a pre-flash to calculate the aperture value. This calculation is based on the distance between the flash and the subject. The calculation concentrates mostly on the area covered by the active focusing point. In Program mode, the camera compares this aperture value to the aperture value calculated from the ambient exposure metering. The smaller value of the two is used for the final exposure. A dedicated sensor reads the flash illumination at the focal plane to control the flash output. These steps ensure an accurate exposure of the subject in any lighting condition.

E-TTL

Canon later introduced Evaluative Through-The-Lens (E-TTL) flash control for some of their external flash units. E-TTL is available on the EX-series of Speedlites. E-TTL exposure measurement starts when the shutter button is fully depressed and the pre-flash fires but before the mirror flips up. The camera uses the evaluative metering sensor to compare the pre-flash illumination and the ambient light exposure, concentrating on the active focus area. The analysis is used to calculate the flash output for the exposure on the subject, which maintains a subtle balance between foreground and background. E-TTL also provides a method to spot meter with flash (Flash Exposure Lock) and provides the ability to use flash at high shutter speeds (FP mode).

Review Enhancement

When the Review option is turned on in the Digital Rebel menu, the camera will automatically display the last shot taken for a period specified by the Review Time menu option. During the display, you can delete the picture by pressing the Erase button (see Figure 6-14). With the original firmware, you would have to press left or right to select OK, and then press the SET button to confirm the command.

FIGURE 6-14: OK is automatically selected when you press the Erase button during the picture review period.

Because the hacked firmware changes the functionality of the left button to AF selection, the left and right arrow buttons no longer work for the delete capability during reviews. Instead, the firmware enhances the process by automatically selecting the OK selection for you. To confirm delete, simply press the SET button. If you would like to cancel the deletion, simply press any other button.

Note This enhancement works only for the picture review right after the picture has been shot. It does not work during Playback mode. In Playback mode, the delete function still work as in the original firmware. See your Canon EOS Digital Rebel instruction manual for more information about deleting pictures in Playback mode.

Custom Functions

Canon's higher-end cameras allow users to further customize the camera using Custom Functions (C.Fn). On lower-end cameras such as the Digital Rebel, custom functions are not available. Wasia's hacked firmware unlocks the custom functions in the Digital Rebel menu. To access the custom functions, press the MENU button, and then move to the last menu tab. Select Custom Functions(C. Fn), which is the last item on the menu (see Figure 6-15), and then press the SET button.

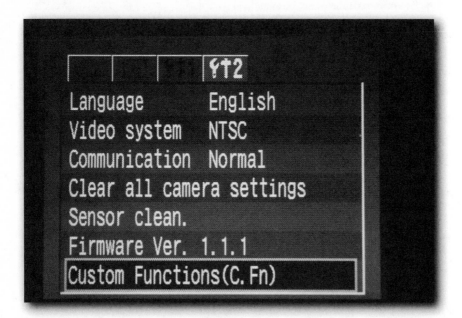

FIGURE 6-15: The Custom Functions menu item

On the Custom Function screen, shown in Figure 6-16, you'll see a number in a yellow box in the top right-hand corner. This is the custom function number, referred to as C.Fn # in Canon's documentation. The up and down arrows next to the yellow box are misleading, because to change the custom function number you will actually have to use the left and right arrow buttons.

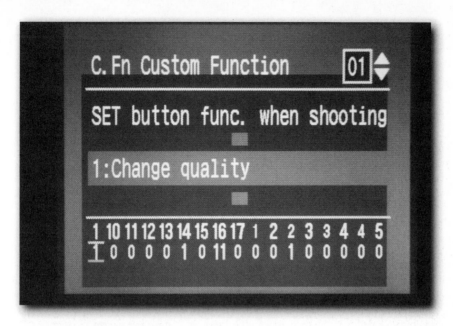

FIGURE 6-16: The Custom Functions screen

The second line of text on the Custom Functions screen is the name of the custom function. For C.Fn 01, the name is "SET button func. when shooting." The next text line shows the current setting for this custom function. To change it, press the SET button. Then use the up and down arrows to scroll through the selections. Once you've made your selection, press the SET button again.

Note You must press the SET button to activate the selection. If you press other buttons, the selection is cancelled.

On the bottom of the Custom Functions screen are two rows of numbers. The first row is the C.Fn number. Unfortunately the list is a little scrambled. It shows 1, 10, 11, 12, 13, 14, 15, 16, 17, 1, 2, 2, 3, 3, 4, 4, and 5. It is best to ignore this row of numbers and concentrate on the C.Fn number shown in the yellow box. An underscore below the number indicates which C.Fn is currently selected.

The second row of numbers shows the selected setting for each C.Fn. "0" is the binary representation for 0. "1" is the binary representation for 1. "10" is the binary representation for 2. "11" is the binary representation for 3. The number "12" and so on is the indication for selection 4 and after. The numbering seems to be inconsistent after 3. But if you just remember what they are, it is still quite useful. An underscore below the number indicates which C.Fn is currently selected.

As potent as the hacked firmware is, there are still a number of custom functions that are not working. Those functions are covered in the "Non-Functional Custom Functions" section later in this chapter.

C.Fn 01: SET button func. when shooting

C.Fn 01 allows you to change the SET button functionality. In shooting mode, the SET button does nothing. With this custom function, you can make the SET button more useful.

```
0:Default (no function)
1:Change quality
2:Change parameters
3:Menu display
4:Image replay
```

Default
```
0:Default (no function)
```

Change quality
When the SET button is associated with this function, the SET button allows you to change the image quality quickly and conveniently. To change the image quality, press the SET button in shooting mode. Use the main dial to scroll through the image quality selections. The selected image quality is shown on the LCD. Press any button to confirm the selection.

Change parameters
This functionality allows you to change the parameter set quickly and conveniently with the SET button. See the Digital Rebel Instruction Manual for more information on parameters. To change the parameter set:

1. Press the SET button in shooting mode.

   The current parameter is displayed on the LCD, such as PA-2. Parameter indications are as follows:

   - PA-0 = Parameter 1
   - PA-5 = Parameter 2
   - PA-A = Adobe RGB
   - PA-1 = Set 1
   - PA-2 = Set 2
   - PA-3 = Set 3

2. Use the main dial to scroll through the parameter sets.

3. Press any button to confirm the selection.

Menu display

This selection causes the SET button to function just like the MENU button in shooting mode. Since the MENU button is readily available on the back of the camera, I found this function to be less useful than the two previous functions.

Image replay

This selection causes the SET button to function just like the Playback button in shooting mode. Since the Playback button is readily available on the back of the camera, I found this function to be less useful than the first two functions.

C.Fn 02: Shutter release w/o CF card

This custom function allows you to decide whether the Digital Rebel triggers its shutter when a CompactFlash memory card is not installed. By default, the Digital Rebel lets you take pictures without the CompactFlash memory card. But the picture is then immediately lost. You can disable this function, so that you would never be confused into thinking that there is a card in the camera when there really isn't.

```
0:Possible without CF card
1:Not possible
```

Default

```
0:Possible without CF card
```

C.Fn 03: Flash sync speed in Av mode

In aperture priority (Av) mode, the camera meters the exposure of the scene and sets the aperture automatically. The exposure creates a pleasing effect of showing the surrounding environment in low-light situations, even when the flash is on. However, if you want to have the subject stand out while the environment is darkened, you will want to fix the shutter speed at $1/_{200}$ second. This custom function applies only to the camera in aperture priority (Av) mode.

```
0:Auto
1:1/200sec. (fixed)
```

Default

```
0:Auto
```

C.Fn 06: Exposure level increments

It is quite impressive that Canon provided exposure level increments in $1/_3$-stops on the Digital Rebel. Normally, $1/_3$-stop increments are only available on high-end SLR models. But what if you rather adjust exposure in $1/_2$-stop increments—maybe because all of your other cameras use $1/_2$-stop increments? The hacked firmware provides that capability in Custom Function 6.

```
0:1/2-stop
1:1/3-stop
```

Default

```
1:1/3-stop
```

The Digital Rebel's exposure level indicator shows only $^1/_3$-stops (see Figure 6-17). Therefore, using it in $^1/_2$-stop mode can be a little tricky. In $^1/_2$-stop mode, the indicator bar only displays on full stops and disappears during $^1/_2$-stop increments. In addition, the bar must still travel through the $^1/_3$-stop increments, but the exposure stays in $^1/_2$-stop metering.

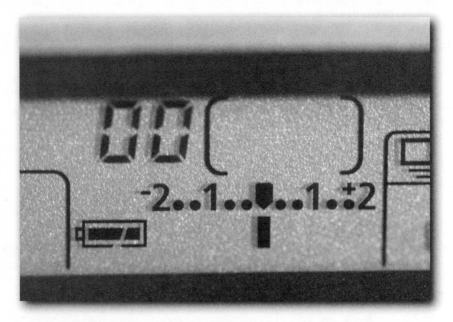

FIGURE 6-17: Digital Rebel's exposure level indicator shows only 1/3-stops.

To adjust the exposure compensation:

1. Hold down the Av+- button while rotating the main dial.

2. Let go of the Av+-button when you have adjusted exposure compensation to the desired amount.

3. Cancel the exposure compensation by moving the indicator bar back to the middle, where exposure compensation is 0.

C.Fn 08: RAW+JPEG rec.

When you capture pictures in RAW mode, the Digital Rebel actually store two versions in the RAW file. The first version is the RAW sensor data. The second version is the JPEG that is generated after applying the white balance and the processing parameters. The stored JPEG file has an image quality of *medium fine* and takes up space in the RAW file. Digital Rebel does not allow you to disable storage of the JPEG version, nor does it allow you to change its image quality. The hacked firmware, on the other hand, lets you choose the JPEG image quality. You can set it to *small normal* to reduce memory usage or set it to *large fine* for excellent JPEG representation.

```
0:RAW+Small Normal
1:RAW+Small Fine
2:RAW+Medium Normal
3:RAW+Medium Fine
4:RAW+Large Normal
5:RAW+Large Fine
```

Default
```
3:RAW+Medium Fine
```

C.Fn 09: Bracket. sequence/Auto cancel

This custom function allows you to change the characteristics of the auto exposure bracketing (AEB). It allows you to change the order at which the bracket exposes the pictures. It also allows you to change whether turning off the power switch automatically cancels AEB.

Note

Before I get your hopes up, I should warn you that this custom function does not fully work. However, half of the function does work (as described below) and the portion that works is very useful.

In this release of the firmware, the change AEB order does not work. Even though the LCD may indicate that the order is changed while you shoot, when you review your pictures, you will see that the order has not been changed.

However, the function that works is the ability to disable AEB automatic cancel when the power is turned off. If you use AEB, you'll find that whenever you turn the camera off with the power switch, by opening the CF slot cover, or by opening the battery cover, AEB will be cancelled. The AEB will also be cancelled if you change the lens. This can become a nusianceif you always use AEB as part of your work or if, in the middle of an AEB shoot, you have to change CF cards, batteries or lenses. This custom function allows you to disable the automatic cancellation of AEB.

```
0:0,-,+/Enable
1:0,-,+/Disable
2:-,0,+/Enable
3:-,0,+/Disable
```

Default
```
0:0,-,+/Enable
```

0,-,+/Enable

In this mode, the first shot is the standard exposure, the second is the underexposure, and the last is the overexposure. Power off automatic cancellation is enabled in this mode.

0,-,+/Disable

In this mode, the first shot is the standard exposure, the second is the underexposure, and the last is the overexposure. Power off automatic cancellation is disabled in this mode.

-,0,+/Enable

In this mode, the first shot is the underexposure, the second is the standard exposure, and the last is the overexposure. Power off automatic cancellation is enabled in this mode.

 Note The order of the exposures in this mode does not work.

-,0,+/Disable

In this mode, the first shot is the underexposure, the second is the standard exposure, and the last is the overexposure. Power off automatic cancellation is disabled in this mode.

 Note The order of the exposures in this mode does not work.

C.Fn 12: Mirror lockup

Mirror lockup is a feature that is used often in astronomical photography, where extremely long telephoto lenses are used, or in close-up macro pictures, where extreme magnification is produced on the subject. In both cases, just a slight vibration could cause minor blur in the image. With most SLRs, the mirror (see Figure 6-18) moving out of the way (mirror slap), could cause vibrations that translates into the picture. To alleviate this possibility, high-end cameras generally provide the mirror lockup feature, which allows the mirror to be locked in the out-of-the-way position prior to releasing the shutter for the picture. The Digital Rebel does not provide this feature off-the-shelf. However, the hacked firmware unlocks this capability in C.Fn 12.

 Note When the flash is used during mirror lock, the flash will fire when the mirror is lifted. Then it will fire again when the shutter is released. This seems to be hardly a bug at all, because the picture is taken fine with the flash. The pre-flash may be of minor inconvenience. If your subject is a person, you should consider warning the subject so that he or she will not think that the photo has been shot on the pre-flash.

```
0:Disable
1:Enable
```

Default
```
0:Disable
```

FIGURE 6-18: The SLR mirror

Caution

In the *Canon EOS D30 Camera User's Guide,* Canon warns that the sun's heat could burn and damage the shutter curtain. Canon advises the user to not point the camera at the sun during mirror lockup. Since the mirror lockup concept is the same in the D30 and the Digital Rebel, you should heed this advice with your Digital Rebel as well.

This mirror lockup works differently with the different Drive Modes, described in the following sections.

Single Drive Mode

In the Single Drive Mode, the mirror lockup features work as intended. When the shutter button is pressed down fully, the mirror swings out of the way (see Figure 6-19). After the mirror lockup pause time (see "C.Fn 17: Mirror lockup pause time"), the shutter curtain is released and the picture is captured. Finally, the mirror swings back down.

Continuous Drive Mode

The mirror lockup function is disabled in the Continuous Drive Mode. In this drive mode, the camera operates normally as if mirror lockup has not been enabled.

Tip

If you use the Continuous Drive Mode all the time (as I do), you might consider leaving the mirror lockup function enabled. When you want to use the mirror lockup function, simply press the drive mode button to switch the camera to Single Drive Mode or Self-Timer/Remote Mode. Enabling mirror lockup this way is a lot more convenient and quicker than going through the Custom Function menu screens.

FIGURE 6-19: The mirror in the locked up position

Self-Timer Operation

In the Self-Timer Operation mode, the mirror lockup also works. When the shutter button is pressed down fully, the camera starts the 10 second self-timer count down. At the end of the count down, the mirror swings out of the way. After the mirror lockup pause time (see "C.Fn 17: Mirror lockup pause time"), the shutter curtain is released and the picture is captured. Finally, the mirror swings back down.

Wireless Remote Control

The wireless remote control works as the shutter button. Therefore, the mirror lock-up function works as indicated earlier with the wireless remote control.

C.Fn 17: Mirror lockup pause time

The mirror lockup pause time determines how much time to wait, after the mirror is swung out of the way, before the shot is taken by releasing the shutter curtain.

```
0:1.5 Sec
1:3 Sec
2:4.5 Sec
3:6 Sec**
4:7.5 Sec *
5:10 Sec
```

Each * denotes an unprintable character. The characters are meaningless artifacts that remained in the hacked firmware from previous versions.

Default
```
0:1.5 Sec
```

Known Issues

The hacked firmware is not without bugs. Fortunately the bugs seem minor and do not render the camera unusable. The bugs listed here are only minor inconveniences, and will likely not hinder the joy of using the hacked firmware.

Language

The firmware seems to work well when the language is set to "English" as some features do not seem to work correctly in other languages. After you've installed the hacked firmware, trying to change from one language to another will cause the camera to lock up. If your camera is locked up, it will not respond to any button commands, not even the power switch. Reset the camera by removing the battery and putting it back.

To change the language without locking up the camera, reinstall the official firmware version 1.1.1 first. Change the language, and then reinstall the hacked firmware.

Older E3kr111B71 Firmware

Two versions of the E3kr111B71 firmware are distributed on the Internet. The newer version shows the C.Fn 17 options as described in this chapter. The older version shows the C.Fn 17 options as follows:

```
0:1,5 SEC

1:3 SEC

2:4,5 SEC

3:6 SEC**

4:7,5 SEC *

5:10 Sec
```

Each * denotes an unprintable character. The characters are meaningless artifacts that remained in the hacked firmware from previous versions.

Really, the only difference between the new and the old version of the E3kr111B71 firmware is whether there's period or comma at the decimal point location, and whether "sec" is all caps or lowercase.

AI Servo AF

See "Auto-Focus Modes" for information about this issue.

Auto Exposure Bracketing

See the "C.Fn 09: C.Fn 09: Bracket. sequence/Auto cancel" section for information about this issue.

Mirror Lockup with Flash

See "C.Fn 12: Mirror Lockup" for information about this issue.

Non-Functional Custom Functions

While an impressive number of custom functions are available on the Digital Rebel after you install the hacked firmware, a number of them are not yet functional. These custom functions may become operational in the future with the help of clever people, or they may never be functional because of hardware limitations of the Digital Rebel. These custom functions are described here in detail in case you wonder what they should do.

C.Fn 04: Shutter button/AE lock button

This custom function allows you to change the operation of the shutter button and the * button (also called AE lock button). It proves to be quite useful for action shots in AI Servo AF mode, where you want to determine when auto-focus/auto-exposure (AF/AE) is activated and when the shutter is triggered independently.

```
0:AF/AE lock
1:AE lock/AF
2:AF/AF lock, no AE lock
3:AE/AF, no AE lock
```

Default
```
0:AF/AE lock
```

AF/AE lock

Pressing the shutter button down halfway starts auto-focus (AF) and auto-exposure (AE). Pressing the * button causes AE to be locked. This is the default behavior on the Digital Rebel.

AE lock/AF

Pressing the shutter button down halfway causes AE to be locked. Pressing the * button starts AF and AE.

AF/AF lock, no AE lock

Pressing the shutter button down halfway starts AF and AE. Pressing the * button causes AF to be locked. AE lock is not available in this mode.

AE/AF, no AE lock

Pressing the shutter button down halfway starts AE. Pressing the * button starts AF and AE. AE lock is not available in this mode.

C.Fn 05: AF-assist beam/Flash firing

The Digital Rebel does not have a dedicated AF-assist beam. However, it does fire a brief burst of flashes to assist AF.

```
0:Emits/Fires
1:Does not emit/Fires
2:Only ext. flash emits/Fires
3:Emits/Does not fire
```

Default

```
0:Emits/Fires
```

Emits/Fires

The built-in flash fires a brief burst of flashes to assist AF. If an external flash with AF-assist beam support is mounted, the external flash emits the AF-assist beam. This is the default behavior on the Digital Rebel.

Does not emit/Fires

The built-in flash does not fire to assist AF. If an external flash with AF-assist beam support is mounted, it also does not emit the AF-assist beam.

Only ext. flash emits/Fires

The built-in flash does not fire to assist AF. If an external flash with AF-assist beam support is mounted, it emits the AF-assist beam.

Emits/Does not fire

This emits the AF-assist beam to assist AF. It does not fire the AF-assist flash.

C.Fn 07: AF point registration

With this custom function, the Assist button on some EOS SLRs can be used to change the AF point quickly (see Figure 6-20). Since the Digital Rebel does not have an Assist button, this custom function does not work with the Digital Rebel. The following list is the translation of the graphical options:

```
0: Center point
1: Lower point
2: Mid-right point
3: Right-most point
4: 7 points
5: Left-most point
6: Mid-left point
7: Upper point
```

FIGURE 6-20: This custom function uses a graphical representation of the AF points.
Note that the custom function actually displays the point in graphical representation.

Default
0: Center point

C.Fn 10: Superimposed display

Canon calls the red dot that lights up on the AF points in the viewfinder the superimposed
display. This custom function allows you to turn on and off those red dots. However, it does
not work on the Digital Rebel.

0:On
1:Off

Default
0:On

C.Fn 11: Menu button display position

This custom function allows you to change the characteristic of the MENU button.

0:Previous(top if powered off)
1:Previous
2:Top

Default
0:Previous(top if powered off)

Previous (top if powered off)

When the MENU button is pressed, the selection returns to the previous menu option. When the power is turned off, the selection returns to the menu top. This is the default behavior on the Digital Rebel.

Previous

When you press the MENU button, the selection always returns to the previous menu selection.

Top

When you press the MENU button, the selection always returns to the top of the menu.

C.Fn 13: Assist button function

This custom function allows you to change the characteristic of the Assist button. Unfortunately, the Digital Rebel does not have an Assist button. Therefore, this custom function serves no purpose.

```
0:Normal
1:Select Home Position
2:Select HP (while pressing)
3:AV+/- (AF point by QCD)
4:FE lock
```

Default

```
0:Normal
```

C.Fn 14: Auto reduction of fill flash

When the subject is in front of strong backlighting such as sunsets, auto reduction of fill flash prevents underexposure of the subject. When enabled, the auto reduction helps synchronizes the flash to the backlight.

```
0:Enable
1:Disable
```

Default

```
0:Enable
```

C.Fn 15: Shutter curtain sync

This custom function allows you to change the flash synchronization to shutter curtain.

```
0:1st-curtain sync
1:2nd-curtain sync
```

Default

```
0:1st-curtain sync
```

1st-curtain sync

The flash is fired immediately after the shutter curtain is fully open.

2nd-curtain sync

The flash is fired immediately before the second curtain closes.

C.Fn 16: Safety shift in Av or Tv

In shutter priority and aperture priority mode, the Digital Rebel locks the AE when it achieves focus. When the lighting of the scene changes, the exposure does not automatically change. Using this custom function, you can enable the camera to automatically shift the exposure.

```
0:Disable
1:Enable
```

Default
```
0:Disable
```

Reverting to Canon's Firmware

With all the nice features provided by the hacked firmware, you have to wonder why anyone would ever want to revert back to the Canon's official firmware. However, there are a couple of reasons that you might want to do just that:

- In the future, Canon might release a newer version of the firmware to fix bugs or add new features. If that happens, it is highly likely that Canon's firmware will not support features from the hacked firmware. However, you might be inclined to install this new version if it fixes a bug that hinders your workflow.

- You might want to send your camera to Canon's Service Center for inspection, cleanup, upgrade, or troubleshooting. Reverting to the original Canon firmware will prevent possible misunderstanding or misassumption of the issue at hand.

If you do revert to Canon's official firmware, you need to remember to restore the default settings first. In the Digital Rebel, there is an option to Clear All Camera Settings. However, this does not help you, because it does not reset the custom functions and it does not reset the options that are available in the hacked firmware. You must reset those new features manually. The following checklist will help you reset all the options:

- ISO—Set ISO to a value below 3200.
- FEC—Set FEC back to 0.
- AF—Set AF to One Shot
- C.Fn—Set all C.Fn to the default value. Cheat sheet: change all the numbers on the bottom of the Custom Functions screen to 0,0,0,0,0,1,0,11,0,0,0,0,0,0,0,0,0.

When you have completed the reset, you can update the firmware to another version. Follow the instructions presented previously in "Updating the Camera Firmware."

Hacking Lenses

Using Accessory Lenses

When you purchase a camera, whether it is point-and-shoot (P&S) or single-lens-reflex (SLR), it likely comes with a built-in or detachable lens that is either a single-focal lens or a zoom lens. This lens is the camera's primary lens (see Figure 7-1).

At first, the new camera and its primary lens are going to feel exhilarating, but the more you use your camera, the more limitations you will discover. Not that your camera is no good, but there are limitations to each piece of photographic equipment. For example, your primary lens may not zoom far enough to capture the woodpecker in a tree. Or maybe it is not wide enough capture your entire family in the restaurant. And maybe it can't focus close enough to capture the magnificent colors of a butterfly.

On cameras with detachable lenses, you can always detach the primary lens and attach another one that suits your particular need. Even if you have a non-detachable lens camera, there is a whole world of accessory lenses to enlarge the potential of your primary lens. Different types of accessory lenses may include telephoto to get you closer to the action, wide-angle to take in more of the environment, macro to focus closer to small objects, and anamorphic to reshape the scene to fit a 16:9 wide-screen display (see Figure 7-2).

This chapter explores the different types of accessory lenses, when you use them, and how you attach them to the primary lens on your camera.

FIGURE 7-1: This Sony DSC-P92 point-and-shoot digital camera has a built-in zoom lens. This built-in lens is the primary lens.

FIGURE 7-2: Assorted accessory lenses

External Anatomy of an Accessory Lens

Figure 7-3 shows two accessory lenses. The lens on the left is upside down. The lens on the right is right side up. The glass optic on the front side of the accessory lens is called the front lens element. The glass optic on the rear side of the accessory lens is called the rear lens element. The female screw thread on the front side of the lens is the filter thread. The filter thread allows you to attach filters, lenses, hoods, and other accessories. The male screw thread on the rear side of the lens is called the mounting thread. The mounting thread allows you to mount the lens on the filter thread of another lens.

FIGURE 7-3: The external anatomy of an accessory lens

Understanding Magnification

Magnification is the change in object size from the physical world to the image world. For example, when you stand in front of a simple plane mirror, the image of yourself in the mirror is the same size as the real you (see Figure 7-4). There is no magnification. But if you look at yourself in a funhouse mirror at a carnival and your mirror image is half as tall as you, the mirror has changed the magnification of your mirror image (see Figure 7-5).

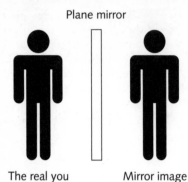

Plane mirror

The real you   Mirror image

FIGURE 7-4: The image in the plane mirror is the same size as you.

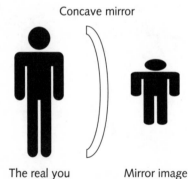

Concave mirror

The real you   Mirror image

FIGURE 7-5: The image in the concave mirror is smaller than full size.

In mathematic terms, magnification is defined as the image height divided by the object height. In the case where the mirror represents your height as your real height, magnification is 1 (image height and object height are the same).

$$Magnification = \frac{Image\ Height}{Object\ Height}$$

In the case where the funhouse mirror changed your image height to half as tall as the real you, your magnification is ¹/₂. The following equation assumes that you are six feet in height:

$$Magnification = \frac{Image\ Height}{Object\ Height} = \frac{3\ feet}{6\ feet} = \frac{1}{2}$$

Camera lenses work the same way as a mirror; they create an image from a physical object. Every lens changes the magnification of the physical object when creating the image. Inside a camera, this image is captured on photosensitive material, such as film or digital sensor. A lens that records a physical object the same size on film is a lens with a magnification of 1. These lenses are generally called 1:1 macro lenses because they allow you to represent small objects, say a butterfly, on film in life-size.

However, most camera lenses de-magnify so that they can fit an entire scene into a single film frame. A 35mm film camera has a frame dimension of 36mm × 24mm (about 1" measured diagonally). Consider how many frames it would take to capture an entire tree if you use a non-magnifying 1:1 lens.

The amount of lens magnification depends on its focal length relative to the image plane and the size of the photosensitive material. Assuming that the size of the photosensitive material is constant, the only variable that changes magnification is the focal length of the lens. This means that when you change the focal length setting on a zoom lens, you are really changing the amount of magnification.

When you increase the focal length (moving the focal point away from the image plane), you are really increasing the magnification of the object image. This effect is demonstrated in Figure 7-6. Think of a telephoto lens. The further you zoom, the bigger your subject looks in the viewfinder.

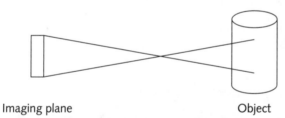

Imaging plane   Object

FIGURE 7-6: When the focal point is moved away from the image plane, the object looks bigger in the picture.

When you decrease the focal length, you are decreasing the magnification of the object image. This effect is demonstrated in Figure 7-7. Think of a wide-angle lens. The shorter focal length de-magnifies the subject, allowing the lens to miniaturize everything in the scene. In turn, you can fit more objects in a single frame of your photograph.

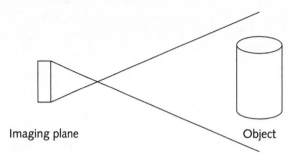

Imaging plane   Object

FIGURE 7-7: When the focal point is moved toward the
image plane, the object looks smaller in the picture.

Understanding Perspective

Imagine you are taking a picture of a cluster of leaves on a tree. Taking into account the relationship between lens and magnification, what do you think happens when you change the focal length of your lens?

Figures 7-8 and 7-9 are pictures of a leaf cluster. The relative sizes of the leaves, in the picture frames, are the same. However, one picture is taken with a 35mm wide-angle lens. The other picture is taken with a 200mm telephoto lens. Observe the two pictures closely. Note that although the leaves in the two pictures are the same size and are shot from the same angle, the backgrounds are different. What you're seeing in these pictures is called a change in perspective.

FIGURE 7-8: Leaves, taken with a 35mm lens

FIGURE 7-9: Leaves taken with a 200mm lens

When you change focal lengths with lenses, you are changing the relative size of the foreground object in relationship to the background object. In the example, when a wide-angle lens is used, the foreground leaves are rendered larger, while the tree trunk becomes smaller. In the telephoto lens picture, the foreground leaves are rendered smaller, while the tree trunk becomes large enough to fill the frame.

Perspective is best described with a diagram. In Figure 7-10, imagine that the tree is the subject. At different distances, the tree will fill the entire viewfinder at different focal lengths. With a wide-angle lens, such as a 28mm lens, you will have to move very close to the tree to fill the entire viewfinder.

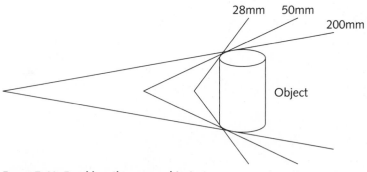

FIGURE 7-10: Focal length versus subject

Through the use of different focal length lenses, you can change the audience's perspective of the portrayed subject. This effect is particularly important when you are shooting portraits of people. If you use a wide-angle lens, a person's nose becomes much larger relative to the face. This may be desirable when you shoot a clown, but it is otherwise undesirable.

Using Wide-Angle Lenses

Wide-angle accessory lenses are one of the most popular lens types, second to telephoto lenses. These lenses are great at shooting indoor environments where the space is limited. Unless you have a mansion, it is impossible to move backward very far to get everything into your picture frame. Maybe you want to take a picture of your entire family at a restaurant. Wide-angle lenses can help you capture everything in the scene.

A trait of wide-angle lenses (shorter focal length) is that they provide greater depth-of-field than telephoto lenses (longer focal length) at the same aperture setting. Depth-of-field is the range of distance at which objects are within focus. A greater depth-of-field means that objects are in focus within a larger range of distance. A smaller depth-of-field means that objects are in focus within a smaller range of distance. Using a wide-angle lens, it is possible to have all objects within 3' to infinity in focus.

Along with the ability to provide great depth-of-field, wide-angle lenses widen the angle-of-view, allowing you to widen the space in your picture. These two traits combined makes wide-angle lenses good candidates for shooting landscape pictures, such as the one shown in Figure 7-11.

Most wide-angle accessory lenses are specified with a demagnification number, such as 0.5x. This number is the multiplier to the focus length of your primary lens. Therefore, if you mount a 0.5x wide-angle accessory lens on your 28mm lens, you end up with a focal length of 14mm.

When you mount wide-angle accessory lenses, make sure you zoom the primary lens out to the widest setting. This prevents your picture from having light fall off at the corners. Plus, you want to maximize the widest angle-of-view anyway.

In most cases, you want a wide-angle lens that can fill the entire picture frame. However, there are specialized wide-angle lenses to create special effects. One such wide-angle lens is the fisheye lens. The fisheye lens gets its name from the way fish sees the environment around them. These lenses generate a circular image that is warped. The image has a large angle of view to capture up to 180 degrees or more. The fisheye lens generally creates a circular vignette around the picture, as shown in Figure 7-12.

There are also some semi-fisheye lenses. The semi-fisheye lenses are like the fisheye lenses, except they are not so extreme. Some of them can provide the warping effect but still fill the entire picture frame with images from the scene. The semi-fisheye can be a good compromise between a wide-angle lens and a fisheye lens if you don't like the black corners in your pictures.

FIGURE 7-11: A wide-angle lens is perfect for landscape photography.

FIGURE 7-12: A circular fisheye picture

Using Telephoto Lenses

Telephoto lenses are the most popular accessory lens type. The first thing that most photographers do when they try to take pictures of flighty animals is to use long telephoto lenses. These lenses allow your camera to magnify subjects so that they appear larger in your pictures. They are a necessity for capturing wildlife images. The general rule of thumb is that the longer focal length the better. Using a telephoto accessory lens is the easiest and most inexpensive method to increase the focal length of your primary lens.

In addition to capturing wildlife, telephoto lenses have a few traits that make them good for other purposes as well. With their narrower angle-of-view, telephoto lenses have a tendency to flatten the subject. The flattening is called the compression effect. Figure 7-13 is a good example of the compression effect. By using a telephoto lens, the skyscrapers in Seattle are flattened into a 2D image.

Telephoto lenses also make the subject stand out by blurring the background (see Figure 7-14). This effect is caused by the narrow depth-of-field in pictures generated by telephoto lenses. Knowing this background blurring effect, the narrow depth-of-field, and the compression effect, many professional model photographers take advantage of long focal length telephoto lenses (sometimes 300mm and 400mm lenses) for model shots.

FIGURE 7-13: The Space Needle and surrounding buildings in Seattle are flattened by a telephoto lens. The effect makes the city look two-dimensional.

FIGURE 7-14: A telephoto lens keeps the subject sharp but blurs the background.

Most telephoto accessory lenses are specified with a magnification number such as 2x. This number is the multiplier to the focal length of your primary lens. Therefore, if you mount a 2x telephoto accessory lens on your 200mm lens, you end up with a focal length of 400mm.

When you mount telephoto accessory lenses, make sure your primary lens is at the longest focal length setting. This would prevent any vignette that may occur. Plus, you want to maximize the magnification.

Optical Teleconverter vs. Digital Zoom

Quite often, digital cameras are offered with a digital zoom to boost their zoom capability to 2x, 4x, 6x, or even more. The digital zoom is just a marketing ploy to persuade the uninitiated camera buyers to pick the highest digital magnification camera over other competing digital camera models. There is absolutely no advantage to using the digital zoom function on your digital camera.

When you set a digital camera to digital zoom, the camera actually shoots the picture at its full optical zoom setting (full zoom with the physical optics). Once the picture has been shot, the camera magnifies the digital image internally to match the digital zoom setting. Then it outputs the final digitally magnified image to storage. When it digitally magnifies the images, it has to make every object in the scene bigger than it was originally shot. To do so, it expands each object by the digital zoom factor and fills in the missing new details with the color of the adjacent pixels. This process of generating additional image data is called interpolation. Figure 7-15 shows an image that was shot with a Nikon COOLPIX 950. The camera was set to a 2x digital zoom to boast the image to twice its original magnification.

Interpolation is the reason that digital zoom is useless. The camera did not really zoom in to the subject and acquire the additional data from the scene. It is making up new data from already captured data. You can perform this process easily through photo-editing software on your computer. Think of it as enlarging your image in your photo-editing software, and then cropping out the desired frame. In fact, on your computer, you can magnify the image as large as you want: 2x, 10x, or 100x. The amount of magnification is limited only by the amount of memory in your computer.

On the other hand, when you use an optical teleconverter lens, you are actually magnifying the scene with a physical optical lens. As you zoom toward your subject through optics, the scene is examined anew each time. The camera sees the new data, the smaller details, from the actual scene through the optical lens. The camera can capture as much detail as the lens and the digital sensor can resolve. Then the data is captured permanently on the digital sensor for storage. Figure 7-16 is a picture shot with an Olympus 1.9x teleconverter. The lens is mounted on the Nikon COOLPIX 950 digital camera set at full optical zoom.

Continued

Continued

Figure 7-15: Picture shot with 2x digital zoom

The pictures shot with the digital zoom and the optical zoom have the same magnification (very close anyway); each object in the scene is the same size in both pictures. Although the digital zoom and the optical lens have slightly different magnification factors, changing the camera distance to the subject slightly eliminated that variable in these pictures.

Looking at the digital zoom version, the white flower on the party favor seems to lack detail and is a little washed out. That is the symptom of a digital zoom. It could also be the symptom of a poorly made optics that doesn't resolve enough resolution. But in this case, we know the picture is shot using 2x digital zoom.

In the second picture, shot with the telephoto lens, the same white flower shows a lot of detail. You can see each petal. In fact, you can see the texture of the fabric that made up those petals. The ability to resolve details is the power of using a good optical teleconverter over the digital zoom feature.

FIGURE 7-16: Picture shot with a 1.9x telephoto lens

Filter Thread

On some primary and accessory lenses, you may see a screw thread on the front face (see Figure 7-17). This screw thread is called the filter thread. The filter thread allows you to attach filters to create different effects on your pictures. (Various filter hacks are covered later in this book.) In addition to filters, you can also mount hoods, accessory lenses, and other camera gear.

You can determine the filter thread size by looking at the filter thread indicator on the lens, as shown in Figure 7-18. Unless you have specialized equipment, the filter thread pitch is 0.75mm.

Your P&S camera and its primary lens may not have a filter thread. A lens that has a filter thread is more versatile than a lens without it. Generally the lower-end camera models lack the filter thread. However, don't let the fact that your camera lacks a filter thread be the end of your adventure. You can still modify your camera to support accessory lenses. See Chapter 8 for details about those modifications for your camera and lens.

FIGURE 7-17: The lens on the left does not have a filter thread, while the lens on the right does have a filter thread.

FIGURE 7-18: The filter thread size indicator

Mounting Thread

When investigating accessory lenses for your camera, you will frequently come across the phrase "for 52mm camera." This phrase means that the accessory lens has a 52mm mounting thread at the rear of the lens. This measurement allows you to determine whether this lens is suitable for use with your camera gear. If the primary lens on your camera has a 52mm filter thread, you can mount a 52mm accessory lens to it.

Step-Up and Step-Down Rings

At some time, you may find a really nice accessory lens with a mounting thread that doesn't fit your camera's filter thread. You can still adapt the lens to the camera through the use of step-up and step-down rings. A step-up ring is a ring with a smaller screw thread on the filter thread side and a larger screw thread on the mounting thread side. A 37–52mm step-up ring allows you to mount a 52mm accessory lens on a 37mm filter thread. As you might suspect, a step-down ring has a larger screw thread on the filter thread side and a smaller screw thread on the mounting thread side. A 58–52mm step down ring allows you to mount a 52mm accessory lens on a 58mm filter thread. Figure 7-19 shows examples of step-up and step-down rings.

FIGURE 7-19: A step-up ring and a step-down ring

A step-up ring is generally more useful than a step-down ring. Usually, you will be able to install an accessory lens with larger diameter optics on a primary lens with smaller diameter optics without any side effects. In many cases, when you try to step-down the attachment (mounting a smaller accessory lens on a larger primary lens), the smaller optics won't cover the full image circle on the larger lens. The effect is vignette around all four corners (see Figure 7-20) or even the entire image.

FIGURE 7-20: Vignette caused by mounting a smaller accessory lens on a larger lens

Step-up rings and step-down rings come in limited sizes. There may not be a ring for stepping 37mm up to 77mm. But you can accomplish the same thing by stacking step-up rings. You can combine a 37–58mm step-up ring with a 58–77mm step-up ring to achieve the 37–77mm step-up you want. Figure 7-21 is a step-up ring composed of three step-up rings. Make sure you test your combination before you commit it to a shoot. When you stack too many rings, the thickness may cause vignette around the corner of your pictures. This problem occurs more often with wide-angle lenses than telephoto lenses.

Tip   When I built up my SLR gear, I had lenses with filter threads ranging from 52mm to 77mm in diameter. Because I wanted to buy only one set of filters for use with all my lenses, I decided to standardize on 77mm filters. Then I bought a step-up ring to 77mm for each of my lenses. A step-up ring for each lens is a lot cheaper than a filter for each lens.

FIGURE 7-21: Stacking step-up rings

Mounting to a Point-and-Shoot Camera

Years ago, most P&S cameras were manufactured with built-in filter threads. Now, P&S cameras with built-in filter threads are as rare to find as dinosaur fossils. But as a result of the popularity of accessory lenses, many camera manufacturers designed accessory lens adapters for their digital cameras, such as the Sony VAD-PEA shown in Figure 7-22. These adapters attach to the digital cameras and provide a filter thread for the front of the camera lens.

Even if the manufacturer does not produce a lens adapter for your camera, or if they have stopped supplying it, many times you can find third-party versions. A good example is when Sony discontinued the VAD-PEA lens adapter for the Sony Cyber-shot DSC-P92. Many photographers wrote to me asking where they could obtain the lens adapter. Later, someone informed me that he found third-party version on eBay, the online auction marketplace.

Cross-Reference After exhausting all of these routes on sourcing a lens adapter for you camera, you can still make one yourself. In Chapter 8, I show you how to make your own lens adapter.

FIGURE 7-22: The Sony Cyber-shot DSC-P92 has a specially designed VAD-PEA lens adapter.

Mounting to an SLR Lens

Virtually all SLR lenses have filter threads on the front. Accessory lenses are particularly useful on SLRs with non-detachable primary lenses (such as Olympus ZLR cameras). All you have to do is screw the accessory lens onto the primary lens (see Figure 7-23). Although most SLRs have detachable lens mounts for you to mount the right lens for the right situation, accessory lenses could come in handy for these cameras as well. Accessory lenses are generally cheaper than an SLR lens. Accessory lenses can be mounted on different SLR systems (when you buy an SLR lens it works only with a particular manufacturer's SLR). Accessory lenses are generally smaller and lighter to carry around.

Differences between an SLR Lens and an Accessory Lens

Conceptually, there are no differences between an SLR lens and an accessory lens; both types of lenses serve the purpose of delivering the kind of picture you want. So why would you pick a SLR lens over an accessory lens, and vice versa? That's a good question, and the answer depends on a number of advantages and disadvantages of each type of lens.

SLR Lens

SLR lenses are always made for a particular camera system. The newest SLR lenses all come with bayonet mount connectors for easy attachment and detachment from the cameras. The mounts include a specialized electrical interface to facilitate communication between the camera and lens. The interface is proprietary to each brand. Therefore, you won't be able to use one brand of SLR lenses on another brand of SLR. (Adapters do exist but I won't go into details on those adapters in this edition of the book.)

Because SLR lenses are made for a particular brand of camera system, the lens designers can optimize the lens optics to provide the best image quality and provide the best compatibility for the particular system.

Accessory Lens

Accessory lenses are made to fit on particular filter thread diameters. Because of the standardization of filter threads, you can mount accessory lenses on a variety of P&S cameras, SLR lenses, and camcorders. For the same reason, the lens designers are unable to optimize the accessory lens design for all camera lenses. Generally, the accessory lenses produce decent pictures in combination with other primary lenses. But in some cases, the combination fails miserably. Compatibility testing between primary and accessory lenses is a burden on the user's shoulders.

FIGURE 7-23: A Kenko 0.5x wide-angle lens mounted to the front of a Canon 28mm SLR lens

Mounting to a Camcorder

Most camcorders have filter threads on the front of their lenses. They generally have small primary lenses, because of their small sensor sizes. Many times, the lenses are even smaller than those on P&S digital cameras. Therefore, their filter thread diameters are small as well. Some camcorders have filter sizes down to 26mm. Despite the difference in filter thread size, everything mentioned in this chapter for P&S digital cameras applies to camcorders as well. Use step-up rings to attach your camera filters and lenses to your digital camcorder.

Making an Accessory Lens Adapter

In Chapter 7 you learned how to change the perspective of your pictures by using different accessory lenses. Now you just have to mount these lenses to the filter thread on your camera. That's easy if your camera came with filter threads. But it is a little more difficult if it doesn't have built-in filter threads, the camera manufacturer doesn't produce a lens adapter for your camera, and you can't find a third-party lens adapter. The good news is that you can make one yourself. This chapter shows you how you can modify the camera so that it has a filter thread. Once you have modified your camera with this hack, you can mount all sorts of stuff to your digital camera, such as filters, a lens hood, a macro ring flash, and other accessories.

I will use a Sony DSC-P92 Cyber-shot digital camera as an example. The concept can be applied to any film or digital camera, but there are some minor differences between the two types, which I will point out later.

Parts You Need

Here are the parts you will need to complete this project:

- PVC pipe
- Step-up ring

Most point-and-shoot (P&S) cameras have a retractable lens, especially those with a zoom lens. When the camera is turned off, the lens retracts and is flush with the body. For these types of camera, you'll need a PVC pipe to extend the filter thread out as far as the lens could ever extend.

PVC stands for PolyVinyl Chloride, a type of plastic commonly used in plumbing pipes. These pipes come in various sizes at home improvement stores. The pipe to use for this project doesn't necessary have to be made from PVC, as long as it is made out of rigid plastic that has enough strength to hold up your accessory lens.

The size and length of the pipe you need depends on the lens on your camera. The diameter should be large enough for the lens barrel to pass through, and long enough for the lens to extend without ever touching the accessory lens. PVC pipes are sold by the foot. Buy one that is about 1' in length so that there will be plenty to allow you to cut it down to the length you need. After cutting it down in length, try it on your camera and make sure it doesn't vignette the corners of your picture.

Tip

The plastic tube I used in this project may be a little different from yours. This tube came with the tweeter speaker for my car. I didn't need this tube when I mounted the speaker in the car, so it has been lying around my home. It turned out to be a perfect fit on my Sony DSC-P92, both in diameter and length. You might consider looking for spare parts around your home as well when you are building projects in this book.

Once you have a PVC pipe that fits well over your camera lens, find a step-up ring that fits the PVC pipe. The pipe that I am going to use in this chapter is 1 ¹/₂" in inner diameter. Since step-up rings are measured in millimeters, you'll have to measure the pipe in millimeters or do a simple mathematic conversion (1" is equal to 25.4mm). My PVC pipe is 38mm, so I chose a 37mm–52mm step-up ring. This ring will provide a 52mm filter thread when the project is complete.

Tools You Need

- Hacksaw
- Flat metal file
- Round metal file
- 5-minute general-purpose epoxy
- Cardboard
- Toothpick

You might have a specialized pipe-cutting tool. If not, you can cut the pipe with a hacksaw. Then use the metal files to smooth off the edges. The epoxy will be used to glue everything together. You'll need a disposable piece of cardboard and a toothpick to apply the epoxy.

Assembly

After gathering your parts and tools, you are ready to assemble the lens adapter on your camera. The total assembly requires just a few steps.

Measuring and Cutting the Pipe

The first thing you need to do is cut the plastic pipe down to size. It needs to be long enough so that your camera lens will never reach the end of it. You can determine the length of your lens barrel by extending it to its fullest length. With your camera turned on (in camera mode), play with the zoom buttons until the lens is fully extended. Measure the length with a ruler. My Sony DSC-P92 extends to about 21mm in length (see Figure 8-1).

FIGURE 8-1: Measure the lens barrel with a ruler.

Some fixed focal length P&S cameras extend the lens slightly farther during focusing or snapping of the picture, so after you measure the fullest zoom length, try focusing (by pressing the shutter button down halfway on most cameras) and snapping a picture. See if the lens extends any farther than its fullest extension. If it does, you will have to estimate the extra length. Make sure you cut the plastic pipe long enough to cover this extra length.

After you determine the length of the pipe, mark the plastic pipe with a ruler and a pencil or marker. On a workbench, hold the pipe steady as you position the hacksaw. Line up the hacksaw with the mark. Slowly pull the hacksaw toward yourself, while the teeth of the hacksaw are planted firmly on the plastic pipe. Repeat this several times to make a nice groove in the plastic pipe. If you don't make this groove, the hacksaw will jump over the plastic pipe. Using the groove to guide the hacksaw, cut the plastic pipe with a back-and-forth motion. Cutting the plastic pipe is easy and won't take more than a minute or so.

After you cut the pipe to length, the edge of the pipe is going to be a little fuzzy. The heat generated from the friction between the metal hacksaw and the plastic pipe causes tiny strands of plastic to melt and deform. File the edge down with a flat metal file. Because the inner surface of the pipe is round, you may find the round metal file beneficial.

Test Fitting

After you cut the pipe clean off the edge cleaned, test-fit the pipe on the camera and make sure it fits and it is long enough for the lens. Holding the pipe onto the camera, turn the camera on, extend the lens to its fullest, and snap a picture. Make sure the lens doesn't protrude out of the pipe end. Figure 8-2 shows my Sony DSC-P92 lens flush with the plastic tube when the lens is fully extended. Figure 8-2 shows that the tube is a perfect fit on the Sony DSC-P92.

FIGURE 8-2: The lens is flush with the plastic tube when fully extended.

Next, test-fit the step-up ring on the plastic tube. If it doesn't fit, you'll have to find another step-up ring that will. And test the tube and ring combination to make sure they still fit over the camera lens. In my case, I found the 37mm-52mm step-up ring works great. I even mounted a teleconverter lens onto the ring and made sure that the picture doesn't vignette while using the combination.

Gluing Everything Together

After satisfying yourself that everything fits together, it's time to make the permanent modification to your camera. First, glue the step-up ring to the plastic tube. I found that the 5-minute general-purpose epoxy works wonders. It is strong and durable. You can also try superglue, but it's brittle and cracks over time. It also produces a fume that turns its surroundings white. Thus, it is somewhat dangerous to use around lens, because you won't want your lens optics to turn white and obscure its vision.

The epoxy is slightly harder to use than superglue. You'll need to find a piece of cardboard to mix the chemicals and a toothpick to mix and apply the chemical to your project. Both the cardboard and toothpick will have to be thrown away afterward.

When you are ready to glue, squeeze equal amounts of the two chemicals in the epoxy container onto the cardboard. Mix the two chemicals together with the toothpick. Give the resulting epoxy about 30 seconds to react. Then apply the epoxy to the surfaces between the step-up ring and the plastic tube. Now press the two pieces together firmly, as shown in Figure 8-3.

FIGURE 8-3: The 37mm–52mm step-up ring glued to the plastic tube

If you are quick, you can also apply the same epoxy to the plastic tube and glue it to the camera. Otherwise, you'll have to mix a new batch of epoxy to glue the tube to the camera. It might not be a bad idea to take your time anyway, because it's easy to make a mistake if you're under pressure and trying to do things too fast.

Leave the camera, tube, and ring sitting on the workbench and don't touch it. Give the epoxy about an hour to dry completely (see Figure 8-4).

FIGURE 8-4: The tube and step-up ring glued to the camera

Fixing the Sony VAD-PEA Lens Adapter

Sony makes a lens adapter for the DSC-P92 Cyber-shot digital camera. The model is VAD-PEA. I bought one of these early on and have been very happy using it with my digital camera. Some of my web site's fans have written me and mentioned that Sony has discontinued this lens adapter. So I decided to write this chapter and suggest to the fans that they make their own adapter.

During the process of writing this book, my girlfriend accidentally sat on my precious Sony VAD-PEA lens adapter. It caused the lens adapter to split in two, as shown in Figure 8-5. I was quite disappointed, because Sony no longer makes this adapter and the third-party version costs three times as much as the Sony adapter.

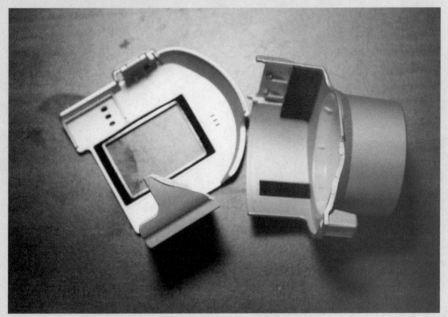

FIGURE 8-5: My split Sony VAD-PEA adapter

I was quite bummed, but I thought maybe it could be glued back together. Whether the glue would be strong enough to handle the weight of my heavy Kenko Video Wide Converter KVC 0.5x Pro lens was the question. The lens adapter was already broken, so I figured that I had nothing to lose by trying. I applied the epoxy to the inside and outside surface of the seam and let it dry overnight (see Figure 8-6).

The next morning, I played around with the adapter. It seemed quite strong. And after putting the adapter on the camera, it was able to hold up the heavy lens without problem. But I am still very careful with it, because the lens, by itself, is heavier than the digital camera. So, it turned out that the 5-minute general-purpose epoxy is far more versatile and stronger than I expected. The moral of this story: Don't throw away your lens adapter if it is broken—try fixing it first.

Continued

Continued

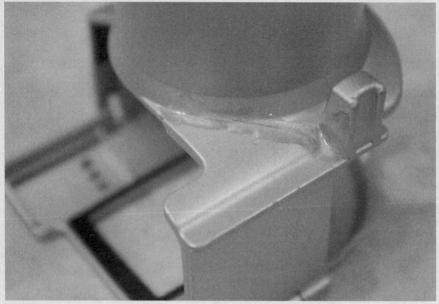

FIGURE 8-6: Apply epoxy to the seam.

Trying Out the Lens Adapter

After the modification has fully dried, take a look at the camera. Make sure everything is securely glued. You don't want to put an expensive accessory lens on there only to have it fall off the next second. When you are sure everything is solidly glued together, you can begin experimenting with it.

This is the most exciting part of the project. You can finally attach accessories to your camera. Try it with a lens, a filter, or whatever else you've got. You may need additional step-up rings to attach bigger or smaller accessories. Take a few pictures and review them. Make sure there is no vignette around the corners of the pictures.

I used an Olympus C-160 1.45x teleconverter when I tested my set-up (see Figure 8-7). It is a light lens with a 52mm mounting thread. It can be attached to the lens adapter directly. Its light weight allows me to test the lens adapter without a huge risk of breaking the epoxy bond.

Cross-Reference

As I mentioned before, there are many potential uses for a lens adapter. For more ideas, take a look at Chapters 7, 9, 12, 18, and 19.

FIGURE 8-7: The Olympus C-160 1.45x teleconverter mounted on the lens adapter

Using a P&S Camera like an SLR

On a P&S camera, the optical viewfinder sees out of a different optical window than the lens, creating a parallax effect. The parallax effect causes your framing of the scene to be slightly off. When you use a lens converter, such as a teleconverter or wide-angle converter, the magnification in the optical viewfinder is off by the same amount as the magnification lens converter applies. In addition, lens converters are generally quite large and stick out in front of the camera. In many cases, the lens converter will block the optical viewfinder window.

On an SLR, the optical viewfinder sees exactly what the lens sees. The best way to use your P&S digital camera, with accessories for your lens, is to turn on the electronic viewfinder (when you use the LCD as the viewfinder) during composition. The electronic viewfinder allows you to see the scene as the lens sees it (see Figure 8-8) after filter, lens converters, and other accessory effects have been applied. This characteristic is similar to the way an SLR works.

Unfortunately for P&S film cameras, there is no LCD and no electronic viewfinder for these cameras. If you modify a P&S film camera, you will have to shoot using the optical viewfinder. Your framing will be based on trial-and-error and by studying the prints afterward. But your guesses and estimations will get better and better over time.

FIGURE 8-8: The LCD being used as an electronic viewfinder

Changing the Lens Magnification

In Chapter 7 you saw how magnification and perspective changes the observer's viewpoint. It's easy to see that your zoom lens not only helps you get closer to the action but can help you portray your subject differently as you set the zoom lens to a particular focal length and move physically closer or farther away. The magnification, and therefore perspective, is changed.

Sometimes you'll want to extend the zoom range or change the magnification on your fixed focal length lens. You can do that with wide-angle and telephoto accessory lenses as described in Chapter 7. But if you understand lens elements and groups, you can even take your accessory lens apart and recombine elements from multiple lenses to achieve the desired magnification. In this chapter, you'll learn about lens elements, groups, and how to reconfigure your lenses.

Understanding Lens Elements and Groups

A very basic lens, such as the lens found in a common magnifying glass, is called a simple lens. A simple lens has only one lens element, generally made out of a spherical glass. The simple lens in the magnifier is a converging lens, where the lens is thicker in the center than at the edge (see Figure 9-1). A diverging lens, on the other hand, is thicker at the edge than at the center. A diverging lens will make the subject you're observing appear smaller.

Even though today's camera lenses are based on the simple lens concept, they are far more complicated. Today's camera lenses have multiple lens elements in multiple groups. The lens elements could be made out of spherical glass, aspherical plastic, or combinations of the two. A lens group is a group of lens elements either cemented together or which travel together within the lens throughout the zoom/focus range.

By combining multiple lens elements and groups, you can create a diverse range of telephoto and wide-angle lenses. Telephoto lenses are generally composed of multiple converging lenses. Wide-angle lenses are generally composed of multiple diverging lenses.

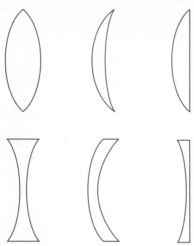

FIGURE 9-1: Converging and diverging lens shapes. Converging lenses are shown on the top row; diverging lenses are shown on the bottom row.

Note The lens makers' equation is covered in physics books, in optics-related chapters. The equation is useful if you want to design your own lens. But it's not very practical if you just want to figure out the specifications for the lenses you own.

Stacking Lenses

It's pretty much agreed upon that the more lens elements you have between your subject and the imaging material (film or sensor), the more likely that the resulting image is going to be degraded. The cause of this problem is the slight transmission loss as light travels through each lens element. This is true even in cases where all of the lens elements are optimized to work with one another, as they are in commercially manufactured lenses. The problem becomes worse when you stack multiple lenses on top of one another that weren't designed to work together.

There are many valid situations where you must stack multiple lenses and teleconverters because you won't be able to get the image you want any other way. For example, if you are shooting in narrow quarters, you might need to stack several wide-angle lenses to fit everything in one photo frame. And if you are shooting ducks on the other side of a pond that doesn't allow you to wade in its water, then you may need to stack several telephoto and teleconverter lenses.

The point is, avoid stacking lenses, but don't make it your life's mission. When you need it for getting the perspective you want, stack them.

Reconfiguring the Cokin 0.5x Wide-Angle Lens

The Cokin 0.5x Wide-Angle Lens (model 10440) is an accessory lens to supplement a camcorder or a digital camera. As its name implies, it changes the magnification of the primary lens by 0.5 times. If the primary lens's focal length is 20mm, this accessory lens converts its field-of-view to that of a 10mm lens.

Upon closer examination of the lens, and owing mostly to the fact that "macro" is stamped in red on it, I found that the Cokin 0.5x Wide-Angle Lens is actually composed of two separate lenses: a wide-angle lens and a macro lens. When unscrewed from each other, the macro lenses worked quite well when mounted on a camera. On the other hand, the wide-angle lens mounted on the camera, by itself without the macro lens element, did not allow the camera to focus at any distance. Nevertheless, I am quite pleased that the Cokin 0.5x Wide-Angle Lens serves two purposes: wide-angle and macro.

Intrigued by the way the macro lens element complemented the wide-angle lens element, I decided to disassemble the lens further, extracting all of the lens elements.

Disassembling the Lens

The front element is held with an aluminum ring that screws onto the front of the silver lens casing. Unscrew the aluminum ring from the silver external casing to disassemble the wide-angle lens. Once the lens has been disassembled, you can remove the two diverging lens elements from the casing (see Figure 9-2). Be careful not to touch the face of any lens element, which could scratch it.

FIGURE 9-2: The Cokin 0.5x wide-angle lens disassembled

Reconfiguring the Lens Elements

The two diverging lens elements work together to create the 0.5x magnification. Each, by itself, produces more magnification than the two combined. The smaller diverging lens element produces a wider angle-of-view than the larger diverging lens element. It turns out that each of the lens elements works with the macro lens element to produce a different wide-angle magnification. So by reconfiguring the lens element, you can have a 0.5x lens and two additional wide-angle possibilities.

What's Next?

You might have other accessory lenses lying around. Try to take those apart. You might try to combine lens elements from different accessory lenses to see what kind of results you get. You might find that you could end up with more wide-angle or telephoto capabilities than you think you have.

Making Your Own Pinhole Lens

Pinhole photography is the same as "normal" photography in every respect but one: No lens is used in the process of taking the picture. A pinhole camera has a very small hole, called an *aperture*, which projects an image onto film or a digital sensor. So, if photography is the art or process of producing images on photosensitive surfaces, then pinhole photography is photography using a tiny hole.

Several characteristics of a pinhole photograph are important because they are the reasons a photographer chooses to shoot with a pinhole:

- Pinhole pictures are generally not as sharp as pictures made with a lens.

- The pictures have an infinite depth-of-field.

- The pictures have straight lines that are always straight (rectilinear), with no barrel or pin-cushion distortion from a conventional lens.

- A pinhole lens is cheap and easy to make at home.

Why Does It Work?

The pinhole is the grandfather of all lenses. The basic concept of how any lens works is the same as how a pinhole lens makes images. The concept is best described with a diagram, shown in Figure 10-1. The picture is always generated upside-down because light travels in a straight line.

FIGURE 10-1: Light travels in straight lines through the pinhole onto a photosensitive surface.

Making the Pinhole Lens

From the moment I first learned about it, I have been fascinated with the art of pinhole photography. The possibility of creating an image using the tiniest hole is amazing to me. I read about how to make a pinhole camera out of a 35mm film canister—it seemed easy enough. But despite my fascination, I have never involved myself with pinhole photography. Although the process of making the camera is easy, loading and processing the film is extremely cumbersome. To use a film canister-based pinhole camera, one frame of film has to be loaded in the dark, exposure has to be calculated, the picture has to be exposed by uncovering the pinhole, the pinhole has to be covered, and the film has to be unloaded in the dark. All that work for a *single* exposed frame! But that is not the end, because the frame has to be processed in a personal darkroom, since it is extremely hard to find a place to process one frame of 35mm film at a time.

As I thought about the difficulties, this occurred to me: "Wouldn't it be nice if I could have a pin-hole camera that has a built-in exposure meter, uses 35mm film or a digital sensor, and comes with auto frame advance? Then I could concentrate on creating pinhole art, instead of concentrating on processing it." After a few years (yes, I am a tad slow) I thought, "Wouldn't it be nice if I could have a pinhole lens on my EOS camera—that has auto-exposure, uses standard 35mm film, and has an automatic film winder?" Wow!

Although the rest of this chapter uses the Canon EOS SLR system as its example, the same concept can be applied to any film or SLR from any manufacturer (Nikon, Olympus, Pentax, Kodak, Sigma, and so on.) with a body cap. Throughout this chapter, I'll use SLR to mean any single-lens-reflex film or digital camera.

Parts and Tools You Need

Here are the parts and tools you will need to complete this project:

- Camera body cap
- Needle
- Small drill bit
- Electric drill or electric screwdriver

The material needed to make this lens is inexpensive—in fact, this is probably the cheapest lens available for an SLR because the only material needed is the camera body cap (see Figure 10-2). Often, these caps can be found for a dollar or two in the clearance bin at a camera store. You might want to pick up several spare body caps.

FIGURE 10-2: A camera body cap is all you need to make a pinhole lens.

This project requires a slow, low-torque electric drill. A heavy-duty, industrial drill is overkill and will make the task a lot harder. Manual drills will also work, but they generally require two hands and will make the process tedious. A simple and cheap electric screwdriver with a drill bit made for it works well for this task.

Measuring the Cap

The first thing to do is to find the center of the body cap, which is where you drill the pinhole. To find the center, draw two perpendicular lines, each cutting the circle exactly in half—the intersection of the two lines marks the center of the circle.

Start by moving the ruler across the body cap as shown in Figure 10-3, looking for the widest part of the cap, which is the cap's diameter. Draw a straight line with a pencil on the body cap. Do the same to draw the second line perpendicular to the first, as shown in Figure 10-4. The center of the cap is where the two lines intersect.

FIGURE 10-3: Using a ruler, measure the inside diameter of the body cap.

FIGURE 10-4: Once you've measured horizontally, measure vertically to find the center.

Drilling the Preliminary Hole

After you mark the center, it's time to drill the pinhole. Use the smallest drill bit you have, but be careful; even the smallest drill bit can make a pinhole far too big, so use the drill bit only to start the hole. For the examples shown in this chapter, I used a $^1/_{16}$" bit. From inside the lens cap, drill a hole down to the other side (see Figure 10-5), *but do not drill all the way through.*

FIGURE **10-5: Drill the hole in the center of the camera body cap with the smallest drill bit and a low-torque electric screwdriver.**

Be sure to drill on a suitable surface and not on your executive desk, in case the drill bit punches through. Although you don't want to drill all the way through the camera body cap in this step, there is always Murphy's Law.

Drill slowly and constantly check to see if the hole is getting close to the other side. There are two ways you can check. The first is to look at the hole and estimate its depth relative to the thickness of the cap. This method requires intuition on your part but is not difficult.

The second method is to constantly check the other side and see if a dimple has formed. (As your drill bit comes closer to the other side, the material becomes thinner and the surface deforms slightly into a dimple.)

Creating a Pinhole Using a Needle

The hole drilled in the previous step with the $^1/_{16}$"drill bit is far bigger than a pinhole, so get out your next tool, the needle.

Note	You can use a shirt-pin (see Figure 10-6) instead of a needle. I buy dress shirts for work and have tons of these pins lying around. I always wondered what purpose they might serve for me in the future. Afraid that they may stab the trash man or some other unfortunate soul, I have been reluctant about throwing them away. But in this project, the shirt-pin serves a significant purpose.

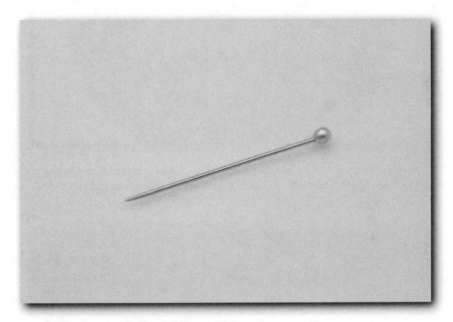

FIGURE 10-6: A shirt pin is a great tool for making a pinhole.

Using the needle, start working on the pinhole at the center of the drilled hole, as shown in Figure 10-7. Work slowly and keep the hole small. When you begin to see that the needle is making a little bump on the other side of the camera body cap, turn the cap over and start working on the outside of the body cap, using the needle on the center of the bump. This way you can be sure of making a tiny pinhole (see Figure 10-8).

FIGURE **10-7:** Drill slowly with the needle on both sides of the body cap, remembering to constantly check whether a pinhole has been made—you don't want to make it too big.

FIGURE **10-8:** A completed pinhole lens. The pinhole is extremely small and could only be captured with a 1:1 macro lens in the photograph.

Trying It Out

The pinhole is so small that only a minute amount of lights passes through it. Thus, when you look through the optical viewfinder of an SLR with the pinhole lens cap, you won't see anything—at first. However, your eye will adjust, just like when you first turn off the lights at home at night. Eventually you will see a dim image, representing the scene your camera sees.

Before starting to use the pinhole lens for photography, it is worthwhile to check it first. The best way to see if the pinhole covers the entire picture frame is to point the camera and the pinhole at a bright light source. As Figure 10-9 shows, I prefer to use a light bulb; it's readily available in a controlled environment, your home. Looking through the viewfinder of your camera, with the pinhole lens mounted on the camera, get very close to the light bulb of a lamp. Examine the edge of the frame: If you can see distinct edge lines, then the frame is covered and you are ready to experiment with pinhole photography.

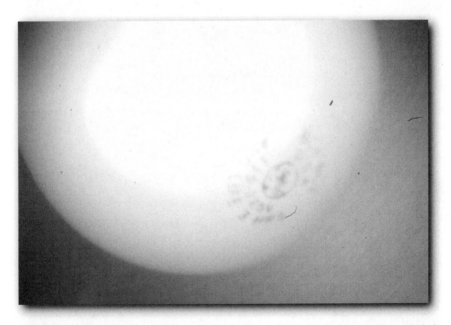

FIGURE 10-9: A light bulb provides an excellent source of light for checking your pinhole lens.

Lens Comparison

Of the following pictures (Figures 10-10 and 10-11), one was taken with the EOS pinhole lens, the other picture was taken with the Canon EF 50mm f/1.8 II lens at f/22, the smallest aperture for this lens. Can you guess which picture is taken by which lens without peeking at the caption?

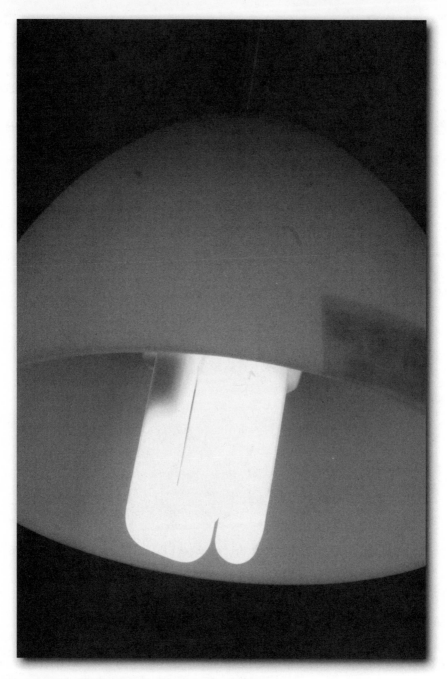

FIGURE 10-10: A picture taken with the Canon EF 50mm f/1.8 II lens at f/22

FIGURE 10-11: A picture taken with the EOS pinhole lens

Shooting with the Pinhole Lens

For some photographers, taking pictures is a form of art. The artistic expression in the result, the photograph, is to them the most important element. These photographers may not care about how the picture is taken or what photographic gear is used in the process. For other photographers, the process of shooting the photograph and the gear used are equally significant or even more significant than the final art. They want to know what settings made the effects. They want to know what focal length, what aperture, and what shutter speed were used to shoot the picture. Both of these preferences are equally valid. There are professional photographers in both camps, and they all produce exceptional photographs that inspire and are admired by many.

This section is for the second type of photographers: the photographers who want to know the pinhole's focal length, aperture, and depth of field, and the exposure needed to shoot different types of pinhole photographs.

If you are the first type of photographer, you need read no further. You are ready to experiment with your new pinhole lens and learn to shoot pinhole pictures. Use the automatic exposure feature of your SLR to guide you. You can always come back later to read about the concept behind the process.

Focal Length

The focal length is defined as the distance between the lens and the film/sensor plane. On Canon EOS SLRs, you can see a little mark that looks like a circle with a vertical line drawn through it, as shown in Figure 10-12. The mark indicates the position of the film plane. The focal length can be determined by measuring from this mark to the pinhole, generally in millimeters. The focal length of the EOS pinhole lens is 50mm.

Aperture

To calculate aperture, divide the focal length by the diameter of the pinhole. The unit (inches, millimeters, or whatever you decide to use) of the focal length and pinhole diameter must be the same. The resulting aperture number is unit-less, and is referred to as the f-number, or f-stop.

$$f-stop = \frac{focal\ length}{aperture\ diameter}$$

For this example, I estimated the diameter of the pinhole on my lens cap with an imprecise ruler. In my estimation, the pinhole I made is about 0.2mm. The focal length is 50mm.

$$f-stop = \frac{50\ mm}{0.2\ mm} = 250$$

An f-stop of 250 requires *a lot of light* to make an exposure. Enlarge the pinhole slightly if you do not want to wait so long for an exposure. But keep in mind that the larger the aperture, on a pinhole lens, the softer the image.

FIGURE 10-12: You can measure the focal length of the pinhole lens with a ruler. Measure from the film plane mark to the end of the camera body cap.

Determining Exposure Time

Cameras create pictures by exposing a photosensitive surface such as film or digital sensor to light. The amount of detail depends on the amount of light striking the surface and on the sensitivity of the surface. Since a pinhole restricts the amount of light passing through it, pinhole photographs generally take a relatively long time to expose compared to other types of photographs. Depending on the lighting conditions and the size of the pinhole, exposure time may range from a few tenths of a second to a few hours.

An SLR with an automatic exposure metering system makes exposure time determination easy because the on-board computer calculates the setting for you. But what if you are using film with reciprocal failure? Most films are designed to be exposure for a fairly short period of time, such as $1/10000$ second to 1 second. If you use these films outside the design range, the film will not be properly exposed, which is called reciprocal failure. Different films have different exposure ranges. You'll have to look at the reciprocal failure section on the specification sheet for your particular film. The specification sheet will help you determine how to adjust the exposure for your film.

Checking Your Digital SLR Sensor for Dust

If you own an SLR, you will find that a pinhole lens can help you check for dust on the digital sensor. With a regular lens and limited depth-of-field, specks of dust are usually blown so out of focus that they don't show up in the picture. The large depth-of-field provided by the tiny aperture of a pinhole lens causes even the tiniest dust speck on the sensor to show, thereby allowing you to detect dust for cleaning (see Figure 10-13).

FIGURE 10-13: Dust shows up as dark anomalies in your picture that are not in the physical scene.

Start by finding a fairly bright scene or light source. Take a picture of the scene with your digital camera set at the highest resolution. Then bring up the picture on the camera's LCD or on your PC at home. I prefer a PC so that I can see the entire picture in full resolution at 1:1 ratio. Sometimes the reduction of resolution on the camera's LCD can hide dust specks. Dust shows up as dark anomalies in the picture that are not in the physical scene. Once you have determined that there is dust on your sensor and you have located it, follow the sensor cleaning instructions in your camera's instruction manual.

Tips on Shooting a Pinhole Photograph

The best place and time to shoot pinhole photographs are outdoors and on bright sunny days. These conditions let you shoot with the fastest shutter speed, and may even allow you to hand-hold your camera without blurring the image. Nevertheless, you will encounter times when the exposure time for a scene is so long that you can't eliminate camera shake, not to mention that your arms will get very tired during long exposures.

One way you might achieve shorter exposure times is by using more sensitive film or by increasing the sensitivity of the digital sensor. You can do this by using higher ISO film or by using the highest ISO setting on the camera. See Appendix D for more information on ISO speed.

If you don't want grainier images or more digital noise—side-effects of using more sensitive material—you will want to get a tripod. By placing your camera on a tripod, you can get rid of camera shake and your arms won't have to carry the weight of the camera during a long exposure. You can also place your camera on the ground, a chair, a table, or even a bean bag. In essence, use anything available to keep your camera steady.

Most SLRs today allow you to set long exposures—up to 30 seconds. But if the exposure is any longer, you will have to use the *bulb* mode, where you manually control the camera to open and close its shutter. Some cameras are engineered so that when you push the shutter button once, the shutter opens, and when you push the button a second time, the shutter closes. Other cameras open the shutter when you push the shutter button and close the shutter when you release the button. Both have advantages and disadvantages, but if you have the second type, it will get tiring very quickly when you try to make an hour-long exposure.

To overcome that problem, use a remote shutter release. The remote shutter release attaches to the camera and moves the shutter button off the camera. Most electrical shutter releases have a lock feature so you don't have to hold it during a bulb exposure. But most mechanical shutter releases do not. You can easily mitigate this with masking tape.

Extending the Lens on Canon EOS Cameras

As camera technology becomes more sophisticated with auto-exposure, auto-focus, image stabilization, and optical zoom, its lens technology must keep up as well. One result is that the lens-to-camera communication is far more sophisticated than before. Gone are the simple mechanical lenses that attach to single lens reflex (SLR) camera bodies. Today's lenses and cameras have sophisticated electrical and mechanical contacts that facilitate communication between the two parts.

As a result of the sophistication in lens-to-camera interfaces, interesting phenomena occur when you are trying to hack the system to your advantage. One good example is when you attach a T-mount lens to a T-mount adapter to an auto-focus (AF) teleconverter to a Canon EOS camera body. In many cases, the Canon EOS camera faults and reports an error to you, preventing you from shooting the picture.

In this chapter, I explain the differences between Canon EOS manual and automatic lenses, and show you how to circumvent the problem and how to modify your commonly used lenses permanently so that you don't have to deal with this issue often.

The Problem

A few years ago, my friend was working for Mead, the telescope company. One night, he brought home a 1200mm telescope so that we could examine the face of the moon. Using a T-mount adapter, we were able to mount it onto my Canon EOS Elan IIe SLR. We were able to shoot some really nice pictures of the moon and see some cool craters. We got even closer by mounting both of my 1.4x and 2x EOS automatic teleconverters for a total focal length of 3360mm. The view was spectacular; we were able to fill the entire 35mm film frame with half of the moon's face. Both large and small craters showed up clearly. We clicked the shutter release to capture this grand exhibition and, behold, the battery symbol continuously flashed on the LCD while the camera went into an error state.

Cross-Reference

See Chapter 9 for information about changing magnification.

After experimenting with the camera, teleconverters, and lenses, I realized that the automatic teleconverters must be used with automatic lenses. Automatic teleconverters with pass-through contacts cannot be used with manual lenses, such as my friend's telescope. As much as I like camera equipment, I did not want to spend more money on manual teleconverters. Plus, I don't think manual teleconverters are even available for Canon EOS cameras. Luckily, I discovered how the Canon EOS cameras determine whether an automatic or a manual lens is mounted.

Note

Automatic lenses are EF-compatible lenses, which can communicate with the EOS camera body via the electrical EF interface. Manual lenses can be mounted to the EOS body directly or through a T-mount adapter but do not communicate with the EOS camera body.

The EOS SLRs monitor a mechanical switch on the lens mount. Each lens has three tabs for mounting to the camera body's bayonet mount. On auto lenses, the tab is longer (see Figure 11-1), thus triggering the switch. The tab is shorter on a manual lens (see Figure 11-2) and will not trigger this switch. When the switch is triggered, the EOS camera body attempts to communicate with the lens upon activation of the AF/shutter button. If the switch is not triggered, the EOS cameras assume that a manual lens or no lens is mounted and therefore does not communicate to the lens at all.

T-Mount

Each SLR manufacturer designs its cameras around its own mounting system. Therefore, a Canon EF lens will not mount to a Nikon camera body, and vice versa. However, there are a number of manual lenses out there that don't need to take advantage of the sophisticated electrical communication system of any particular camera manufacturer. These lenses can be used on any SLR in manual mode. These lenses utilize a lens mount called a T-mount.

The T-mount lenses can be mounted to any SLR system with a T-mount adapter. A T-mount adapter is made for each camera system and can be purchased from your local photography store for about fifteen bucks. See Chapter 12 for pictures and technical specifications of a T-mount adapter.

FIGURE 11-1: The tab on an automatic lens is longer.

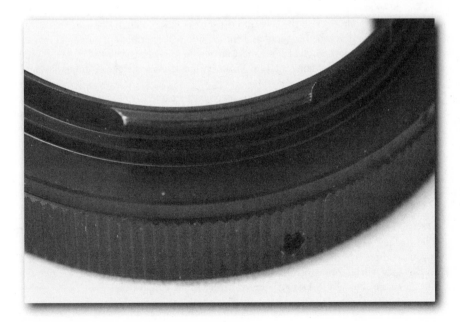

FIGURE 11-2: The tab on a manual lens is shorter.

New EOS Design

The new EOS design doesn't include this mechanical switch. The Digital Rebel (also known as the 300D and the Kiss Digital), for example, doesn't come with this switch. It could determine whether an automatic or manual lens is mounted by communicating through the electrical EF interface. If the lens responds, the camera determines that the lens is automatic. If the lens doesn't respond, the camera assumes that it is manual.

In the telescope situation, we mounted the telescope (manual) onto the T-mount adapter (manual), then onto the two teleconverters (automatic), and then onto the EOS camera body. The automatic teleconverter, the one closest to the camera, triggered the mechanical switch and passed the electrical EF signals to the second teleconverter. The second teleconverter also passes the signals to the T-mount adapter, where the signals are dropped, because the T-mount adapter is a manual mount. The camera didn't see a return signal and therefore went into an error state.

Jury-Rigging the Lens

To use automatic teleconverters with manual lenses on Canon EOS SLRs, mount the manual lens to the teleconverter as normal. But when mounting the teleconverter to the camera body, do not turn the teleconverter all the way into the lock position. When done correctly, the mechanical switch will not be triggered and the camera will operate as if a manual lens is mounted. Using this method, my friend and I were able to shoot wonderful close-up pictures of the moon that night. The same method works with automatic extension tubes also.

Caution Realize that when using the equipment in this manner, the camera is not locked to the teleconverter and lens pair. Rotation to either could cause them to detach from each other, causing one of the parts to drop to the ground. If you choose to use your equipment in this manner, be very careful.

Modifying the Lens Permanently

If you often need to jury-rig your set-up because you shoot a lot of astrophotography, you might consider making a permanent modification to your teleconverter or lens. Keep in mind that when you do, these teleconverters or lenses will not work in automatic mode on the older EOS SLRs. But they will continue to work in both automatic and manual modes on the newer EOS SLR (refer to the "New EOS Design" sidebar earlier in the chapter).

Tools You Need

Here are the tools you will need to complete this project:

- Metal file
- Precision screwdriver
- Permanent marker
- Vise

The best way to make the permanent modification to your lens is with a metal file. A small round one works best. The precision screwdriver helps you remove the lens mount so that it's easy to file. You use the permanent marker, such as a Sharpie, to mark the modification location. The vise is not absolutely necessary, but it helps hold the mount steady as you file. You can pick up all of these parts at a home improvement store for a few bucks.

Modifying the Lens Mount

Before proceeding, examine the bayonet mount on the lens and the camera to determine which tab to modify. Also, you need to determine which side of the tab to hack. Use a permanent marker to mark the location.

Next, dismantle the lens mount from the lens, teleconverter, or extension tube. The modification process will be a lot smoother with the mount removed. Chapter 12 provides instructions on the dismantling process.

Mount the lens mount to the vise. Now you are ready to file the mount. With the round file, move the file back and forth on the corner of the tab to be modified. Start by filing slowly, and steadily increase your pace. You will soon notice that the tab has gotten a bit shorter. Check the mount periodically to see if you have filed away enough metal for your set-up to work. Stop as soon as you have filed away enough metal.

Reassemble your lens, and it will work as a manual lens.

Making Reverse Macro Adapters

H ave you ever wanted to capture a flower really close up—maybe even get the texture of the flower petal and the little tiny ant to show up in your pictures? Flowers, petals, and ants are just a few of the fascinating subjects in a small world. This small world is the beautiful garden in your back yard.

You've probably tried to capture this small world before, and if so, you have probably found that the general-purpose lens that came with your camera has a minimum focus distance the size of a football field in this small world. You've probably been frustrated just trying to shoot rose petals. To capture the beauty of this small world, you can buy some fancy extreme close-up equipment.

That specialized equipment is expensive. Most of it can only give you a magnification of 1:1. A magnification of 1:1 means that the actual size of the subject is captured on film. A magnification 1:4 means the subject is rendered $1/4$ its actual size on film. A magnification 4:1 means the subject is rendered on film is four times its actual size. What most manufacturers don't tell you is that with a simple adapter, you can make your general-purpose lens a very good accessory for macro photography. With a simple adapter, you can even magnify to a scale greater than 1:1. The simple adapter is a lens reversal adapter, which will enable you to shoot extreme macro photography, as you can see in Figure 12-1.

In this chapter, I explain how to make two different types of lens reversal adapters. One, the manual lens-reversal adapter, is extremely simple and easy to make. You can make one in 15 minutes. The other one, the automatic lens-reversal adapter, is a lot more involved and will probably take you a few nights to get right. But the automatic adapter will work with all the neat electronic features on your camera. And it may be the one you have to make if you have to change lens aperture through your camera.

FIGURE 12-1: An extreme close-up of a flower

Parts You Need

This section has two parts, one for building a manual adapter and one for building an automatic adapter. The manual adapter is extremely easy to build and is generally enough for most macro photography. Macro photography uses an extremely short range-of-focus; therefore AF is not necessary and could sometimes even get in the way. For the ultimate macro photography experience, build the automatic adapter and you will be able to control AF as well. If you have an SLR system that doesn't have a mechanical aperture ring on every lens, the automatic adapter will allow you to change the aperture electronically.

Manual Adapter

You need only two parts to build the manual adapter:

- T-mount adapter
- 52mm-58mm reversal ring

You can buy the T-mount adapter at a camera shop for about $15. It is possible to find the reversal ring, but it is not as easy as it used to be. If you can't find one locally or online, you can make your own (see the "Making Your Own Lens-to-Lens Reversal Adapter" sidebar for instructions). The size of the reversal ring should be determined by the lens you want to use for macro photography. You can also use step-up and step-down rings to adjust the size for different lenses in your collection.

Making Your Own Lens-to-Lens Reversal Adapter

It used to be easy to find a lens-to-lens reversal adapter. This type of adapter allows you to reverse a lens onto the front of another lens. There is a male lens thread on each side of the adapter, as shown in Figure 12-2.

FIGURE 12-2: A 52mm–58mm reversal ring

When I was writing this chapter, I looked to purchase more lens-to-lens reversal adapters. Much to my surprise, the largest professional camera equipment resellers are no longer carrying these reversal rings. I was fortunate to have a 52mm–58mm reversal ring on hand.

Continued

Continued

Fortunately, step-up and step-down rings are in abundant supply. You can build your own lens-to-lens reversal adapters with step-up and step-down rings. Take two rings and place one on top of the other in reverse, as shown in Figure 12-3. Glue the two rings together. Now you have your own reversal ring.

FIGURE 12-3: A 52mm–55mm step-up ring glued to a 55mm–58mm step-up ring. The result is a 52–-55mm reversal adapter.

Automatic Adapter

The automatic adapter requires the following parts:

- 12mm automatic extension tube
- 20mm automatic extension tube
- 10" ribbon cable
- 52mm–49mm step-down ring

Extension tubes come in many sizes. The length, as shown in Figure 12-4, specifies their sizes. The difference between an automatic extension tube and a manual extension tube is that the automatic version retains the electronic communication between your camera and your lens. Automatic extension tubes of any size can be used for this project. If you buy a set, it will cost less than purchasing each one individually.

FIGURE 12-4: Auto extension tubes: 12mm, 20mm, and 36mm

Ribbon cables are commonly used in electronics and computers. You can find them at electronic parts stores. If you have a lot of old computer ribbon cable lying around, you can also use this. (See the "Scavenging the IDE Ribbon Cable" sidebar later in this chapter.) Canon EOS cameras have an 8-pin electrical connector. Therefore, the ribbon cable has to have a minimum of eight wires. For other brands, you may need more or fewer wires in your ribbon cable. It is better to use a ribbon cable with more wires than you need; you can always strip away the extras.

I used a 7.5" ribbon cable for this project. It was barely long enough for my Canon EF 50mm f/1.8 and my Canon EF 28mm f/2.8 lenses. To be safe, you'll want to use a 10" ribbon cable. And if you really want to use big lenses, you should use a 20" ribbon cable.

For Canon EOS cameras, I have found that the 52mm–49mm step-down ring fits perfectly on the lens mount. This step-down ring provides a 52mm reverse mount, which is the standard diameter for many of Canon's standard and wide-angle lenses. You can then use other step-down and step-up rings to mount other lenses in your collection. You'll have to do some experimentation to find the right size for other SLR brands.

Macro Focus Accessories

Reversing the lens with an adaptor is not the only way you can achieve macro focus on your subject. There are numerous other accessories to help you get close.

A **close-up lens** is basically a magnifying glass. By placing close-up lenses in front of your existing lenses, you can focus much closer to the subject than normal. Close-up lenses are available in +1, +2, and +4 diopters. You can create different diopter combinations by combining multiple close-up lenses. For example, combining +1 and +2 lenses makes a +3 diopter close-up lens. There are two types of close-up lenses: standard and achromatic diopters. A standard close-up lens has a single element, and generally renders an image that is sharp in the center, but that sharpness quickly falls off around the edges. The uncorrected distortion also introduces color fringing around the edges. An achromatic close-up lens has two elements. The two lens elements are highly corrected and work together to produce extremely sharp images from edge-to-edge without color fringe. The nice thing about a close-up lens is that it does not reduce the amount of light reaching your digital sensor.

Extension tubes are basically empty tubes that extend the lens farther away from the film plane. These tubes can be attached between your SLR lens and your SLR. When the lens is extended away from the film plane, it becomes short-sighted, allowing it to focus much closer than it could normally. In turn, this increases magnification. Because extension tubes are simply extensions without any lens elements, they do not affect the optical quality and resolution of the original lens. However, the longer the extension tube, the less light reaches the film plane, meaning you have to use a longer exposure.

A **bellows** is basically a flexible extension tube. Instead of being hard and rigid, like a plastic extension tube, the tube of the bellow is made out of soft material. The material could be paper, cardboard, fabric, or other soft non-transparent material. The bellows can be lengthened or shortened. It acts as an extension tube that has a continuously adjustable length.

Macro lenses are also widely available for SLRs. Most macro lenses can focus to a 1:1 magnification. Some macro lenses are just lenses with built-in extension tubes. Higher magnification macro lenses are rare, but they do exist. They are also far more expensive than normal macro lenses.

A **microscope** can help you see a world of tiny objects. They can magnify far greater than 1:1. Some microscopes have special camera attachments. Look for microscopes that support the use of a T-mount adapter.

Tools You Need

The tools you need differ depending on whether you are making a manual or an automatic adapter.

Manual Adapter

The manual adapter is easy to make, so the number of tools needed is minimal.

- 5/64" slotted precision screwdriver
- 5-minute general-purpose epoxy

Automatic Adapter

Don't let the size of this tools list scare you. These are all very basic tools that can be found around your home or a home improvement store.

- #1 Phillips precision screwdriver
- Tweezers
- $\frac{1}{4}$" drill bit
- $\frac{1}{16}$" drill bit
- Wire stripper
- 15 watt soldering iron
- 0.32"-diameter standard 60/40 resin core solder
- 5-minute general-purpose epoxy

Optional Tools

If you are building an automatic adapter, some additional tools may help you but are not required.

- Multimeter
- Soldering helper

The multimeter is not required to complete this project, but it helps diagnose electrical problems with any electronic project. I have an $80 digital multimeter that can measure volts, ohms, amps, and many other things. But an analog multimeter or a simple continuity checker costs only a few dollars at a home improvement store.

Although it's not a necessity, the soldering helper is a great time-saving investment if you do much soldering work. It acts as basically third and fourth hands (see the claws in Figure 12-5). This tool can be found at an electronic parts store. The soldering helper has speeded up many of my soldering projects. It also works great when you're gluing a part that you don't want to put down while it is drying.

FIGURE 12-5: Soldering helper

Extreme Macro Photography with Your Point-and-Shoot Camera

Don't feel left out if you have a P&S digital camera and not an SLR. You can take extreme macro photographs as well by reversing SLR lenses onto your P&S camera. You'll need a lens-to-lens reversal ring that matches the filter thread on your camera and the SLR lens you want to use. Refer to Chapter 8 for information about how to make a lens adapter if your P&S digital camera doesn't have a filter thread at all. Of course, if you don't have an SLR lens already, you'll have to get one.

In Figure 12-6, I have attached a Canon EF 85mm f/1.8 SLR lens to my Sony Cyber-shot DSC-P92 digital camera. The Sony VAD-PEA lens adapter has a 30mm filter thread and the Canon 85mm lens has a 58mm filter thread. I also wanted to use the 52mm–58mm reversal ring so I stepped-up the 30mm filter thread using two step-up rings: 30mm–37mm and 37mm–52mm. Figure 12-7 shows the components that went into this setup. The picture shown in Figure 12-8 was shot with this setup.

FIGURE 12-6: Canon EF 58mm f/1.8 SLR lens reversed on a Sony Cyber-shot DSC-P92 digital camera

FIGURE 12-7: Components that went into this rig: Sony Cyber-shot DSC-P92 digital camera, Sony VAD-PEA lens adapter, Canon EF 58mm f/1.8 lens, 30-37mm step-up ring, 37-52mm step-up ring, and 52mm-58mm reversal ring

Continued

Continued

I tried using the Canon EF 50mm f/1.8 lens earlier. The Canon 50mm lens is an all-plastic lens, which makes it very light. Combined with its small size, it would have been a perfect companion for the Sony Cyber-shot DSC-P92. Unfortunately, the Canon 50mm lens element is too small to cover the entire image circle of the DSC-P92. The result is vignette on all four corners. The vignette may work for some low-key pictures, such as the picture shown in Figure 12-9. It's hard to see the vignette corners because of the low-key nature of the photograph.

The first rule of thumb when you choose a lens for your extreme macro photography is to choose one large lens elements. The lens elements should be big enough to cover the entire imager area of your P&S camera. This will eliminate vignette. Trying the lens on your camera is the easiest way to see if your image vignettes. If you see black corners, then it does and you will probably want to choose a different lens

It is a pity that the Canon 50mm lens cannot be used. As you can see, it has greater magnification on the subject than the Canon 85mm lens.

The next rule of thumb is to find the shortest focal length lens you can get away with that still covers the entire image circle on your P&S digital camera. The shorter the focal length, the more extreme you can get with your macro photography.

FIGURE 12-8: The Sony DSC-P92 was able to focus extremely close to the M-key with the assistance of the Canon 85mm lens.

FIGURE 12-9: This picture was shot with a Canon EF 50mm lens reverse mounted to the Sony DSC-P92. The lens element was too small and caused vignette on all four corners.

Making a Manual Adapter

A T-mount is an adapter for attaching universal manual lenses to a camera. Many of these universal manual lenses are specialized equipment, such as telescopes, microscopes, and slide film duplicators. These universal manual lenses attach to the T-mount adapter via a 42mm diameter thread with 0.75mm pitch (see Figure 12-10), which can be specified as M42-0.75. On the other side of the T-mount adapter is the mount specialized for your camera (see Figure 12-11).

Tip A manual reversal adapter may already exist for your camera. Some of these adapters cost less than the parts that would go into making your own, depending on the camera. But making your own manual adapter is really worth it if an adapter is not already available or simply costs too much.

Figure 12-10: The T-mount adapter has an M42-0.75 thread on the lens side.

Figure 12-11: On the other side, the T-mount adapter is either bayonet (pictured) or machine thread, depending your camera's lens mount type.

Disassembling the Sacrificial T-Mount Adapter

There is a T-mount adapter for every type of SLR out there. To simplify manufacturing, the T-mount adapter is composed of two metal pieces. The outer piece is specialized to the SLR. The inner piece has the M42-0.75 thread and is universal. Three tiny screws hold the universal piece within the inner circle of the outer piece, as shown in Figure 12-12. Unscrew each of the three screws. The inner piece can be easily removed, as shown in Figure 12-13.

FIGURE 12-12: A tiny screw is located at the deep end of this hole.

Note If you have a T-mount adapter that cannot be disassembled, skip the next step. You can still make a manual adapter with step-up and step-down rings.

Gluing the Reversing Ring to the T-Mount

With the inner metal piece removed, the 52mm end of the reversing ring fits perfectly on the T-mount (see Figure 12-14). Mix the chemical from your general-purpose epoxy with a toothpick. Be sure to follow the instructions on the label of your adhesive. Apply the epoxy to the 52mm side of the reversal ring, and then affix the reversal ring to the T-mount adapter. When the glue has set, in about a half hour, you'll be able to try out the adapter.

FIGURE 12-13: The inner piece can be easily removed.

FIGURE 12-14: The reversing ring glued to the T-mount adapter

Substitute with a Step-Up/Step-Down Ring

If your T-mount adapter can't be disassembled, you can still complete this project by gluing a step-up or step-down ring, in reverse, to it. It will work exactly the same as if you had used a reversing adapter. Figure 12-15 shows a step-up ring glued to a T-mount adapter. An added bonus to modifying the T-mount adapter this way is that the T-mount can still serve its original purpose, depending on the size of the T-mount lens.

FIGURE 12-15: A step-up ring glued to a T-mount adapter

Making an Automatic Adapter

The automatic lens reversal adapter retains all electrical communication between the camera body and the lens, even though the lens is reversed. For many camera brands, such as Canon EOS, it means that you will be able to retain control of the aperture and auto-focus through the camera body. Some cameras control lens aperture and auto-focus through mechanical means. This adapter won't benefit those mechanical camera and lenses. If you own mechanical camera and lenses, it's easier and cheaper to build the manual adapter as described earlier in this chapter.

This section shows you how to build an automatic lens reversal adapter for Canon EOS SLRs. But the concept can be applied to building automatic lens reversal adapters for other SLR systems. The steps are practically identical, but require a little more experimentation on your part. And that is part of the fun of hacking your camera equipment.

Dismantling the Sacrificial Extension Tubes

The extension tubes are composed of three major parts: the front lens mount, the rear lens mount, and the plastic tube. The metal mounts are attached to the plastic tube via four small machine screws. A #1 Phillips precision screwdriver will help you dismantle these mounts. Before you try to remove the mounts in haste, see Figure 12-16. I tried to disassemble the mounts on my 12mm extension tube too quickly and ended up with lots of parts all over my work area. These parts are tiny and when they go flying, they are hard to find.

Figure 12-16: If you are not careful removing the mount from the extension tube, you will have a mess of tiny parts on your workbench.

The best way to dismantle the EOS extension tubes is to remove the front lens mount first, then the rear lens mount. The front lens mount holds the lens locking switch and a black spring. When you remove the rear lens mount, place the extension tube flat on the table and lift up the rear lens mount slowly. When both mounts are removed, you will see the parts shown in Figure 12-17.

FIGURE 12-17: The 12mm extension tube after you have taken apart the front and rear mounts

You will also have to dismount the electrical connector from the rear lens mount. A black screw secures the connector, as shown in Figure 12-18. Remove these two black screws with the #1 Phillips precision screwdriver. Then slowly pull the electrical connecter out as shown in Figure 12-19.

FIGURE 12-18: Electrical connector screw

FIGURE 12-19: Electrical connector removed

Next, take the front lens mount off the 20mm extension tube. Remove the lens locking switch, black spring, and brass spacer. Then take the rear lens mount off as shown in Figure 12-20, but remember to keep the parts between the two extension tubes separate. A felt cardboard is placed behind the electrical contacts on the rear lens mount to prevent internal reflection (see Figure 12-21). Remove the felt cardboard carefully. You will have to place it back in position later. I was a lot more careful taking apart the 20mm extension tube, so the springs and the contact pins are still in place (Figure 12-22)

FIGURE 12-20: The 20mm extension tube taken apart

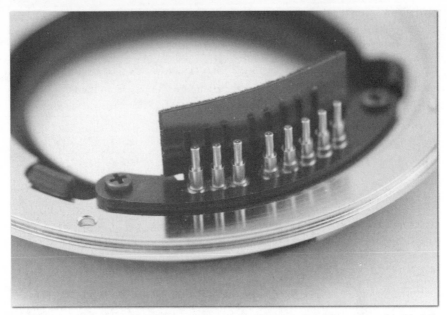

FIGURE 12-21: The electrical contacts on the rear mount. Note the felt cardboard behind the contacts.

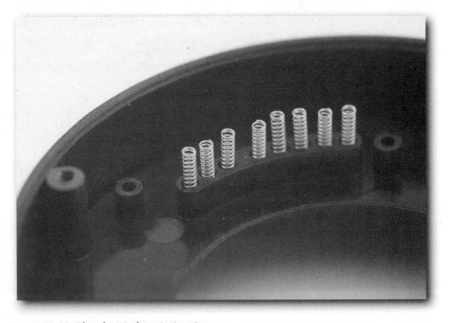

FIGURE 12-22: The electrical contact springs

Modifying the Extension Tubes

In this step, you'll have to make a few holes with your drill bit. The holes are for routing the ribbon cable. Use a $1/4$" drill bit and drill a hole on the side of the plastic tube, next to where the electrical contacts are located. On the 12mm extension tube, drill behind the front lens mount but in front of the electrical contact (see Figures 12-23 and 12-24).

FIGURE 12-23: Drill a hole on the side of the extension tube.

On the 20mm extension tube, the ribbon cable is going to reside on the inside of the plastic tube. Therefore, drill a $1/4$" hole between the electrical contact holes and the rear lens mount.

Now, take the 12mm plastic extension tube and enlarge the electrical contact holes with a $1/16$" drill bit as shown in Figure 12-25. These contact holes have to be enlarged in order to thread the ribbon cable through. Do not enlarge the holes on the 20mm extension tube.

FIGURE 12-24: The hole for the electrical cable

FIGURE 12-25: Enlarge the electrical contact holes with a drill bit.

Threading the Ribbon Cable

The Canon EOS electrical connector has 8-pins. Therefore, if you have a ribbon cable with more than eight wires, strip away the excess. You can strip them away easily with your finger-nails or an X-acto knife. Still working on the 12mm extension tube, thread the ribbon cable through the ¼" hole that you made. The ribbon cable has to be bent slightly, as shown in Figure 12-26.

FIGURE 12-26: The ribbon cable threaded through the hole on the side of the extension tube

Once the ribbon cable has been threaded through the large round hole, use your fingernail or an X-acto knife to separate the ribbon cable into individual wires. Feed each wire into the small holes on the extension tube (see Figure 12-27).

On the other side, use the wire stripper to strip the insulator off each wire. The ribbon cable wires are 22-gauge. They are extremely small. Use caution when you strip the insulator away, because you can easily pull out the metal wires inside the insulation. Thread the ribbon cable through the 20mm extension tube the same way as the 12mm extension tube. Also remember to separate and strip each individual wire (see Figure 12-28).

FIGURE 12-27: Thread each of the cables through the small contact holes.

FIGURE 12-28: Strip the wire insulator. Tin each wire with solder.

Scavenging the IDE Ribbon Cable

Having built many computers myself, I have a lot of old computer ribbon cable lying around. The internal IDE ribbon cable is a common standard in personal computers. I have quite a few of these. So I scavenged one of them for this project.

The computer ribbon cables have ribbon connectors on both sides. The IDE ribbon cable even has a connector in the middle. Use an X-acto knife to slide off the ribbon cable at the edge of the connector, as shown in Figure 12-29. The IDE ribbon cable has 40-pins, so strip off the extra wires that you don't need.

FIGURE 12-29: Slice the ribbon cable off the IDE connector with an X-acto knife.

Soldering the Wires

When you have successfully stripped all of the insulators from the wires, tin the wires with solder. Consult Appendix A if your soldering skills are rusty.

Next take the electrical connector for the 12mm extension tube and solder a tiny blob on the end of each electrical contact with a 15-watt soldering iron. Do not use a bigger soldering iron. I used a 30-watt soldering iron at first, but it was too hot, causing the plastic around the electrical contacts to melt. I had to do a lot of work to get the connector back in shape.

Solder each wire to the respective electrical contact. The contacts are extremely small, so you can only solder the tip of the wire to the contact. Start from one side on the connector and work your way to the other side (see Figure 12-30). When you're done, you should end up with a connector that looks like Figure 12-31. Check to make sure no wire is touching any other wire.

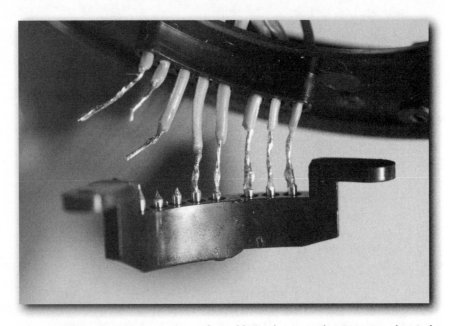

FIGURE 12-30: For the 12mm extension tube, solder each wire to the respective electrical contact.

The 20mm extension tube has longer gold electronic connector. You'll need to solder the ribbon cable to the side of the connector, between the rear lens mount and the gold spring contact. Start by placing a solder blob on each gold contact (see Figure 12-32). Be careful that you don't get any solder on the notch for the gold spring. It is very difficult to remove solder. I had to shave some off slowly once with an X-acto knife.

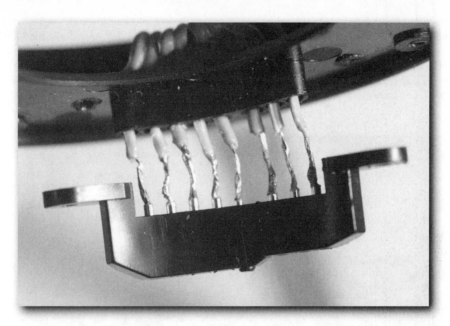

FIGURE 12-31: The connector should look like this after you have soldered all of the wires.

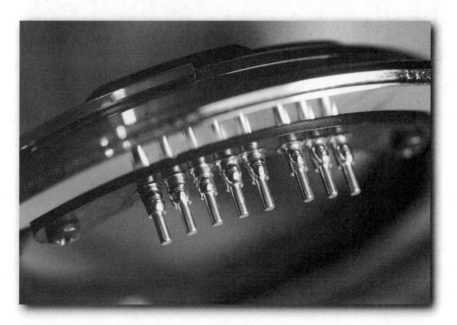

FIGURE 12-32: For the 20mm extension tube, place a solder blob on each gold contact.

Once you have placed a solder blob on each contact, it's easy to solder the wires to the solder blobs. Before you solder the wires, make sure you know which wire is soldered to which connector on the other extension tube. You will have to solder them to the matching contacts. The wires and contacts are small, so solder the wire ends to each solder blob (see Figure 12-33). Start from one side of the connector to the other side. When you are done, your contact should look like Figure 12-34. Check each wire to make sure it is not touching any other wires.

FIGURE 12-33: Solder each wire to a solder blob.

Tip You can use a multimeter or a continuity checker to make sure your solders are making good electrical contact.

Putting the Reverse Macro Adapter Together

Now you're ready to reassemble the extension tubes. Start with the 12mm extension tube. Push the electrical connector back into the rear lens mount (see Figure 12-35). Be careful that you don't break any of the solder connections that you've made. If you do, you will have to go back to the previous step and re-solder the broken connection. Secure the connector with the two black screws.

FIGURE 12-34: The 20mm extension tube connector should look like this after you have soldered all of the wires.

FIGURE 12-35: Install the connector back onto the rear mount.

With the connector securely mounted on the rear lens mount, carefully push the rear lens mount onto the plastic extension tube. Watch the wires while you are pushing to make sure they slide back through the electronic contact holes. Make sure you push slowly, but steadily. Don't break any of the solders that you've made. When the rear lens mount is firmly seated on the extension tube, screw it in with the four silver machine screws.

The front lens mount is a lot easier to install than the rear mount. Insert the black spring back onto the round hole for the lens-locking switch. Then put the lens-locking switch back in place. Attach the front lens mount and screw it down with the four silver machine screws. Make sure the front lens mount is not placing any stress on the ribbon cable.

You reassemble the 20mm extension tube slightly differently than the 12mm extension tube. Place all of the contact pins back into the plastic tube (if you have taken them out). Then place all of the gold springs in place on top of the contact pins. Looking between the rear lens mount and the plastic extension tube, put them together while making sure each gold pin is inserted into the correct gold spring. When they are all correctly inserted, secure the rear lens mount on the plastic extension tube with the four silver machine screws.

Turn the 20mm extension tube over. It's time to reassemble the front lens mount. Insert the brass spacer into the hole for the lens-locking switch. Place the black spring on top of it. Then place the lens-locking switch in place. Attach the front lens mount with the four silver screws, and the automatic lens reversal adapter is reassembled (see Figure 12-36).

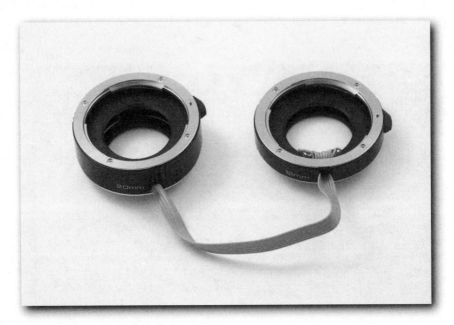

FIGURE 12-36: Reassembled extension tubes

Reverse Engineering Adapter

The automatic lens reversal adapter you just built can also serve as a lens communication reverse engineering adapter. The 20mm extension tube is fully functional, and you can still use it as an extension tube. With the lens mounted correctly on the 20mm extension tube, and the extension tube mounted correctly on the camera, the tethered 12mm extension tube serves as a reverse engineering tool. You can use digital multimeters, oscilloscopes, and other electronic tools to monitor the communication between the camera and the lens.

The Canon EOS-EF communication protocol has long been a mystery in the camera hacking community. Using the automatic lens reversal adapter as a reverse engineering tool, it may be possible to decipher the code. This application works for other camera systems as well.

To get you started, the following list shows the Canon EOS-EF signal names on the front of the camera body, reading from left to right. On the lens, pin 2 and 3 (P-GND) are one big contact. The camera hacking community derived the following data. This information may or may not be accurate.

- VBAT—Auto-focus motor power

- P-GND—Auto-focus motor ground

- P-GND—Same as above

- VDD—Logic circuitry power

- DCL—Data from camera to lens

- DLC—Data from lens to camera

- LCLK—Data clock

- D_GND—Logic circuitry ground

Gluing the Step-Down Ring

The last step is to glue a reversal ring onto the front of the 12mm extension tube. For the Canon EOS lens mount, I found that the 52mm–49mm step-down ring fits perfectly (see Figure 12-38). Use the 5-minute general-purpose epoxy on the three tabs of the bayonet lens mount. Then place the step-down ring in the center of the lens mount over the three tabs (see Figure 12-37). In half-an-hour, the epoxy will dry and your automatic lens reversal adapter will be ready for use.

FIGURE 12-37: The 52mm–49mm step-down ring is a perfect fit on the Canon EOS mount.

Trying Out Your Adapters

With the manual lens reversal adapter, you can attach your lens and camera in any combination you like. You can attach the lens to the adapter first, and then attach the adapter to the camera. Or you can attach the adapter to the camera, and then attach the lens to the adapter.

It's a little more difficult with the automatic lens. The best way is to mount the 12mm extension tube to the camera first. Screw the lens to the 12mm extension tube. Then attach the 20mm extension tube to the rear of the lens. Figure 12-38 shows a 50mm lens reverse-mounted on the reversal adapter, which is attached to an SLR.

With the lens and adapter attached to your camera, you are ready to shoot some close-up pictures. Using the manual adapter and the automatic adapter is fairly similar. The automatic adapter gives you the ability to auto-focus and change aperture electronically. But with the manual lens on the manual adapters, you should be able to change aperture with the mechanical adapter ring. In either case, you will be doing most of the focusing manually by moving forward and backward relative to the subject. The depth-of-field (DOF) is so shallow when you shoot at high magnification that the auto-focus won't work until you move the camera within the DOF range of the subject.

FIGURE 12-38: A Canon EF 50mm f/1.8 lens mounted in reverse on the automatic lens reversal adapter

Lens Selection

Find the lens with the shortest focal length possible. When you reverse-mount a lens, you reverse the magnification characteristic of the lens. In a normal setup, the longest telephoto lens provides the greatest magnification. However, when you reverse mount the lens, the telephoto lens provides the least magnification. So in extreme close-up photography, you will want to use a short focal length. A 50mm lens is a good one to start with. Try 28mm, another common lens, as well.

Angle Finder

Many small-world wonders live close to the ground. You will find yourself having to crawl on the grass or in the dirt just to capture them in your picture. You might be tempted to capture the wonder from atop, being too lazy to get down low. But you will only lose the opportunity to capture the wonder as you originally intended. The secret to getting the picture you want without crawling around is getting an angle finder for your camera.

An angle finder is an attachment that redirects the optical viewfinder of your camera by ninety degrees. It allows you to look through the viewfinder from the top of your camera. Some angle finders can be rotated, allowing you to shoot vertical as well as horizontal pictures.

Modifying the Canon EF-S Lens for Use on Canon EF Mounts

In 1987, Canon released a revolutionary new lens mount design. This new design allowed the camera body to communicate to the lens through electrical connectors only. This electrical communication controlled the mechanical features of the lens, such as auto-focus and closing the aperture diaphragm. Canon called this new mount the Electro-Focus mount, or EF mount. Thus, the Electro-Optical System (EOS) camera series was born.

Recently, digital SLRs (DSLRs) have become popular. Other than the highest-end professional cameras, most DSLRs have CCD or CMOS sensors that are smaller than a 35mm film frame (36mm × 24mm); often referred to as *full-frame*. While the EF lens's image circle covers the entire 35mm film frame with its 43.2mm diameter, it is oversized for the smaller sensor DSLR. The current EOS DSLR line-up—the Digital Rebel, D30, D60, 10D, and 20D—uses the smaller 22.7mm × 15.1mm sensor; often referred to as the 1.6x sensor because of its magnification difference compared to the full-frame.

A smaller 27.3mm-diameter image circle is all a lens needs to cover the smaller sensor, so a photographer who does not shoot film or a high-end full-frame DSLR will not benefit from the extra weight and cost of an EF lens. To help ease the burden on these photographers, Canon created a new mount for a new series of lenses, called EF-S. As its name implies, it is based on the original EF mount. The *S* in EF-S means short back focus. An EF-S lens has shorter back-focus distance (the distance between the rear of the lens and the focal plane) than an EF lens. Thus, the rear lens element protrudes and will contact the mirror in a full-frame camera. The Canon EF-S design includes a protective plastic and rubber ring to prevent the damage that would be caused by mounting this type of lens to EOS cameras that are not designed to accept EF-S lenses. Figure 13-1 shows the difference between the mounting surfaces of the two lens styles.

FIGURE 13-1: Canon EF 50mm f/1.8 lens on the left; Canon EF-S 18-55mm f/3.5-5.6 lens on the right

Canon designed the EF-S mount after releasing D30, D60, and 10D DSLR. Therefore, the EF-S mount made it onto the body of the Digital Rebel, the Digital Rebel XT, and the 20D only. Theoretically, since these cameras all use the same-size sensors, EF-S lenses should work on D30, D60, and 10D as well. In practice they do, with some help—this chapter will show you how to modify your EF-S lens to fit an EF lens mount.

Why would you want to use an EF-S lens on a non-EF-S camera? When you own:

- A small sensor DSLR with an EF mount, such as D30, D60, or 10D
- An EF-mount APS film camera
- A full-frame SLR or DSLR, but you want to use portion of the focal range that does not interfere with the mirror of your camera

Physical Differences between EF and EF-S

Canon first introduced EF-S mounts on the Digital Rebel. Now the Digital Rebel XT and the 20D have them as well. These cameras have 1.6x magnification sensors. The 1.6x magnification sensors are smaller than full-frame sensors; therefore, the camera bodies also have smaller mirrors. EF-S lenses are made for these smaller sensor cameras. The EF-S lenses are also smaller, more compact, and lighter. As a result of the smaller lens elements, they are also cheaper to produce and purchase. It is foreseeable that Canon will continue to introduce EF-S lenses for future 1.6x magnification sensor cameras. Theoretically, the EF-S lens should work on older 1.6x magnification sensor cameras such as the D30, the D60, and the 10D, but they do not because of physical differences between the EF mount on the camera body and EF-S mount on the lens. Figures 13-2 through 13-5 show the differences between the mounts on the camera body and the mounts on the lenses.

FIGURE 13-2: EF mount on a camera body

Continued

FIGURE 13-3: EF-S mount on a camera body. Note the indented circle.

FIGURE 13-4: EF mount on a lens

FIGURE 13-5: EF-S mount on a lens. Note the surrounding rubber that protects the lens and the body when the lens is accidentally mated to an EF camera.

Tools You Need

The following tools will help you modify your EF-S lens. Figure 13-6 shows the basic tools that are useful on a plastic lens mount. Read further for tool substitutes if you are modifying a metal lens mount.

- Precision screwdriver with a large handle
- Small precision screwdriver set
- Metal file
- C-clamps (2)
- Hobby saw

C-clamps are not required but may be useful to hold down the lens mount while you saw.

I found the hobby saw simple and easy to work with on plastic mount lenses. If you are working with a metal mount, you will probably want to use a hacksaw instead.

The file is not necessary unless you are working with a metal lens mount.

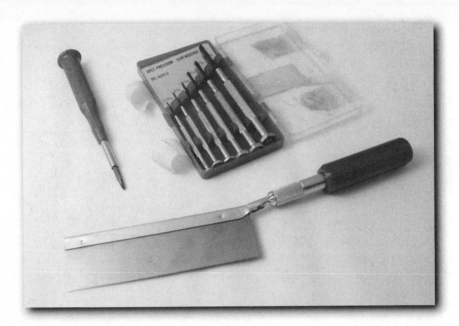

FIGURE 13-6: A precision screwdriver with a large handle, a small precision screwdriver set, and a hobby saw

Hacking Away

This example uses the Canon EF-S 18–55mm f/3.5–5.6 lens, but the concept can be applied to any EF-S lens. To keep the cost low and weight light, Canon decided to implement a plastic EF-S mount on this lens. On other EF-S lenses, the mount may be metal. But you can make the same modification, except that you might need to use a hacksaw instead of a hobby saw.

Disassembling the Lens

Start by unscrewing the two black screws holding the electrical contact strip to the lens mount (see Figure 13-7). Next, unscrew the four larger black screws on the lens mount (see Figure 13-8). The screws are fairly tight. Make sure you use a precision screwdriver with a large handle, so that proper torque can be applied; without the right tool, you can strip the head and make it very difficult to remove the screw later.

FIGURE 13-7: Two very small Phillips screws hold the electrical contact block to the lens mount.

FIGURE 13-8: Four bigger Phillips screws hold down the lens mount.

Carefully pull the lens mount upward. The electrical contact strip is soldered onto the circuit board below and should detach from the lens mount. If it provides resistance, make sure you've removed the screws (having done this operation so many times, sometimes I forget to unscrew it). You don't want to damage the contact strip. After pulling off the plastic lens mount and the paper ring under it, you will end up with the parts in Figure 13-9.

FIGURE 13-9: Lens mount, ring, and EF-S lens

Sawing the Plastic Mount

Saw the protruding rear plastic and rubber ring off. Saw it down to the level below the electrical contract. Use one of your EF lenses for comparison. If you don't have one, look at the pictures in the "Physical Differences between EF and EF-S" sidebar earlier in this chapter. I used C-clamps on a tool bench to secure the lens mount for sawing (see Figure 13-10). Because the lens mount includes an internal plastic cylinder to protect the lens element and circuit board, it is easier to saw around the cylinder instead of sawing through it. You might also consider removing the rubber ring from the plastic so that it doesn't get in the way.

Substituting the EF Lens Mounts

The thought has occurred to me that, rather than modifying the EF-S mount, it might be possible to substitute EF mounts from other EF lenses, thus allowing EF-S and EF mounts to be switched rather than permanently modified. After looking through my EF lens collection (of both Canon and third-party lenses), I rejected this idea. It turns out that the screw patterns on most EF lenses are different. And when the screw patterns are the same, the electrical contact locations, relative to the screw pattern, are different. It would require a lot more modification to the EF mount than to modify the EF-S mount itself.

FIGURE 13-10: The EF-S lens mount held down by C-clamps for easy sawing

Reassemble the Lens

After you have sawed the protruding plastic ring off the lens mount, clean the mount to remove burr. The plastic mount can be easily cleaned with your finger. If you are working with a metal mount, use a round file. The result is shown in Figure 13-11.

FIGURE 13-11: Modified EF-S lens mount, rubber ring, and plastic piece that was cut off from the mount

You are ready to put the lens back together. Line up the internal paper ring to the screw holes. Then carefully put the lens mount back on the lens. Be careful with the electrical contact strip. Screw the two small screws onto the lens mount and into the electrical contact strip. Then screw the four large screws into the lens mount. The lens is ready to use.

The newly modified mount, on this particular lens, does not protect the internal lens components as well as the original mount did. As shown in Figure 13-12, the circuit board and internal lens barrel components are fully exposed. So be careful when you handle the lens while it is detached from the camera. This cautionary note may or may not apply to other modified EF-S lenses.

FIGURE **13-12:** Once the EF-S mount has been modified to fit on EF cameras, the circuit board and lens internals may be exposed.

Trying the Lens on EOS SLRs

The EF-S lens is designed for EF-S compatible cameras, so there is no guarantee that the modified version will work with non-EF-S compatible cameras. Take care when you first try it out. On some cameras, the mirror might contact the rear lens element (see Figures 13-13 and 13-14). The modified lens will continue to work with EF-S compatible cameras, such as the Digital Rebel, the Digital Rebel XT, and the 20D.

FIGURE **13-13**: The rear lens element on an EF lens does not protrude from the mount.

FIGURE **13-14**: The rear lens element on an EF-S lens protrudes from a modified mount.

Digital SLRs

Theoretically, the modified lens should work with other 1.6x sensor DSLRs, such as the D30, the D60, and the 10D. I've tested the modified lens on my D30 (see Figure 13-15), and it works fine. I've heard that it also works with a 10D.

FIGURE 13-15: Modified EF-S lens mounted on a non-EF-S compatible camera

APS SLRs

The APS SLRs have a slightly bigger film frame than the 1.6x digital sensors. The APS film-frame dimension is 30.2mm × 16.7mm. The Canon EF-S 18–55mm f/3.5–5.6 lens has been tested to work on my Canon EOS IX APS SLR. There is no rear lens element to mirror contact throughout the entire focal range. Therefore, it should work with all EOS APS cameras.

Full-Frame SLRs

The rear lens element on the Canon EF-S 18–55mm f/3.5–5.6 lens retracts progressively into the lens barrel as the lens is zoomed out to 55mm. Observing the retraction, it seemed to me that this lens would work on 35mm and digital full-frame cameras, at least for a portion of the zoom ranges. It turned out that the result is better than I expected.

At the widest zoom setting (18mm) the mirror contacts the rear lens element, causing the LCD indicator on my Canon Elan IIe to flash the empty battery indicator, meaning a camera error. Pressing the shutter button halfway resets the error. Examination of the camera mirror and the rear lens element showed no damage. However, I would advise against inducing this failure; over time, the continuous striking of the mirror on the rear lens element may crack the mirror or the lens element.

At around 19mm (see Figure 13-16), the mirror no longer strikes the lens element, rendering this lens quite useable on a full-frame camera. The only catch is that because this lens was designed for a smaller image circle than the full-frame sensor requires, the image vignettes until 24mm. Therefore, the modified version of this lens could serve as a fully functional 24mm–55mm lens.

FIGURE 13-16: The threshold at which the mirror will no longer strike the rear lens element

Creative Photography Hacks

part

Hacking with Filters

W hen you first got your camera body and your camera lens, you
were probably looking forward to shooting some awesome pictures like the ones you see in the magazines. You probably wanted
to shoot the beautiful landscapes where the blue sky is perfectly exposed with
white fluffy clouds against a perfect city skyline. Except when you shot it,
you exposed the city skyline correctly and blew out the exposure on the sky.
Or you might have exposed the blue sky and white clouds correctly, but the
city skyline was way too underexposed to match the saturated sky.

In another instance, you might have purchased the sharpest lens in the
world, a prized possession. Then you tried to shoot portraits with it, only to
find out it is so sharp that it resolved every single blemish on your model's
face. The result is far from the glamour pictures that you are familiar with in
your favorite magazines. Why did the most capable lens provide the least
desirable result?

In both shooting situations, you assumed the most capable camera and
the most capable lens would yield professional quality results. They might
produce the quality you expect under some optimal conditions (such as
Figure 14-1), but a real professional knows a secret that you do not: to get
the pictures that you want consistently, it takes more than just a capable
camera and a capable lens—you need filters as well.

Before digital cameras came along, one of the most popular and most effective ways of adding special effects to photographs was with filters. Filters
are generally made out of glass or plastic, and they attach to the front of the
lens. A filter can make subtle or flamboyant changes to your picture. A filter
can soften your sharp lens for a dreamy model shot. A filter can introduce
fog on a bright sunny day. A filter can bring the exposure of the bright sky
down to the same level as the city skyline, giving you the perfect exposure
balance.

Sometimes filters are used to depict color more accurately under difficult
lighting conditions, although today, with the ability to automatically adjust
white balance on digital cameras, the color-correction filters are losing their
luster. You can even use the white balance function to create special effects
with colors. But you must not forget that filters are still one of the most
effective ways of creating special effects in your pictures.

FIGURE **14-1: This picture of downtown Seattle has a balanced exposure between the buildings and the sky because of the overcast. Without the cloudy sky, a graduated filter would have been needed to bring the exposure on the sky down to the same level as the buildings.**

Color Correction

Since I mentioned correcting color with filters, I should give you a better understanding of how to correct for different lighting conditions for different films. Most of the films available at local stores, such as Kodak Gold and FujiFilm Superia, are daylight-balanced films. When you use them indoors at home, you'll need to correct the color balance with filters. The information in Table 14-1 is particularly useful if you ever go back to using film or if your digital camera's white-balance function is broken. In the table, find the light source that fits your scene (left two columns), then cross-reference it with the type of film you are using (right three columns across the top). The result is the filter or filters you need to use for that scene.

For example, if you are using daylight film under a 100-watt incandescent lamp, you need an 80A and an 82B filter to compensate.

When you use these filters, they will decrease the light reaching your film or digital sensor. You will have to make exposure adjustments in manual mode (see Table 14-2). If you use automatic exposure mode on your camera, the camera will do the metering for you. If you stack multiple filters, the exposure adjustment is additive.

Table 14-1: Color Correction Filters

Light Source	Temperature (Kelvin)	Daylight (5500 Kelvin)	Tungsten A (3400 Kelvin)	Tungsten B (3200 Kelvin)
Clear skylight	12000	81A + 81C	85B + 85C	81A + 85B + 85C
Hazy skylight	9000	85C	81EF + 85B	85 + 85C
Shade on a clear day	9000	85C	81EF + 85B	85 + 85C
Light overcast	7000	81D	81A + 85B	81D + 85B
Heavy overcast	6500	81C	81 + 85B	81B + 85B
Electronic flash	5500		85	85B
Blue photoflood lamp	4900	82A	81 + 85C	85
Clear flashbulb	4200	80D	81EF	81A + 81EF
Photoflood lamp	3400	80B		81A
Photographic lamp	3200	80A	82A	
100-watt incandescent	2900	80A + 82B	80D	82B
75-watt incandescent	2800	80A + 82C	82A + 82C	82C

Table 14-2: Exposure Compensation for Filters

Filter	Exposure Increase (Stops)
80	1 ⅔
80A	2
80B	1 ⅓
80C	1
80D	⅔
81	⅓
81A	⅓
81B	⅓
81C	⅓
81D	⅓
81EF	⅓

Continued

Table 14-2 (continued)

Filter	Exposure Increase (Stops)
82	$\frac{1}{3}$
82A	$\frac{1}{3}$
82B	$\frac{1}{3}$
82C	$\frac{2}{3}$
85	$\frac{2}{3}$
85B	$\frac{2}{3}$
85C	$\frac{2}{3}$

Physical Characteristics

Many different types of filters are used in the photography and cinematography industry. Each type differs only in its physical properties and how it is made.

Note Most SLR lenses, point-and-shoot (P&S) cameras with lens adapters, and accessory lenses have filter threads built into them for attaching filters. If your P&S camera doesn't have an available lens adapter, see Chapter 8 to make your own lens adapter.

Circular Screw-On Filters

The most popular type of filter on the consumer market is the screw-on filter. It has a glass or plastic filter element encased in a metal ring. The metal ring also provides the male screw thread and the female screw thread. Figure 14-2 is an example of a screw-on filter. The male screw thread is the mounting thread to the front of a camera lens. The female screw thread on the front side serves as a filter thread for additional filters and accessory lenses.

Screw-on filters are popular because they can be fitted onto the front of single-lens reflex (SLR) lenses and video cameras. Many P&S digital cameras have special lens adapters that can be used with these screw-on filters. They are available from 26mm diameter thread to 87mm diameter thread to suit all applications. Most SLR lenses use screw-on filters with a thread range of 52mm–77mm. P&S digital cameras typically use a thread range of 30mm–49mm. Video cameras typically use a thread range of 26mm–37mm.

FIGURE 14-2: This 77mm red circular screw-on filter is large enough for most applications.

It's possible and sometimes wise to get the biggest screw-on filters and then use step-up rings to adapt the filter to your photographic gear. Filters could be quite expensive, sometimes hundreds of dollars. But step-up rings only costs $5–10. For example, if you have an SLR, a P&S digital camera, and a digital video (DV) camcorder. If your SLR lens has a 58mm filter thread, you can get a 58mm circular polarizer and several step-up rings so that the filter can be used with your SLR, P&S, and DV camcorder (see Figure 14-3). This strategy makes sense if you want to use the filter with all three gears at different times and when the filter is expensive.

See Chapter 7 for a thorough discussion about P&S lens adapters and step-up and step-down rings.

FIGURE 14-3: A 77mm red filter mounted on this DV camcorder with 37–52mm, 52–58mm, and 58–77mm step-up rings. The red filter boosts the contrast when the DV camcorder is shooting in black-and-white mode.

Square and Rectangle Filters

Cokin, Lee, and several other filter manufacturers make square and rectangle filters. These filters are sometimes less expensive than the circular screw-on filters because they lack a metal ring and screw threads. The filter can be made out of glass or plastic. Its straightedge shape also eases manufacturing, reducing the cost further. To mount these filters on your camera, you'll have to purchase a filter holder. The filter holder has a male screw thread for mounting to the front of your lens or your camera. This single filter holder generally holds up to three filters and can be used with all square and rectangle filters that are of the same size (see Figure 14-4).

Cokin makes two types of filter systems: System A and System P. The System A filters and holder can be used on smaller lenses and cameras. The System A threaded rings come in the following diameters (in millimeters): 36, 37, 39, 40.5, 41, 42, 43, 43.5, 44, 46, 48, 49, 52, 54, 55, 58, and 62. The System P filters and holder are generally used on larger camera lenses or wide-angle lenses where the smaller filter holder may cause vignette. The System P threaded rings come in the following diameters (in millimeters): 48, 49, 52, 55, 58, 62, 57, 72, 77, and 82. If your camera gear has a filter thread diameter that is not listed, you can use step-up and step-down rings to mount the holder to your gear.

FIGURE 14-4: Cokin A and P-series filter holders

System A and System P filters come in both square and rectangle shape. They can be slipped onto the filter holder quite easily. The System A filters are approximately 65mm across and can be any length. The System P filters are approximately 83mm across and can be any length. The filters can be up to 2mm thick, but 1mm thick filters are easier to install into the holders.

Gelatin Filters

Gelatin filters are more commonly called gel filters. They are used widely in the movie and photography industry because they are made out of gelatin. The result is clear flexible film filters that are available in various colors. They are light and easy to carry around. The filter can be easily cut into different shapes. Although there are special gelatin filter holders that fit over camera lenses, their thin and flexible characteristics are extremely convenient for taping to electronic flashes, photographic lamps, and lenses. Because of the material they are made out of, they are cheaper to manufacture and purchase than glass filters. Their only drawback is that they are more fragile than glass filters. And the characteristic of the dyes used in the gelatin filters may change under heat and light, both abundant in photography. The gelatin filters should be replaced periodically.

How Gelatin Filters Are Made

The process of making color gelatin filter starts by dissolving organic or synthesized dyes in liquid gelatin. The correct amount of gelatin is then coated onto a flat surface, such as glass. After the coat of gelatin has dried on the preparation surface, the gelatin film is removed and then coated in lacquer. Gelatin filters have a thickness of 0.1mm, plus or minus 0.01mm. With their uniform thickness, gelatin filters have an excellent optical quality.

Putting a Filter Thread on an Accessory Lens

Most accessory lenses have a front filter thread. However, I see more and more consumer accessory lenses that lack this thread. This section explains how you can add a filter thread to your accessory lenses.

My idea for this hack started on a spring weekend back in 2001. I wanted to shoot some special-effects pictures with my filters on my Olympus C-2500L digital camera. The camera has a focal length range of 9.2–28mm (which is equivalent to a 36–110mm on a 35mm camera). In order to get the perspective I wanted for the scene, I had to use the Olympus 1.45x teleconverter in front of the C-2500L digital camera. Unfortunately, the Olympus 1.45x teleconverter has no front filter thread.

After thinking about the problem for a while, I thought maybe step-up ring could be screwed onto the front of the teleconverter.

Tools You Need

Here are the tools you will need to complete this project:

- Ruler
- 5-minute general-purpose Epoxy

A regular wooden ruler is good enough for this project. You can pick one up for about 25 cents from the local department store. While you are there, pick up some 5-minute general-purpose epoxy as well. This type of epoxy is generally located in the home maintenance section for around $5.

Parts You Need

Here is the part you will need to complete this project:

- Step-up ring

Step-up ring sizes are specified by the mounting thread diameter and the filter thread diameter of the ring. A 52–58mm step-up ring has a 52mm mounting thread and a 58mm filter thread. The size of the step-up ring you need to mount to the front of your accessory lens depends on two things: the size of your accessory lens and the size of the filter you want to use with the lens. To determine the size of your accessory lens, measure the front of it with a ruler, as shown in Figure 14-5. Next, determine the size of filters you want to use. Your decision might be affected by whether you have existing filters for your other camera equipment.

FIGURE 14-5: Measure the diameter of the accessory lens with a ruler.

I picked a 58–77mm step-up ring for mounting on the teleconverter to my Olympus 1.45x teleconverter. I had several reasons why I wanted to mount such a large adapter ring:

- Most of my filters are 77mm, because most of my Canon EOS SLR lenses have 77mm filter threads. All filters that I buy in the future are going to be 77mm or larger.

- I do not want to vignette my pictures. The bigger the filter, compared to the lens element, the more filters I can stack in front of the lens without vignette.

Gluing the Step-Up Ring to the Lens

Test-fit the step-up ring to the front of your lens and make sure it fits the way you want it to. Make sure you take your time during the test-fit. There is no turning back after you actually glue the ring and lens together. When you are ready to glue, start mixing the 5-minute general-purpose epoxy by following the instructions that came with it.

Tip

The epoxy is a good adhesive to use because it creates a good, strong bond. The filters and additional accessory lenses you mount in front of your lens could get quite heavy. Using a weaker adhesive increases the risk to your precious filters and accessory lenses.

Modifying the Step-Up Ring

Some accessory lenses have a flat front surface, such as the Cokin 0.5x Wide-Angle Lens shown in Figure 14-6. Normally it's not an issue to glue the mounting thread of the step-up ring directly to the front surface of a telephoto lens. However, the Cokin 0.5x Wide-Angle Lens is so wide that any additional thickness in the front causes vignette. The only solution is to saw the mounting thread off a 52-77mm step-up ring.

FIGURE 14-6: The Cokin 0.5x Wide-Angle Lens has a flat front surface.

The best way to saw the mounting thread off a step-up ring is to have it securely mounted on a vise. Use a hacksaw to saw off half of the mounting thread. Then rotate the step-up ring 180 degrees on the vise and saw off the other half. Use a metal file to clean and smooth off the edges. Make sure the edge is smooth, flat, and free of metal shavings. Any extra material will show up in the Cokin lens' angle-of-view. Once the step-up ring modification is complete, glue the flat surface flush to the surface of the Cokin lens and wait for it to dry.

Generally, the epoxy comes in a syringe-like plastic container with dual chambers. When you squeeze the syringe, two different chemicals are dispersed. Mixing the two chemicals starts the adhesion process. After mixing the two chemicals, you generally have to wait one minute before actually applying the epoxy to your parts.

Line the edge of the lens front with epoxy. Then press the step-up ring onto the front of the lens.

Tip

After the filter thread has been added, the lens cap that came with the Olympus 1.45x lens no longer fits over the lens. But I had a spare generic 77mm lens cap sitting around my home, so this was a perfect application for it. You can find lens caps for your own modified accessory lenses at a camera store.

Making Filters Out of Plain Glass

For the remainder of the chapter, I will talk about making different types of filters. In each case, you will be making these filters out of plain glass (see Figure 14-7). You can buy plain glass in sheets at a home improvement store. A glass cutting tool that costs $5 at the same home improvement store can help you cut the glass into square or rectangle shapes (see Appendix C for instructions on glass cutting and where to get tools). Then you just have to invest in a rectangular filter holder to attach these homemade filters to your camera.

I bought a 10" × 12" glass pane for less than $3 at Lowes. This pane can be made into 9 Cokin System P size filters or 12 Cokin System A size filters. The glass pane I bought was $3/32$" thick, which is exactly 2mm. It's a little too thick to fit in my newer System A holder, and it just barely fit in my older System P holder. You can also use glass panes from picture frames. Those are generally thinner than window glass panes and work better with the filter holders.

Before cutting the glass pane to size, use a ruler and a thin permanent marker to draw the lines. After cutting the glass pane apart, you can wash the line markings off with rubbing alcohol.

Caution

<CAUTION>

Freshly cut glass edges are sharp, and it's easy to get cut by them. In fact, they are so sharp that you won't even feel it when your skin is cut. I have been cut by the glass a few times while washing off the line markings. Use a carborundum file to smooth off the sharp edges.

When you buy the glass pane at a home improvement store, the employees will tape the edges with blue masking tape. The masking tape prevents the edge from cutting you. But it also protects the glass from breaking and shattering into million of pieces. You can tape the glass yourself when you transport it from one place to another.

FIGURE 14-7: A Cokin rectangle filter and a homemade plain glass filter

When you bring the glass pane home, it will be dirty from dust and fingerprints. You can clean it by washing it with water. If it is particularly dirty, use some hand soap as well. Then dry it with a towel.

Tip It is hard to make round screw-on plain glass filters. But you can buy cheap UV or skylight filters. These filters don't change the image too much, and they don't reduce the amount of light reaching the photosensitive material. Once you have the filters, you can make them into whatever type of filters you want. These filters are so common that you may already have a few of them in your possession. If not, you can always find used ones at camera stores.

Diffusion Filters

It turns out that glamour models are very much like the rest of us. They may have minor blemishes on their skin that would distract from glamour photographs. Most lenses are made to resolve as much detail as possible, so the sharp lenses work against the photographer's desired effect in a glamour shot. In many instances, the blemishes can be hidden by make-up, as shown in Figure 14-8. In other instances, the glamour photographer will have to use a soft-focus lens or a soft-focus filter, otherwise known as a diffusion filter. A soft-focus lens or filter will obscure detail slightly, smooth out the blemishes, and, under the right lighting conditions, cover the model in an intriguing haze. It creates soft, pleasing portraits that are very attractive in glamour shots.

FIGURE 14-8: A glamour shot without using a soft-focus filter

Diffusion filters work by diffracting, or bending, some of the light rays passing through the filter. The light rays that pass straight through the filter create the sharp image on the photosensitive material. The bent rays cause additional image information to gather at random locations on top of the sharp image, creating a second, un-sharp image. The combined sharp and un-sharp images result in the soft-focus effect. Figure 14-9 is a diffused photo.

FIGURE 14-9: A glamour photograph shot with the Tiffen Soft/FX diffusing filter

Soft-focus lenses can be quite an expensive investment; especially considering that you can only use the lens in limited situations. However, soft-focus filters are relatively inexpensive and are, in fact, very easy to make for hardly any cost. One reason you can make them so easily and cheaply is the large number of simple materials you can use for making them. Anything that can obscure the lens somewhat can be used. For example, you can wrap women's nylon stockings around your lens, spray hairspray or paint on a plain glass, or smear petroleum jelly (such as Vaseline) on plain glass.

The materials you use may create different soft-focus effects. When you use white stockings or white paint mist, the soft-focus filter will lighten the shadows. If you use black stockings or black paint mist, the soft-focus filter will reduce highlights. If you use a clear transparent material, such as a mist of hairspray or Vaseline, the image will soften, but the shadow and highlight details will be reproduced faithfully.

Tip If you want to make your glamour photographs feel warmer, stack an 81B filter onto your soft-focus filter. Or better yet, buy an inexpensive 81B filter and turn it into a warm soft-focus filter by applying the techniques in this section.

Spray Paint

It's easy to find spray paint at your local stores. Buy the fast-drying, water-based versions. They are easy to paint with and to clean up after. Flat white and flat black spray paints are common and abundant, but you can try other colors as well and see what kind of effects they make in your pictures.

Before you spray, make sure your filter surface is free of dirt and grease. Make sure your work area is protected with drop cloth or newspaper and spray where you don't mind getting a little paint in the environment. Find a well-ventilated location. You should consider wearing a mask over your nose and mouth as well.

Shake the spray paint can vigorously for one minute. The metal ball inside the can will rattle against the inside of the can, mixing the paint. When you spray, keep the can about a foot away from your filter. The more spray paint you get on the filter, the softer the image and the more you'll obscure the subject. Spray just a fine mist on the filter to start—this small amount goes a long way with softening. You can always add more paint later. If you make a mistake, use some thinner to clean the paint off the filter and start over.

When you are done with the spray paint, clean the spray button immediately by turning the can upside down and pressing the spray button for five seconds or until no more paint comes out.

Fog Filter

The fog filter is a close cousin to the soft-focus filter. It can create a fog effect on a bright sunny day. But to use it correctly is tricky, as our brain is conditioned to expect fog only on a hazy, cloudy day. Strong lighting from automobile headlights, a home window, or sunrays breaking through the cloudy sky creates visible flare and increases the fog effect. But in a scene with no highlights, the fog filter will provide barely any effect.

You can try making some fog filters by spraying bug spray or deodorant onto a plain glass filter. Although this quick-and-dirty technique tends to reduce picture sharpness, it's fun and interesting to try on your homemade filter.

Tip By changing exposure and lens aperture, you can vary the fog effect. Increasing the exposure will enhance the fog effect. Using a wide-open aperture also enhances the fog effect, while a using a stop-down aperture reduces the fog effect.

Note Real fog shows its presence by scattering light, which softens the light, lowers the contrast, mutes color transmission, and produces halos around highlights in the scene. Professional fog filters have particles and patterns that scatter the light in the same way that fog scatters light.

Color Filters

As I mentioned before, color filters are generally used to depict the color of the scene correctly on different types of photosensitive material. However, different colors can add to the emotion of the scene. For example, using a red filter, you can depict a heated discussion. Or you might want to use a bluish filter to emphasize an ice-cold glass of water. A color filter works by absorbing a portion of the light spectrum. A yellow filter absorbs all portions of the light spectrum that don't make up the color yellow. It lets only the yellow spectrum through the filter. That process is called transmission.

If you happen to come across some colored transparent wrapping paper, found in gift shops and craft stores, you can make some color filters yourself. Simply glue or tape the wrapping paper to the plain glass filters you made for a long-lasting color filter. When the wrapping paper wears out, remove it from the plain glass filter and put on a new sheet. A roll of this wrapping paper costs only a few dollars. Keep in mind the wrapping paper isn't made for photography, so the image quality may not be optimal. And color consistency probably shouldn't be mentioned in the same sentence with wrapping paper.

Sometimes the colored transparent wrapping paper can be hard to find. The demand for it changes like fashion. But professional camera shops carry color gelatin filters made specifically for photography. They are already rated specifically for this purpose so the color is always consistent. They are made to produce the best image quality, but cost just a little more than wrapping paper. You can cut them into shape and paste them onto your plain-glass filter.

Professional Diffusion Filters

Quite a number of professional diffusion are filters on the market. Each filter manufacturer produces its own series of them, and each series has a different name. Some of these filters have similar characteristics, while others are totally different. In this sidebar, I describe a few of Tiffen's diffusion filters.

Tiffen Pro-Mist

The Tiffen Pro-Mist filter is an excellent diffusing filter that eliminates sharp edges without adding the undesirable out-of-focus effect. Highlights in the scene end up with more flare. Contrast is reduced only slightly. And colors have a softer, pastel appearance.

The Pro-Mist series of filters are available in three different densities. The lower density Pro-Mist filter can be used to reduce the sharpness and contrast of your photographs. The higher density filter will have you creating surreal glamour shots.

A "Black" version of the Pro-Mist filter is available. It reduces reflectivity and absorbs more light than the regular Pro-Mist filters. The Black Pro-Mist doesn't create as much flare in the highlights as the normal Pro-Mist filter. Contrast is also lower. And the shadow area isn't lightened as much as it is with the regular Pro-Mist Filter.

Tiffen Soft/FX

The Tiffen Soft/FX filter has a pattern of tiny lenslets, or micro-lenses, to diffuse the image. The diffusion is designed to soften any blemishes on the subject's skin while still retaining the image clarity. Thus, the Soft/FX filter is a great tool for glamour shots.

The Soft/FX series of filters are also available in various densities. The lower density version creates subtle diffusion. It generates little flare from highlights. And it doesn't reduce contrast as much as higher density Soft/FX filters. On the other hand, the higher density filter diffuses the subject more and will soften any skin imperfections to a much greater degree.

Warm Diffusers

All of Tiffen diffusing filters, such as the Pro-Mist and the Soft/FX filters, are available in the "warm" version. These warmer filters are basically the regular diffusing filters combined with the Tiffen 812 warming filter. These filters are generally used to eliminate blue cast under shaded conditions outdoors. In addition, these filters can eliminate pale skin-tones created by electronic flash. If you already have a diffusing filter and a warming filter, you can simply stack the two filters, instead of getting a specialized warm diffusing filter.

Star Filter

Star filters are simply plain glass with etched lines. A two-point star filter has parallel lines that result in light streaks in your picture. A four-point star filter has straight etched lines that are perpendicular to each other (see Figure 14-10). An eight-point star filter has perpendicular lines in addition to diagonal lines. Star filters usually come on a rotating mount so that you can orient the star trails in any direction.

Tip Star filters require no exposure compensation. But the effect may change at different aperture settings. It is always a good idea to check the star effect with your camera's depth-of-field preview.

Caution Star filters may reduce image sharpness.

While cutting the plain-glass rectangle filters, it occurred to me that since the glass scoring tool that I was using scored straight lines in glass, I could use this tool to etch my own star filter—and you can, too. You can etch them any way you like—you don't have to be methodical in creating uniform filters like the one shown in Figure 14-10. A random cross here or there will yield interesting and non-conventional results. Just keep in mind that star trails are generally oriented in the same direction. But that doesn't mean a picture with random star trail directions isn't going to be fantastic artwork.

FIGURE 14-10: A four-point star filter. Your homemade version doesn't have to be so uniform.

Tip

When you etch the lines closer to each other, the star becomes fatter. On the other hand, spacing the etched lines farther apart produces stars with delicate thin trails.

Note

I have heard that others have success making temporary star filters by wiping a light film of oil on an UV/skylight filter. Make parallel and perpendicular oil lines with your finger.

White Balance Special Effects

With digital cameras, it is so easy to add color special effects to your photographs. You can always trick the camera's white balance function using the custom mode. But one easy, yet creative, color trick that I like is to expose shaded daylight scenes using the incandescent white-balance mode. This adds a deep blue cast in bright daylight. It creates an emotional mood where there otherwise would be none.

Figures 14-11 shows a good example where this trick is useful. I shot this picture while visiting an old friend up in Seattle. The sunlight glow from downstairs looked intriguing and mysterious. But shooting the picture in daylight mode meant another boring staircase picture. I wanted to emphasize the intriguing and mysterious nature of the scene.

FIGURE 14-11: By shooting the stairway in indoor mode, I produced a deep saturated blue in this picture. This special effect makes the normally boring staircase look intriguing and mysterious.

Continued

Continued

By shooting the same scene in the wrong (incandescent) mode, it created a deep saturated blue cast. The blue cast looks obviously unnatural to us, yet it has a pleasant effect. The result is a more emotional picture that forces you to give it a second look.

Unfortunately, the pictures in this book are printed in black and white. You'll have to experiment with your digital camera to see the effects.

Infrared Filter

In Chapter 15, I discuss using infrared filters to eliminate all visible light from your infrared pictures. It can boost contrast in your scenes. But a decent infrared filter is really expensive. One trick is to take developed slide film (the non-exposed portion) and lay them on the plain glass. The developed, non-exposed slide film is very similar to an infrared filter, where it blocks most visible light and transmits infrared light. Lay them on the plain-glass filter in pieces like a puzzle, and glue them to the glass using white paper glue. Squeeze excess glue out and try to eliminate all air bubbles. Cover all areas and do not let any visible light seep through the edges where two slide film pieces meet. Remember to cut off the film advance sprockets.

Shooting Infrared Pictures with Your Digital Camera

Infrared photography is an area few photographers choose to get involved with, and that's quite understandable. Why? Few photographers can see infrared light with their unaided eyes. But after you've seen the eerie and surrealistic result of capturing infrared successfully in a photograph, with its dark, spooky sky and ghastly, white foliage, you'll want to try it, too. Figure 15-1 shows an infrared photograph that creates a dark and moody landscape.

Capturing infrared is a slightly different type of fine art photography from what you might be used to. Infrared pictures are usually captured as black-and-white photographs. When they're captured with color photosensitive material, they generally render strange colors. Infrared photography requires a lot of experimentation to get right, but with digital cameras, the results can be easily seen on electronic viewfinders and tweaked on your computer.

Note | IR is short for infrared, and the terms can be used interchangeably.

FIGURE 15-1: Example of an infrared photograph

Understanding the Light Spectrum

Infrared light is really the same thing as visible light, which is to say that both are part of the electromagnetic wave spectrum (see Figure 15-2). The figure shows the different wavelengths in nanometers. The entire spectrum is divided into different categories: Gamma Rays, X-Rays, Ultraviolet, Infrared, Microwaves, and Radio. Each of these wavelengths could possibly be captured on photosensitive material. For example, your doctor probably has taken some x-ray images of you. However, this chapter concentrates only on the visible, infrared, and ultraviolet spectrum.

The only difference between infrared and visible wavelengths is that we can see the visible light, but not infrared light. Our eyes are sensitive to electromagnetic wavelengths in the 380–700 nanometer (nm) range (see Figure 15-3). When these wavelengths strike our retinas, their energy stimulates the color receptors in our eyes, and the information generated is passed to the brain for processing.

Note   The range encompassing visible light overlaps a bit with that of infrared light somewhere between 700nm–750nm. Because everyone's physical composition is different, everyone's eyes are also slightly different. Some people can see a wider range of the visible spectrum, while others see a narrower range. Some people can see all the colors in the spectrum distinctly, while others, like me, are color-blind to some degree.

Nanometers (nm)

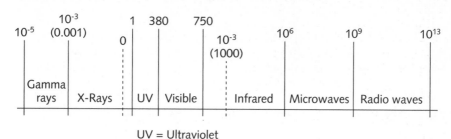

UV = Ultraviolet

FIGURE 15-2: The electromagnetic wave spectrum

FIGURE 15-3: The visible spectrum from 380nm–750nm

The infrared spectrum itself is divided into three chunks: near, mid, and far. Where the divisions occur is not agreed on and may vary. One major factor that determines the boundary of these divisions is the sensor technology used to observe each region. Infrared photography is, generally, done in the near-infrared region. Therefore, this chapter focuses primarily on the near-infrared region, from 750nm–1000nm.

Thermo Infrared

Science fiction writers like to employ thermo infrared radiation detection capability. Quite often, you see movies in which a nice thermo infrared detector or an exoskeleton armor suit can detect thermo infrared. This thermo infrared falls in the mid and far-infrared regions. It is possible to make these detectors for thermo infrared, but they require special sensors that may contain heat-sensitive circuits. These circuits generally contain crystals such as germanium where their electrical resistance property is changed by exposure to heat. Since these sensors detect heat and convert it to colors, the sensors themselves have to be cool. Basically, the sensors have to be cooled to well below 0 degrees Celsius. The cooling is usually done with liquid nitrogen or some type of temperature regulator.

Can My Camera Shoot Infrared Photographs?

All cameras can take pictures of the infrared light. The question is whether the image-capturing material (film, digital sensor, and so on) in the camera is sensitive to infrared light. In the rest of this chapter, you'll find out whether your film or digital camera is suitable for infrared photography, and by the end of the chapter you'll know what equipment to use and the basics of how to compose infrared photographs.

Chapter 16 gives instructions for turning your digital camera into a very good infrared camera.

Infrared Photography with Film

All film cameras can shoot infrared pictures. It is the photosensitive film that determines whether infrared light will be captured. Most color and black-and-white films on the consumer market today are either not sensitive to infrared light or have low infrared sensitivity. The films are made to be insensitive to infrared light so that they capture what we see. Because our eyes cannot see the infrared light spectrum, when color film captures infrared and renders it into colors our eyes *can* see, the picture looks strange and abnormal to us. When you capture your friend's birthday, you typically want to remember it the way your own eyes saw it.

Several film manufacturers produce infrared film. Infrared films were originally made for scientific studies and were never intended for artistic use. But the interesting infrared effects have made it an art form among infrared photographers.

What Infrared Films Are There?

A few infrared films are on the market. Each one has slightly different characteristics.

Exposure index (EI) is the official terminology for film speed. Film sold today is rated with EI. EI is currently synonymous with ISO and ASA. Because both ISO and ASA are really acronyms of different standard organizations, these acronyms are loosely associated to film speed.

ILFORD SFX 200

This ISO 200 black-and-white film has peak red sensitivity at 720nm and an extended red sensitivity up to 740nm. This film shows less infrared effect than other infrared films by limiting the blooming effect when you are shooting infrared highlights. To increase the contrast and enhance the infrared effect of this film, use a yellow, light red, or dark red filter. You can use many black-and-white development processes to develop this film.

Infrared Film That No Longer Exists

Kodak Recording Film 2475 was originally made for military instrumentation. Later it was picked up by law enforcement agencies. Rated at ISO 1000, this film filled the needs of many photo-journalists of the day. It works well in tungsten lighting because of its extended red sensitivity. Because of its grainy effect, this film was highly regarded when grain became a popular artistic expression. The Kodak Recording Film 2475 has a narrow exposure-latitude, so if you are able to find any today, bracket generously (see "Bracketing Your Shots" later in this chapter).

Kodak Ektachrome Professional Infrared EIR

This color-slide film is sensitive to infrared. You can produce different color and effects by using two different methods of film processing. For accurate infrared color, rate the film at EI 100 and develop the film with the AR-5 process. But if you like false color with higher color-saturation and contrast, rate the film at EI 200 and develop it with the standard E-6 process.

Kodak High-Speed Infrared

The Kodak High-Speed Infrared is a black-and-white negative film. It is sensitive to infrared and some visible light. It produces grainy and fairly high-contrast pictures. Any subject that reflects or emits infrared, such as foliage and clouds, appears white on film. Non-infrared reflective subjects such as clear sky and water appear black. Rate this film at EI 50.

Kodak Technical Pan

This black-and-white negative film has extremely fine grain and extreme sharpness. You can change its contrast level from low to high through different exposures and developing. Its extended red sensitivity is excellent for infrared photography. This film has an EI rating from 16–320, which provides a lot of flexibility in development.

Konica Infrared 750nm

This black-and-white negative film has peak spectral sensitivity at 750 nanometers, hence its name. With fine grain, this is a good film for aerial photography, scientific work, and detailed landscape photography. When you use this film without filters, it can reproduce grays faithfully for normal pictorial photography.

Where Can You Buy Infrared Film?

Because of the limited application of infrared photography and because it's a niche market as an art form for photographers worldwide, finding the film can be difficult. Infrared films are not available in electronics stores and supermarkets, where you can usually find color film. A better place to find them is at a professional photography shop. If your local photography shops don't carry them, you can order them online from large professional photography outfits. Two of the largest in the United States are B&H (www.bhphotovideo.com/) and Adorama Camera (www.adorama.com/) in New York.

Tip

The large photography outfits generally stock each type of film in high volume. Because films have expiration dates, any leftover stock is generally discounted heavily when the expiration date gets closer or has expired. You may see photo outfitters advertise films that are about to expire as *short-dated*. These are good times to pick up films when you just want to do some experimentation. Keep your eyes open for these deals.

Loading and Unloading Infrared Film

The general rule-of-thumb is to load and unload all infrared films in complete darkness. Many film canisters are lightproof to the visible spectrum, but not to the infrared spectrum. Film manufacturers have recently improved the design of their canisters to better block stray infrared light. However, to be safe, you should change your film in complete darkness. A darkroom is probably the best place to load and unload your infrared film, or use a film-changing bag. Keep in mind that some film-changing bags are not infrared lightproof. Once your infrared film is unloaded, place it in the lightproof container that came with the film.

Tip

You can check whether your bag or room is infrared lightproof by using an infrared camera and or camcorder. (See "How Well Does Your Digital Camera Perceive Infrared Light?" later in this chapter.)

Film Processing: C-41, E-6, and AR-5

Throughout this section, I have touched lightly on film processing and the names for some types of process and their associated chemistry: C-41, E-6, and AR-5 (there are many more that I haven't mentioned). Film manufacturers invented each of these processes for developing a very specific set of films. For example, the C-41 chemical process is commonly known for developing color negative film. If you have ever dropped off your color negative film at the one-hour photo lab, you have had your film developed using the C-41 process. E-6 chemical process is the standard for developing color slide films. The AR-5 process is a very specialized processing for infrared aerial photography. AR-5 processing labs are rare and only a few exist around the country.

I won't touch on how to develop your own film at home or go into the details of each of these processes, because there are simply too many ways of processing and developing your film. Entire books have been written on this subject. Plus, like photography itself, developing film is an art. A thorough film photographer knows that shooting the picture is half of the art. The second half is developing the film and exposing it on photo paper.

With that said, I can also tell you that processing film in your own personal darkroom can be a fun and exciting experience, especially if you pick a relatively non-toxic chemical process that is fairly easy. E-6 is a good choice for those reasons. Also, it's possible to cross-process C-41 color negative film in E-6 chemicals for interesting creative color effects, which gives you more artistic options.

Where to Get Your Infrared Film Developed

Finding a place to develop your specialized film is not a simple task. One-hour photo developers generally develop only the standard C-41 color processing films. To develop black-and-white and color slide films (which infrared films are based on), you'll have to find a local professional photofinisher. Most of them still develop these specialized films.

Without a local professional photofinisher, you'll have to send your film out for development. You'll generally wait about two weeks before the photos get back into your hands. Most one-hour developers can take your specialized film and send it out for processing. If you can't find anyone locally to help you, you can search online for specialized photofinisher.

Digital Infrared Photography

I was really quite surprised by the sensitivity of digital sensors when I first started infrared photography. Digital sensors, either CCD or CMOS, are very sensitive to infrared and ultraviolet light, making most digital cameras very good candidates for infrared photography. For example, an R72 filter is basically opaque to the naked eye, but, as you can see in Figure 15-4, the digital sensor can see through it easily. (You learn about filters later in this chapter.)

FIGURE 15-4: An IR-sensitive digital camera can easily see through an opaque R72 lens.

In fact, digital sensors are so sensitive to infrared light that digital camera manufacturers have to place an IR-blocking filter in front of the sensor to ensure that non-infrared pictures look normal. An IR-sensitive sensor without an IR-blocking filter would render the color of the scene incorrectly for normal photography, as shown in Figure 15-5.

Because of the IR-blocking filters placed in digital cameras, most digital cameras are not well suited for infrared photography. However, depending on the actual IR-blocking filter installed, some digital cameras are better suited for infrared photography than others. If you have an IR-blocked digital camera, you might still be able to shoot infrared photographs. The IR-blocking filter doesn't block infrared completely; it may just take a longer exposure to capture it. In the following section, you learn how to determine whether your digital camera is suitable for infrared photography. If you determine that it is not suitable, don't despair—Chapter 16 shows you how to make your digital camera suitable.

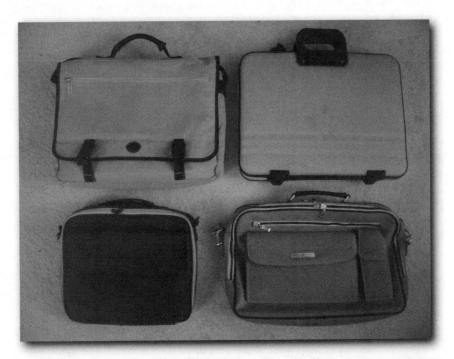

FIGURE 15-5: All four bags are black, but because this picture was shot with an IR-sensitive digital camera, each bag appears in a different color, determined by its IR reflectivity.

How Well Does Your Digital Camera Perceive Infrared Light?

It is actually relatively simple to determine whether your digital camera is suitable for infrared photography. It's quite likely that you have some infrared-emitting devices at home, such as an infrared remote control. Simply aim the infrared LED at the lens and watch the infrared light through your camera. Keep the infrared LED about a foot away from the lens. If you have a digital camera that has an electronic viewfinder or full-time LCD preview, turn it on. You'll easily be able to see the infrared light being emitted. If your digital camera has only an optical viewfinder and no full-time LCD preview, take a picture of the infrared LED and examine the picture to see how well the infrared light is perceived by the digital sensor.

An IR-blocked digital camera does not see any infrared light at all. Therefore, no infrared light shows up in the picture or the electronic viewfinder. However, most digital cameras see some infrared, because the IR-blocking filters generally do not block all infrared light, as shown in Figure 15-6. If your digital camera doesn't have a built-in IR-blocking filter, the digital camera will be practically blinded by the infrared light from the remote control (see Figure 15-7).

FIGURE 15-6: The camera sees the infrared remote control through the IR-blocking filter.

FIGURE 15-7: The camera, without the IR-blocking filter, is virtually blinded by the infrared light from the infrared remote control.

Shooting Infrared Photographs

This section touches on infrared photography for beginners. You don't need to have a modified infrared camera to take advantage of the instructions and techniques presented here. If you have a film camera, get some infrared film. If your digital camera is even slightly sensitive to infrared, you'll be able to follow along. Plus, being familiar with infrared photography will help you modify your digital camera in Chapter 16.

Enhancing Infrared Photography with Filters

All digital sensors and infrared films are sensitive to both visible light and infrared. As you saw earlier, if both visible and infrared light are shot at the same time, the resulting picture will have some interesting effects (see Figure 15-8). These effects are okay if that is what you are after. But most people find these pictures abnormal and distracting. When you shoot infrared, most likely you want to capture just infrared light and not visible light. You can block out the visible light with filters, just as you can block out the infrared light with an IR-blocking filter. When the visible light is blocked out, the infrared spectrum is enhanced and its effects become most pronounced in the photograph.

FIGURE 15-8: This picture was shot with an IR-sensitive camera, without any filters.

Red Filter

For infrared photography, the red filter is a good one to start with. It is relatively cheap compared to other infrared filters, and this type of filter is readily available because most black-and-white photographers use the red filter to increase contrast in their pictures. In fact, it's common enough that you may already have one. As you can see in Figure 15-9, the red filter blocks out the blues and the greens. It lets only the red spectrum and longer wavelengths pass. Since infrared is an extension to the red spectrum, this filter is a good companion for an infrared photographer.

Note Filter names have long been misnomers. Based on its name, a red filter should semantically filter out red light. In reality, it passes red light and filters out blue and green. The reason for the naming convention is that filter names are based on the color of the filter glass. Since the glass passes the color red, the glass looks red. Hence the name *red filter*.

The red filter is easier to shoot with than the infrared filters. The red filter passes red light, which is visible to the naked eye. Thus, a photographer can easily compose and frame the scene through the filter. The ability to see through the red filter is one luxury that other infrared filters do not offer. When you use opaque infrared filters, you will likely need a tripod so your composition isn't changed when mounting the filter. With the red filter, you can easily hand-hold many of your infrared shots.

FIGURE **15-9: The infrared effect is slightly enhanced with the red filter. Some visible light characteristics, in the red spectrum, are also captured.**

Hoya R72

The Hoya R72 infrared filter is a very good next step. Many infrared photographers use the R72 exclusively and are satisfied with the results. As its name implies, it filters all wavelengths below 720 nm. It's quite opaque to the naked eye, but your IR-sensitive film or sensor can see through it just fine (see Figure 15-10).

Note

I ordered an RM72 filter from an online source once, but I received the R72 filter instead. I contacted a Hoya technical service representative to ask about the difference. The representative claimed that there is no difference between the two filter designations. There is no such thing as the RM72 filter on the R72 spec sheet. Hoya's R and IR designations are for IR-transmission filters with sharp IR cut-off. Hoya's RM designation is for IR-transmission filters with smooth and gradual cut-off. Hoya's RT designation is for band-pass IR-transmission filters.

Other Infrared Filters

There are many other infrared filters out there. Usually, they differ only in the wavelength that they transmit and filter. Table 15-1 is a chart of some popular infrared filters. The left-most column shows the transmittance, meaning that light from this wavelength value and above is transmitted through the filter. Any wavelength below the transmittance value is blocked. The next four columns show the manufacturers and respective model numbers.

FIGURE 15-10: The infrared effect is greatly enhanced with the
R72 filter. Most visible light characteristics are eliminated.

Table 15-1: Popular Infrared Filters

Transmittance	B+W	Hoya	Kodak Wratten	Tiffen
600nm	090	25A	#25	25
620nm	091		#29	29
720nm	092	R72	#89B	
795nm			#87	87
850nm	093		#87C	
930nm		RM90	#87B	
1050nm	094	RM100	#87A	

Note The transmittance is only an approximation because the cut-off is not discrete and exact. A 720nm infrared filter generally has a 50% transmittance at 720nm. The slope and cut-off is non-linear. Each manufacturer's filter differs slightly from those of other manufacturers. Table 15-1 should be used only as a general guide. Use the manufacturer's spec sheet for a more detailed analysis of the cut-off points.

Table 15-1 lists the filters in order of opacity to *visible* light, from less opaque to more opaque. Filters with the first two transmittance values (600nm and 620nm) still transmit the red spectrum. The R72 filter and others at the 720nm cutoff transmit very little visible light. The remaining filters transmit no visible light at all and can be considered visibly black. Filters with the last two transmittance values (930nm and 1050nm) even block some infrared light. If you are interested in eliminating all visible light from your photographs, then any of the filters with the last four transmittance values are the way to go. Experimenting with these filters is the key to seeing their effects.

Tip Glass filters can be quite expensive, and glass IR-filters are notoriously expensive. As the filter size increases, its price goes up. While you're experimenting, buy the filters listed in Table 15-1 in their smallest sizes. After you have picked your favorite IR-filter, buy the largest one you need.

Compensating Exposure for Filters

When you start experimenting with infrared filters, you'll find that the exposure recommended by the camera isn't correct. Many times, you'll get a black picture because the scene hasn't been exposed long enough. Because your camera's exposure meter is calibrated for visible light photography, it cannot accurately meter infrared light. It took me quite a few tries to shoot the picture shown in Figure 15-11. The unmodified, IR-insensitive Digital Rebel's exposure meter estimated the scene to 1 second at f/5.6 when the R72 filter was mounted. In reality, the scene had to be exposed for 30 seconds or more.

When you shoot infrared film, change the camera ISO setting to the exposure index (EI) recommended by the manufacturer for the film. The recommendation is on the film box. The EI should get your meter fairly close to the exposure needed for an average scene. Then follow the instructions presented in the "Bracketing Your Shots" section, and you'll find the correct exposure for the effect you want.

With a digital camera, your life should be a little easier because you can see the results immediately after the shot. If the scene is black or too dark, you have to compensate by exposing longer or using a larger aperture. Do this for several different scenes to get an idea of how far off your camera meter is from correctly shooting an average scene. After you become familiar with the difference, you should be able to get pretty close on the first try. When you are close, follow the technique presented in the following section, "Bracketing Your Shots."

FIGURE 15-11: This picture was exposed for 30 seconds. Handholding the camera and the model's slight movement added to the ghost-like effect of this infrared photograph.

Bracketing Your Shots

Most exposure meters are tuned for shooting visible light pictures. When used to measure infrared light, they can be off by a few stops. Sometimes, you think the exposure is spot on, but you'll find out later that it's off. Whether you shoot film or digital, you'll want to bracket your shots. *Bracketing* shots means that you shoot the same picture a number of times using a different exposure (shutter speed and/or aperture change) each time. By bracketing, you can pick the best exposure later, when you can examine each picture closely. Try a three-stop bracket at one-stop intervals. Through experimentation, you can find the best bracket for your camera setup.

Figures 15-12 through 15-14 show a series of a three-stop bracket. The one that is correct depends on your preference and your subject.

 Tip The sun emits stronger infrared light in the morning, in the late afternoon, and at higher altitudes.

FIGURE 15-12: A picture in the series of a three-stop bracket. This picture has a -1 stop underexposure.

FIGURE 15-13: A picture in the series of a three-stop bracket. This picture is the standard exposure.

Framing Your Shot

Since the opaque IR filter blocks all visible light, your eyes won't be able to see through it. Infrared photography is where a digital P&S camera really shines. Most P&S digital cameras have a real-time LCD preview to help you see the scene as the digital sensor sees it. Turn this mode on. It will help you easily frame your shot through the opaque IR filter. The digital sensor can see through the opaque IR filter, and therefore you can see through it, too, with its help.

Some digital cameras and practically all camcorders have electronic viewfinders. The electronic viewfinders work exactly like the real-time LCD preview. These are also good cameras to use for infrared photography.

But what if your digital camera only has an optical viewfinder?

FIGURE 15-14: A picture in the series of a three-stop bracket. This picture has a +1 stop overexposure.

Many digital SLRs, such as the Canon's EOS series of SLRs, do not support any real-time electronic preview mode. Instead, the photographer has to frame through the optical viewfinder. These cameras are a little hard to use for infrared photography, but it's possible. Film cameras are also in this category, because they have no LCD. Nevertheless, infrared photographers have used film cameras for ages. And SLRs have been the primal infrared photography tool since before digital SLRs were available.

When you're creating infrared photographs with an optical viewfinder camera, it is best to use a tripod. Mount the camera on the tripod without the opaque IR filter. Frame the scene to your liking. After you have the scene framed, mount the opaque IR filter on the camera and shoot away. Remove the opaque IR filter when you're ready to reframe the shot.

Focusing on the Subject

Infrared light has a longer wavelength than visible light. When you set the camera to sharp focus, the picture is sharp for the visible spectrum, not the infrared spectrum. When shooting for infrared, you have to readjust the focus to compensate.

SLR Lens

To make your life easier, some SLR lenses have infrared focus marking on them. All you have to do is focus, read the focus mark, and then adjust the focus marking to compensate for infrared. Figures 15-15 and 15-16 show the focus mark window on a zoom lens and a single-focal length lens.

FIGURE 15-15: Focus mark window on a zoom lens. The red markings are the infrared focus settings. Because this is a zoom lens, the manufacturer supplied infrared focus marks for several focal lengths.

The zoom lens shown in Figure 15-15 has infrared markings (in red) for several focal lengths: 28, 35, 50, 70, and 135. So, if the focus mark is on 7' and the focal length is 50, you need to rotate the focus ring so that 7' lines up with the red "50" mark.

In Figure 15-16, the single-focal length lens has a small red mark for sharp infrared focus. Don't confuse it with the aperture depth-of-field marks: 5.6, 11, and 16. When you have achieved focus (say, at 1 meter), rotate the focus ring until 1 meter lines up with the red dot. Now infrared focus is achieved.

Note Surprisingly, the Canon EOS SLRs can auto-focus through an R72 filter. It seems that their AF sensors are as sensitive to infrared as they are to visible light.

FIGURE **15-16: Focus mark window on a prime lens. The tiny red dot is the infrared focus marking. Don't confuse it with the aperture marks in white. The aperture marks are presented on this lens to show depth-of-field at each aperture.**

On SLR lenses that do not have infrared markings, you can readjust focus to compensate for infrared by turning the focus ring. With infrared, focus a little closer to the camera, in front of the subject. Exactly how close to focus depends on the lens, the focal length, and the infrared wavelength your gear is sensitive to. The best way to determine how much to adjust is to experiment.

Tip

Start with one set-up: the same camera you'll be using for your working shots, with a single focal length and one aperture. When you have one set-up figured out, move on to the next set-up. By taking your time to try each set-up, you won't be confused by your experience.

Point-and-Shoot Cameras

Historically, few photographers used P&S cameras for infrared photography. Today, digital P&S cameras are probably the best infrared candidates. However, the manufacturers haven't built infrared-handy features into the digital P&S cameras, so you most likely won't have a digital P&S camera made for infrared photography any time soon, and that means you'll have to deal with readjusting for infrared focus yourself.

Unfortunately, most P&S digital cameras do not allow you to adjust focus, or they allow adjustment in a few discrete chunks. Very few have fine focus adjustment control. The only way to adjust the focus is to achieve focus and then nudge the camera back very slightly so that the focus is slightly in front of the subject. Exactly how far to move depends on the lens, the focal length, and the infrared wavelength you are capturing. The best way to determine how much to nudge is to experiment with your camera.

Moving the camera while holding down the shutter button halfway for focus lock is a tad difficult to accomplish with P&S cameras. It might be easier for you to use the depth-of-field method described in the next section.

Using a Larger Depth-of-Field

Another method to keep your infrared subject in focus is to use a larger depth-of-field (DOF). DOF is basically the range of distance where all objects are in fairly sharp focus. There are two ways to achieve high DOF. First, use a smaller aperture (larger f-number), and second, use a wide-angle lens.

It is generally acceptable to stop down your lens by one, two, or three stops to achieve more DOF. *Stopping down* means making the aperture smaller or the f-number bigger. By limiting yourself to a maximum of three stops, you are using your camera lens at its optimal condition and diffraction is kept at bay.

Wide-angle lenses, by nature, have larger DOF than telephoto lenses. If you have a camera with a zoom lens, set the zoom to minimum (wide-angle). By setting your lens to wide-angle, you have effectively maximized the DOF at any specific aperture.

When both of these ways are combined, you have maximized the depth-of-field and will retain sharpness of your subject.

Picking a Color Mode

As alluded to before, when a digital camera is sensitive to infrared, color will be rendered with unexpected results. And if you use the red filter, your picture will be tinted red. Sometimes the result is interesting; other times it's just weird. Many photographers, including me, choose to just not deal with the color issue at all. We shoot black and white (B&W) instead. It's no wonder that most infrared films are B&W films.

Most of today's P&S digital cameras allow you to select a color mode. Figure 15-17 shows a few selections on one of the digital cameras that I have. If your digital camera has a B&W or sepia setting, it is easy to produce gray-scale images (that is, images without color).

On the other hand, some digital SLRs do not have color mode selection. Interesting how the more professional the camera, the more interesting features it lacks. Nevertheless, you can still create B&W or sepia images in post-processing, which is covered in "Manipulating the Resulting Photograph."

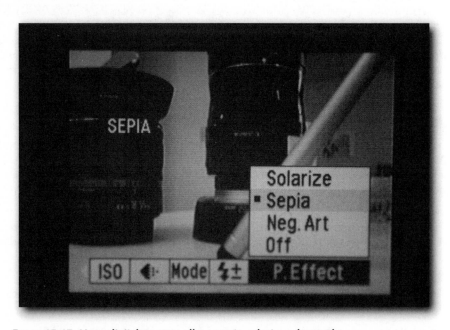

FIGURE 15-17: Many digital cameras allow you to select a color mode.

Color Infrared

Although many infrared photographers choose to shoot B&W infrared photographs, shooting color infrared can be a lot of fun as well. With colors that are less predictable, the result can be interesting and appealing. Also, once the IR-blocking filter is removed, every IR-sensitive digital camera generates different shades of color. This seemingly random permutation of color shift can bring a lot of unexpected marvel to this art form.

It turns out that even though an IR-sensitive digital camera can no longer represent color correctly, its software control algorithm still actively corrects for white balance. In different white balance modes, a different shade of color saturates your resulting image. Don't forget to try different color modes—daylight, cloudy, shades, indoor, and so on—in your infrared photographs.

Manipulating the Resulting Photograph

Even if you have a digital camera that doesn't allow you to change the color mode, you can still turn your color picture into B&W images during post-processing on your computer. Maybe you forgot to set the color mode when you took the infrared image. This happens to me all the time. The camera that I use for infrared photography always resets to color after turning off. To make B&W, Sepia, or other color images in post-processing, all you need is a decent graphics program. You probably already have one that was included with your digital camera. Adobe Photoshop and Corel Paint Shop Pro are also good candidates.

Black and White

To turn your color image into a B&W image, load the picture you want to change in your favorite graphics software. Look for a gray scale function in the menus. Once you select the gray scale function, the graphics software will change your picture into black-and-white.

Eliminating the IR Blocking Filter from Your Digital Camera

Before the popularity of digital cameras exploded, infrared photography was a lot harder. With a film camera, the infrared filter has to be constantly mounted during a shot, but removed between shots for framing. During exposure, the infrared filter also eliminates most visible light, which means that the film has to expose for from a few seconds to a few minutes. This means that a tripod has to be used all the time. The infrared photographer also has to account for reciprocal failure (see Chapter 10) when the film is exposed for such a long period. All of these characteristics mean that shooting infrared photographs is an extremely slow process. In the end, infrared film photography means no instant action shots and sport photography. Digital cameras with infrared sensitive sensors removed these burdens of infrared photography.

Digital cameras are very good candidates for infrared photography because digital sensors are naturally sensitive to the infrared spectrum, which means that the sensors can "see" the invisible wavelengths that your eyes can't see. And unlike infrared film, digital sensors are as sensitive to infrared light as they are to visible light. A digital sensor will see right through an opaque infrared filter, showing you the scene immediately, without your having to unmount the filter. Digital cameras can also display your shots right after you shoot them. Thus, if your infrared exposure is a little off, you can quickly adjust it and shoot again. All these advantages mean that digital infrared photography is suitable for action shots and sport photography, in addition to the traditional still art.

Exclusive IR Cameras

There is a catch to all this digital infrared excitement. Few consumer digital cameras support infrared photography in their native form. Infrared photography is a niche art form and is mostly practiced by photographers with several years of experience. Therefore, manufacturers have been reluctant to offer this capability natively in their digital cameras. Most digital cameras have infrared sensitivity disabled by filtering out most of infrared light reaching the digital sensor. As mentioned in Chapter 15, the manufacturers add this filtering so that you can capture the scene accurately as you originally saw it.

In Chapter 15, I gave you some ideas about how to shoot infrared photographs without modifying your camera. In this chapter, I will show you how to modify your camera so that you can shoot infrared with all the advantages I've mentioned.

Understanding the IR-Blocking Filter

The IR-blocking filter is a glass filter that separates infrared light waves from visible light waves. The glass blocks infrared light, but allows visible light to pass through. Digital camera manufacturers install this glass behind the lens and in front of the sensor to keep the infrared spectrum from reaching the digital sensor. The good news is that the IR-blocking filter is not usually an integral part of the sensor and is relatively easy to remove. The same digital camera was used to take the pictures shown in Figures 15-6 and 15-7 in the previous chapter. In the first picture, before I removed the IR-blocking filter, the infrared spectrum captured from the television remote is limited. In the second picture, after I removed the IR-blocking filter, the camera is so susceptible to infrared light that aiming at an infrared light source caused blinding flare.

Modifying Your Digital Camera

In this chapter, I show you how to remove the IR-blocking filter from a Sony Cyber-shot DSC-P92 digital camera. If you happen to have this camera or a similar Sony Cyber-shot model, following the procedure is a piece of cake. But the procedure in concept can be applied to any digital camera. Even if you have a different brand or type of camera and model, the procedure presented here and your own experimentation will help you create your own exclusive IR camera.

Note   Most digital cameras have the IR-blocking filter. I have seen procedures to remove the IR-blocking filter from Nikon CoolPix 950, Canon EOS Digital Rebel, and Canon PowerShot G-series digital cameras. After removing the IR-blocking filter from my own Sony Cyber-shot DSC-P92 digital camera, I believe that the IR-blocking filter can be removed from almost any digital camera.

Converting the Sony DSC-P92 to Infrared

Caution   Before jumping in, make sure you read this entire section and are familiar with the procedure.

Parts You Need

Here is the part you will need to complete this project:

- 12.5mm × 10mm × 2mm glass pane

The dimensions shown here are for the Sony Cyber-shot DSC-P92 digital camera. If you have a different camera, you won't know the right dimension until you take your digital camera apart.

Sony NightShot Camcorder

Sony's Handycam camcorders have a really interesting feature called NightShot. When NightShot is enabled, the camcorder can see in complete darkness. The Sony NightShot mode works by taking advantage of the CCD's sensitivity to infrared. The camcorder itself emits infrared to light up the scene as shown in Figure 16-1. When turned on, the mechanical NightShot mode switch moves the IR-blocking filter out of the way, a feature that makes these cameras prime candidates for infrared photography. Because the human eyes can't see infrared, it appears that the Sony NightShot camcorder can see in complete darkness.

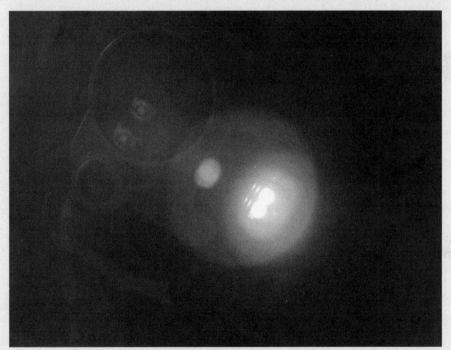

FIGURE 16-1: Sony's NightShot camcorder emits its own infrared light.

Many NightShot camcorders have the ability to turn off the infrared emission through their menu options. By turning off the infrared emission, you can prevent the scene from being polluted by the camcorder's artificial infrared light. This allows you to shoot infrared pictures and videos.

It's also possible to use the NightShot camcorder as an accessory to your infrared camera in complete darkness. Turn on the infrared emitter to light up the scene, and then snap away with your infrared digital camera.

Tip If you don't mind having a shortsighted infrared digital camera, you can forgo the glass. Being shortsighted, your digital camera can shoot close-up infrared photographs, which is a pretty useful photographer's tool as well. I will explain more about that later in this chapter.

You can find glass at any hardware store. They usually sell it in large panes, which is probably a lot more glass than you need. You can also take the glass out of an old photo frame. I found that one of my old photo frames had a glass thickness that was exactly the same as the one in the Sony DSC-P92 digital camera.

Tools You Need

Here are the tools you will need to complete this project:

- Precision tool set
- Glass cutter
- Cutting oil
- Antistatic wrist strap

The precision tool set, glass cutter, and cutting oil cost a few dollars at a hardware store. If you decide to forgo the glass, then you can forgo the glass cutter and cutting oil as well. You can pick up the anti-static wrist strap at an electronics or computer store; it protects your electronic components from being zapped by static electricity.

Disassembling the Digital Camera

The Sony DSC-P92 digital camera has an elegant silver finish, but beneath the silver paint is just ABS plastic. The digital camera is enclosed in a two-piece plastic shell that you can easily pull apart when all of the machine screws are removed. Start disassembling by locating the machine screws (see Figure 16-2) around the plastic case. There are four screws altogether. One of the four screws is hidden in the Memory Stick slot as shown in Figure 16-3.

When all four machine screws are removed, the only thing holding the shell together is a plastic tab, within the plastic enclosure, located at the top of the digital camera. The plastic tab is directly above the DSC-P92 model designation, as shown in Figure 16-4. Carefully insert a small flathead screwdriver between the seams to pry the two halves of the shell apart.

Figure 16-2: Machine screws surround the camera shell.

Figure 16-3: A screw hidden in the Memory Stick slot

FIGURE 16-4: A plastic tab holding the shells together

Be very careful when you pull the two plastic halves apart. Electronic components are on both halves of the shell, and the two halves communicate via a surface mount ribbon cable. If you pull too hard and too far, you will rip the ribbon cable and render your digital camera useless.

The ribbon cable is attached to the circuit board with a surface-mount ribbon connector. To secure the ribbon cable and relieve stress on the ribbon cable and connector, a felt tape is affixed to both the connector and the ribbon cable (see Figure 16-5). Slowly peel the felt tape from the connector. Try not to damage the felt tape; it should be reused to retain the stress relief.

Now that you have peeled back the felt tape, you can unlatch the connector holding the ribbon connector. With your fingernail, or a small flathead screwdriver, pull the latch upward, as shown in Figure 16-6. When the latch is released, you can slide the ribbon cable out of the connector. The two shell halves are now apart, and it will be easier to work on the circuit board.

FIGURE 16-5: Peel off the felt tape carefully until you can get to the latch that holds down the ribbon connector.

FIGURE 16-6: The latching connector is exposed when the felt tape is peeled away.

Before you can get to the IR-blocking filter, you have to detach five additional ribbon cables on the circuit board. Two types of connectors are securing these ribbon cables. You already have experience with the latching type. The second connector type is the insertion type. The insertion type connectors do not have a latch to secure the ribbon cable. Instead, it secures the ribbon cable with friction (see Figure 16-7). To remove the ribbon cables from these connectors, use your fingernails, or a small flathead screwdriver, on the two tabs on each side of the ribbon cable. Pull the two tabs outward, away from the connector. With your thumb and your index finger, you can pull both tabs simultaneously. If you are using the screwdriver, you'll have to alternate working on each side until the cable is completely out of the connector. Proceed slowly and carefully. You don't want to damage any of these cables or connectors. They are not practically repairable at home.

FIGURE 16-7: Insertion type ribbon connectors

Figure 16-8 shows you where the ribbon cables are located, in addition to the four machine screws that are holding down the circuit board. When you have successfully detached all of the ribbon cables, unscrew the four circuit board screws.

The last thing you need to do is to locate the metal bracket with two black machine screws, shown in Figure 16-9. This metal bracket actually secures the digital sensor and circuit board in place. It prevents any motion and relieves any stress placed on the CCD sensor directly beneath it. Unscrew the two black screws and remove the metal bracket.

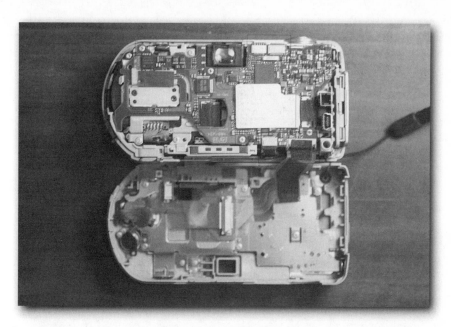

FIGURE 16-8: Circuit board layout showing all of the ribbon connectors and screws

FIGURE 16-9: A metal bracket secures the circuit board and digital sensor in place.

With the metal bracket removed, you are ready to separate the circuit board from the rest of the digital camera. A plastic tab by the shutter release button (see Figure 16-10) is the last circuit board securing mechanism. Simply pull the plastic tab away from the circuit board with one finger and remove the circuit board with your other hand.

FIGURE 16-10: This plastic tab secures the circuit board.

Caution

Handle the circuit board by its edge only. Do not touch any of the electronic components with your hand. Static electricity can zap them. Pick up an antistatic wrist strap at an electronics or computer store and use it religiously when you are around circuit boards.

A set of power wires is attached to the other side of the circuit board, as shown in Figure 16-11. You can choose to disconnect it or not. Either way, you have access to the IR-blocking filter.

FIGURE 16-11: This power cable is attached to the power connector on the circuit board.

Removing the IR-blocking Filter

When you move the circuit board out of the way, either keeping the power cable attached or with it disconnected completely, you can see that the CCD sensor is located on the bottom side of the circuit board (see Figures 16-12 and 16-13). The IR-blocking filter lies directly beneath the digital sensor, as shown in Figure 16-14. Turn the camera upside down and the IR-blocking filter will fall right out. You can then see the rear lens element, as shown in Figure 16-15.

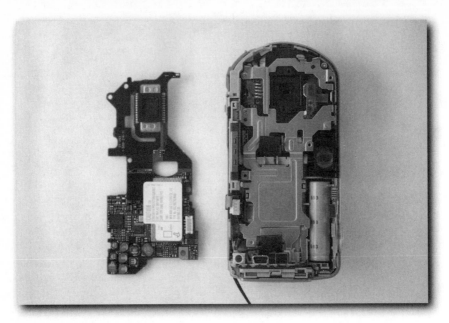

FIGURE **16-12**: The circuit board and camera side by side

FIGURE **16-13**: The CCD sensor

FIGURE 16-14: The IR-blocking filter sits behind the lens, unsecured.

FIGURE 16-15: You can see the rear lens element with the IR-blocking filter removed.

The factory IR-blocking filter is polished on all sides with no jagged edges. The glass filter looks like plain glass; it seems clear when you look through it (see Figure 16-16). You can't tell it is a special filter until you lay it on a white surface and look at it from an angle. When you do, you will see a greenish blue tint (see Figure 16-17) that lets you know this is an infrared blocking filter.

FIGURE 16-16: The IR-blocking filter appears clear when you look at it straight on.

Measure the dimensions of the IR-blocking filter. You'll need this measurement to make a replacement glass filter in the next step. After you're done with the measurement, find a safe place to store the IR-blocking filter. Don't throw it away; you might want to restore your digital camera to its original condition one day.

Cutting Clear Glass

In order for your digital camera to work properly with infrared light and visible light, you have to replace the IR-blocking filter with clear glass. Without replacement glass, your digital camera becomes shortsighted. This means that it focuses only on things that are really close to the lens, and it loses the ability to focus to infinity. So if you want to shoot landscape, scenery, and people pictures, you have to install a piece of plain glass where the IR-blocking filter previously resided.

FIGURE 16-17: You can see the greenish-blue tint when you look at the IR-blocking filter from an angle.

This step is probably the hardest task for most people—it was for me—because most people have no idea how to cut glass. But it is really quite easy after doing it a few times. I learned to cut glass simply by reading the instructions that came with my glass-cutting tool. So, if you are thinking about shying away from this project because of the glass-cutting part, don't.

Note You can learn the basics of cutting glass in Appendix C of this book. Read it a few times and get familiar with the process.

Macro Infrared Photography

Although this trait sounds undesirable, it is actually quite desirable to a close-up photographer. Macro photography concentrates on capturing small things. Most cameras are not very good at taking close-ups of small subjects without help from accessory add-on lenses. Removing the IR-blocking filter is relatively easy and inexpensive. This is a great opportunity for you to make a full-time macro infrared digital camera for yourself.

Continued

Continued

I shot the picture in Figure 16-18 with the Sony DSC-P92 digital camera. I was experimenting without the clear-glass replacement. The digital camera was able to focus on the end of this ruler from ½" to 1" away. When I finally installed the replacement glass, the digital camera's minimum focus distance from the ruler became 4 to 5".

FIGURE 16-18: The camera is excellent at macro photography without the plain glass to replace the IR-blocking filter.

Although cutting glass is fairly easy, your first few tries are bound to fail, especially on a piece of glass that is smaller than your fingertip. My first replacement glass was totally crooked. The second piece I cut wasn't straight and was a little too big on the edge. I used the jaw of the needle nose pliers to chip off the edge slowly. You can see the rugged edge of my glass in Figure 16-19. It is actually a little too small compared to the original IR-blocking filter, but it covered the entire digital sensor and made no difference in the pictures.

FIGURE 16-19: My plain-glass replacement

Putting the Digital Camera Back Together

Unlike other projects in this book, putting the Sony DSC-P92 digital camera back together isn't the reverse of taking it apart. After reconnecting the power cable to the circuit board (assuming you have disconnected it), reconnect the ribbon cable that is next to the USB port. I found that this cable has to be connected before placing the circuit board back in position. It's practically impossible to connect it after the circuit board is in place. Next, put the circuit board back in place and reattach all of the ribbon cables, except for the one that goes to the other half of the plastic shell. Now, secure the circuit board and the metal bracket with the machine screws. Finally, reconnect the last ribbon cable and reassemble the shell. The reassembly is complete when you screw in the four machine screws for the outer shell.

Make Your Own Infrared Emitter

You can get the following parts from an electronics store, such as Radio Shack. Radio Shack part numbers are listed for your convenience.

- High-output, 5mm infrared LED (276-143)

- 10 ohm 1/4W 5% carbon film resistor pk/5 (271-1301)

- AA battery holder (270-401A)

A light-emitting diode (LED) is a semiconductor that produces light when current flows through it. Like a diode, current can only flow through it in one direction. The high-output, 5mm infrared LED has a forward voltage of 1.2v and a forward current of 100mA. The longer lead is the positive lead (see Figure 16-20).

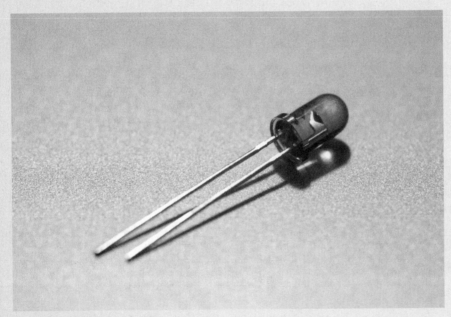

FIGURE 16-20: An infrared LED

Figure 16-21 shows the infrared LED lighted up when 1.2v are applied to it. The picture is captured with an infrared digital camera; you won't see the light with your naked eyes. Rechargeable batteries supply 1.2v and are perfect for this project.

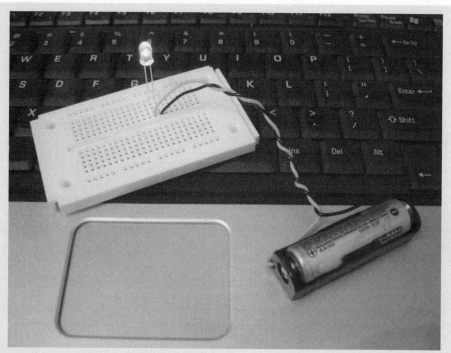

FIGURE 16-21: The infrared LED lights up when 1.2v are applied to it using a NiMH rechargeable battery.

In Figure 16-21, the electricity is supplied directly to the infrared LED. It's ok to do this for a quick test. But during normal operation, the LED will fail prematurely. LEDs have very low internal resistance. Therefore, without a resistor to limit current, the LED will burn out.

The basic electronic equation (resistance = voltage / current) determines the resistor you need to make your own emitter. For the infrared LED being used here, 1.2 volts divided by 0.100 amp equals 12 ohms. A 10-ohm resister is pretty close. You can, of course, make the exact resistor combination by wiring resistors in series and parallel.

Testing the Infrared Digital Camera

Now that you put the digital camera back together again, it's time to test it to make sure it's functional. Turn it on and see if it comes to life. If it does, test its normal functions, such as focus, shoot picture, zoom, and so on. If the camera doesn't turn on, shuts off immediately, or does something strange, chances are you forgot to plug in a cable or a cable isn't seated correctly. Retrace your steps and properly seat all cables and connectors.

Tip When the ribbon cable is secured incorrectly, the Sony DSC-P92 turns on, extends the lens, and turns off. Re-secure the connectors and the Sony DSC-P92 becomes fully operational.

When everything is working, you can satisfy your own curiosity by pointing it at a wireless infrared remote. Press a button on the remote. The remote comes to life with flashing lights that are invisible to your naked eyes. When you are satisfied with your success, give yourself a pat on the back. You have converted your regular digital camera to an exciting infrared digital camera. Now you are ready to shoot infrared pictures.

If you haven't already gotten some infrared filters (after reading the previous chapter), get some now. They will really make your infrared photographs stand out. Figures 20-22, 20-23, and 20-24 show you the difference between having a filter and not having one. Without a filter, the picture looks like one you can make with your original digital camera. Use Chapter 15 as a guide to help you get started with infrared photography.

FIGURE 16-22: Without a filter

FIGURE 16-23: With a red filter

FIGURE 16-24: With an R-72 filter

Ultraviolet Photography

There are many books and how-to guides to fill the infrared photography niche. But few photographers talk about ultraviolet photography. Ultraviolet (UV) photography is quite similar to infrared photography. It is basically the art of photographing the other side of the visible light spectrum. Generally, the IR-blocking filter also serves as a UV-blocking filter. Therefore, most IR-insensitive digital cameras are also insensitive to UV. The opposite is also true: an IR-sensitive digital camera is also sensitive to UV. Therefore, when you made your digital IR-sensitive, you also made it UV-sensitive.

There are three types of ultraviolet lights:

- UV-A: Ranges between 315–400 nm, which is a very safe range.

- UV-B: Ranges between 280–315 nm. This UV range is somewhat hazardous to your health. Very limited exposure is recommended.

- UV-C: Ranges between 100–280 nm. This UV range is dangerous to eyes and tissue.

Figure 16-25 shows a picture taken with the Sony DSC-P92 digital camera that I modified for infrared photography. A black-light bulb, placed to the right of the picture frame, lit the scene. The second picture, shown in Figure 16-26, taken with my unmodified Canon EOS Digital Rebel, was insensitive to UV. The lack of UV-sensitivity caused the exposure of the second picture to be extremely slow compared to the first picture. Even with an exposure almost three-times slower, the second picture is still extremely dark and underexposed. Both pictures were shot at ISO 400 with an aperture setting of f/2.8.

As you might have guessed from the previous paragraph, the common black-light bulb generates ultraviolet light: UV-A to be exact. A handful of these bulbs make an excellent light source to brighten a darkened room for your infrared digital camera and camcorder without ruining the atmosphere.

At the last Halloween party my friends and I threw, I used two bulbs to light up the living room where we told ghost stories all night. I filmed the entire conversation with my Sony Handycam, in NightShot mode, without destroying the spooky mood.

FIGURE 16-25: Shot at ⅟₅₀ of a second under black light

Continued

Continued

FIGURE 16-26: Shot at 1.3 seconds under black light

Shooting Visible Light with an IR Camera

Now that you have an exclusive IR camera, you might wonder how you would be able to shoot regular visible light pictures again, especially if this is your only camera. You can always put the IR-blocking filter back into your digital camera by following the same procedure presented in this chapter. But that's a lot of work. The easier way is to find a hot mirror filter at a camera store. Mount it to the front of the lens, as you do with your infrared filter.

When you use the hot mirror filter, the color in your picture will be fairly normal and accurate. However, because each camera manufacturer's sensor is different, the filter manufacturers make the IR blocking filters specifically for each digital sensor. With a generic hot mirror filter, you won't be able to reproduce the color with the same accuracy as with the IR-blocking filter you removed. But it's a lot easier to install.

Note Hot mirrors and cold mirrors are multi-layer dielectric mirrors for separating infrared radiation from the visible spectrum. Generally, they are used for heat control. A hot mirror blocks and reflects infrared spectrum (basically an IR-blocking filter), allowing visible light to pass through. A cold mirror, on the other hand, reflects the visible wavelengths and allows infrared radiation to pass through. If you mount the cold mirror on the camera without removing the IR-blocking filter, you would filter out both visible and infrared light . . . your camera won't see anything!

Building Fun Camera Tools

part

IV

Building a Car Camera Mount

One reason photography and cinematography are so popular and timeless is that they help you capture your experiences. The photograph or video remembers the event exactly as it happens no matter how much time has passed. Unlike your memory, photographs and videos don't forget or change their perception with time. This trait is why most of us picked up a camera in the first place.

The ability to recall events accurately is why Indy racecar teams mount video cameras, GPS, and vehicle data sensors on the Indy cars. The video cameras record where the car is, where the car is going, and what the driver is doing. The GPS records the exact location on the track. And the data sensor records engine, suspension, and brake parameters at any instant. The race team captures every instance of the action for later analysis, hoping to improve the driver's skills and the car for future races.

Indy racecars have a lot of cool technology. For the rest of us car enthusiasts and wannabe racecar drivers, it is a little difficult to put the same level of technology into our daily driven vehicle. But we can, at least, mount a camera to record our racetrack driving actions for analysis.

Tip Sharing your racetrack video footage could make your audience feel like they are really there. It's the next best thing for people who don't drive their cars on a track.

In this chapter, you make a camera mount for the rear deck of your performance sedan. Figure 17-1 shows the camera mount. At most driving events, loose objects must be removed from the vehicle (plus you don't want them to weigh your car down). The goal is to make a securely mounted camera mount that is safe and legal for the racetrack. The rear deck, with a child-safety seat bracket and far from obstructing the driver, is the best location. If your car doesn't have a rear deck, the camera mount project in Chapter 18 may be suitable for your car.

FIGURE 17-1: Camcorder mounted on the rear deck

 Car and camera manufacturers do not recommend installing your camera gear onto your vehicle. Nor do they recommend the use of your camera during daily drives. Neither the U.S. Department of Transportation (DOT), nor any other local authority approved the instructions presented in this chapter. Therefore, the instructions presented in this chapter should be used only during off-road track events. Use these instructions at your own discretion.

Parts You Need

You need the following parts to build the car mount:

- Mini ball head
- $^3/_8$"-16 bolt
- $^3/_8$"-16 nut
- $^3/_8$" small washer
- $^3/_8$" large washer (2)
- Metal electrical plate

Figure 17-2 shows all of these parts except the ball head. You can purchase these parts at a home improvement store for no more than five dollars.

FIGURE **17-2: Mounting hardware**

The mini ball head, shown in Figure 17-3, is going to be the most expensive part out of the entire rig. If you have a flat rear deck, you may be able to forgo the ball head and use a machine screw, a nut, a washer, and a wing nut instead. (See the "Make Your Own Camera Attachment Head" sidebar in Chapter 22.) My rear deck slopes down towards the front, so I had to use a ball head for leveling the camera.

For this project, I decided to go with a Bogen-Manfrotto Micro Ball Head #482. This micro ball head comes with an oversized ratchet lever for easy locking of the head. It also has two grooves for ninety-degree tilt; most mini ball heads have only one. You can also use a full-size ball head—and I suggest you do for large and heavy camera equipment. I chose a mini ball head because my camcorder is small and light—it fits in the palm of my hand, so the micro ball head is sufficient.

The metal electrical plate is very flexible and useful. You mount this plate to the car. You can then mount the ball head and various other things to this plate. The large flat area allows you to mount anything you see fit.

The screw socket on the bottom of the mini ball head is $^3/_8$"-16; the standard size on all ball heads. The Bogen-Manfrotto Micro Ball Head #482 came with a thread conversion screw, as shown in Figure 17-4. The thread conversion screw converts the $^3/_8$"-16 thread into $^1/_4$"-20 thread. The $^1/_4$"-20 thread is the standard tripod socket size on cameras. However, you should be safe and use the larger, sturdier $^3/_8$"-16 thread to secure the ball head.

FIGURE 17-3: Mini ball head

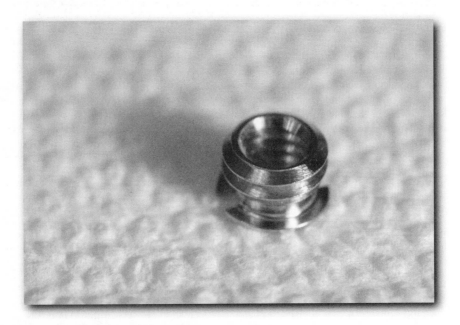

FIGURE 17-4: Thread conversion screw

The $^3/_8$"-16 bolt secures the mini ball head. You can adjust the height of the ball head by using a longer or shorter bolt.

Tools You Need

The tools in the following list will help you build the car camera mount.

- Torque wrench
- Socket wrench (2)
- 14mm socket (2)
- 13mm socket
- Drill press
- $^1/_4$" drill bit
- $^3/_8$" drill bit

You need two socket wrenches and two 14mm sockets because both the bolt and nut are 14mm. You can substitute two 14mm wrenches for the socket wrenches and sockets. You can also pair up a 14mm wrench and a socket wrench with 14mm socket.

In this project, you will need to drill a hole. A drill press will make your life easier on this project, but a hand drill will work. The small drill bit is for starting the hole. The bigger drill bit will finish the job.

Taking Apart the Child Safety Bracket

The child safety seat bracket is standard on today's performance sedans (see Figure 17-5). Three brackets are on the back of a sedan. All of them are covered in plastic. Pick one to convert into your camera mount. Remove the plastic cover to reveal the hex bolt, as shown in Figure 17-6. Use the socket wrench and the 13mm socket to unscrew it.

FIGURE 17-5: The child safety seat bracket is a standard on today's cars.

After unscrewing the bolt, you will end up with the components shown in Figure 17-7. The plastic cover (center) and the metal bracket (left) are not used for this project, but keep them in a safe place in case you want to restore the vehicle to its original condition. Perhaps you might put a kid back there in the future.

The gold screw and bolt set on the right is the hardware that ties down the child safety bracket. You reuse this set of hardware to secure the electrical plate to the vehicle. It includes a bolt, a split lock washer, a flat washer, a spacer, and a cardboard internal tooth lock washer. Your set may be slightly different, and you may need to replace one or more parts in the set for this project.

FIGURE 17-6: The plastic cover pops off, revealing a hex nut.

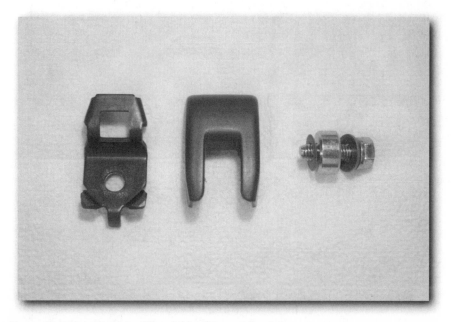

FIGURE 17-7: Components of the child safety seat bracket

Drilling the Mounting Plate

Use the drill press to make a ¼" hole in the metal electrical plate. This plate serves as the mounting place for your camera gear. Place the hole where you want to locate your camera equipment. The bigger drill bit requires more torque and will easily grab the metal bracket, so a smaller ¼" drill bit is a good start. Once you make the ¼" hole, drill the same hole with the bigger ⅜" drill bit. This is the hole where you will mount the bolt for the mini ball head.

If you want to mount other equipment to this plate, you may do so at this time. Some racing organizations require a tethering wire to be installed. You can drill a hole for that as well. The mounting plate in Figure 17-8 has two drilled holes.

FIGURE 17-8: This mounting plate has a ⅜" hole and a ¼" hole.

In my case, I drilled an additional ¼" hole. This hole is reserved for future use, possibly for camera gear to be mounted with a wing nut.

Assembling the Car Camera Mount

Assembling the car camera mount is simple. First, use two 14mm wrenches to secure the $3/8$"-16 bolt and nut to the metal plate.

Then arrange the two larger washers on both sides of the plate, sandwiching the smaller washer. The smaller washer is in place to restrict the mounting plate from moving too much relative to the child safety mount bolt. Once the washers are all in place, re-assemble the child safety bolt set together with the three washers in between.

The configuration of the bolt set, on the mounting plate, should be the same as the configuration on the child safety seat bracket. In my case, the bolt, split lock washer, and flat washer are on top (Figure 17-9), while the spacer and cardboard internal tooth lock washer are on the bottom (Figure 17-10).

FIGURE 17-9: The mounting bolts above the mounting plate

Next, screw the mini ball head onto the $3/8$" bolt securely. You should not be able to see any threads between the mini ball head and the hex nut. If threads are visible, use additional hex nuts to reduce the space. Now, you are ready to install the car camera mount in the vehicle (see Figure 17-11).

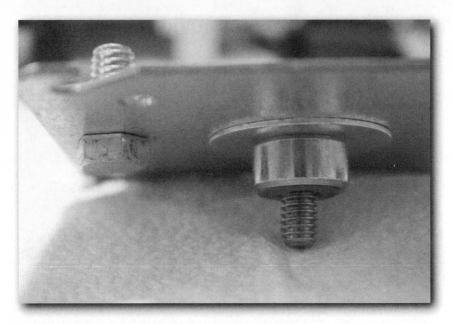

FIGURE 17-10: The mounting bolts below the mounting plate

FIGURE 17-11: The mini ball head attached to the mounting plate

Installing the Camera Mount in Your Car

In my car, there is not enough room to attach the car camera mount to one of the side locations. But the center mount location is roomy and perfect for this installation. Your car may differ.

Using the 13mm socket and torque wrench, torque the bolt down to the chassis with 10 ft-lb of force. Your car camera mount is now complete and should look like the one in Figure 17-12.

FIGURE 17-12: The car camera mount installed in the vehicle

Possible Enhancement

The silver mounting plate and mounting hardware reflect light. I have noticed that it reflects into the rear window. This might be a distraction during track events. A mitigation may be to paint the car camera mount black or to a color similar to the rear deck. A darker color absorbs sunlight and gets warmer than a silver finish. You'll have to make a decision on this trade-off.

Building a Headrest Camera Mount

The car camera mount project in the last chapter is a good rig for cars with a rear deck. But unlike sedans, most sport cars lack this rear deck and the child safety seat brackets. So in this chapter, you'll make a different car camera mount. This camera mount attaches to the headrest metal rods (see Figure 18-1) and is legal for autocrosses and drag strips. Many cars have this kind of headrest on their car seats, so it is likely to be compatible with your car.

Parts You Need

The following list of parts is all you need to make the mount.

- $3/4"\times 3'$ square aluminum tube
- $1/4"$-20 $\times$ 1.5" bolts
- $1/4"$-20 nuts
- $3/8"$-16 hex bolt
- $3/8"$-16 hex nut
- Mini ball head

With the exception of the mini ball head, all the parts in this list can be found at a hardware store such as Home Depot. You can find the mini ball head at a camera store. If you can't find one, you can order them online at B&H (www.bhphotovideo.com/), Adorama (www.adorama.com/), and even Amazon (www.amazon.com/). Most ball heads have a $3/8"$-16 thread on the bottom, hence the same sized bolt and nut listed in the preceding parts list.

FIGURE 18-1: Camcorder mounted on the headrest camera mount

I have a very small camcorder, one that fits in the palm of my hand, so I went with the smallest square aluminum tube that is available at the hardware store. If you have big, bulky equipment, such as an older VHS camcorder, you should use a bigger square aluminum tube. When you step up to a bigger aluminum tube, step up to a bigger fastener as well—$^3/_8$"-16 bolts and nuts are a good choice. This will allow you to use the same size fasteners for everything.

Tip   You want to go as fast as possible at the race track or drag strip. Every ounce of weight counts against your car. I recommend using the smallest and lightest camcorder you can find. This also allows you to use smaller, lighter mounting hardware and ball head.

Tools You Need

The following list of tools will be used for this project. It looks like a long list, but none of these tools is difficult to obtain.

- Tape measure
- L-ruler

- Permanent marker
- Hacksaw
- Sandpaper
- C-clamps
- Hole punch
- Drill press
- $\frac{1}{8}$" drill bit
- $\frac{1}{4}$" drill bit
- $\frac{3}{8}$" drill bit
- Drill gauge
- Metal files
- Screwdriver
- Socket wrench
- 11mm socket
- 14mm socket
- 14mm wrench

This project requires a drill press—it will make your work a lot easier. You can also tough it out with a hand drill, but a hand drill will be less accurate and is slower than a drill press for this project. Borrow a drill press from someone if possible.

Removing the Headrest

The headrest on your car seat is installed via two metal rods as shown in Figure 18-2. The two metal rods allow the headrest to be adjusted up and down. You have probably already adjusted it a few times since the day you bought your car. You can typically move a headrest can moved upward until it reaches a stop. To push it back down or to remove it completely, you have to push in the locking tab. The locking tab is located at the base of one of the metal rod, as shown in Figure 18-3.

FIGURE 18-2: Headrest with metal rods

FIGURE 18-3: The tab locks the headrest in place.

Tip Remove the headrest completely from your car seat (Figure 18-4). You'll have an easier time measuring it.

FIGURE **18-4: The headrest can be detached from your car seat.**

Sizing the Camera Mount

Typically, $1\frac{1}{2}'$ is a good length for this camera mount. It keeps the camera mount short and sturdy. But if you want the camera to be closer to the center of your vehicle, it may have to be a little longer. A three-feet square aluminum tube cut into two halves is perfect. Depending where you want your video camera located, change the length of the square aluminum tube accordingly. Use the tape measure and the permanent marker to mark the length. Then use the L-ruler to draw a line across that mark.

Note You should use bigger square aluminum tubing if you decide to make a long camera mount. The longer bar acts as a long lever arm. The same amount of force applied at the end of a longer bar will apply more torque at the mounting point. When you add your camera gear to the end of the bar, any braking or acceleration forces will be multiplied through the length of the bar. Shorter is better.

Clamp the tube down on your workbench with two C-clamps, as shown in Figure 18-5. Use a hacksaw to cut the square aluminum tube. It is easier for the hack saw to stay on track if you make a notch first. Pull and push the hacksaw slowly several times at the cutting location until the blade digs into the metal. It's likely that the hacksaw blade will jump around the surface of the metal before the notch is made. If it jumps to a different location, bring it back to the mark. Once the notch is made, sawing becomes easier. You can increase your speed steadily then. It takes only a few minutes to saw the tubes in two. After you cut the square aluminum tube in two, don't throw away the second half; in this project, you will be combining the two halves into one strong headrest camera mount. Sand the ends of the tubes with sandpaper to remove any metal shavings.

FIGURE 18-5: The square aluminum tube clamped down on the workbench

Measure the distance between the two metal rods, from the center of one rod to the center of the other rod. Mark this distance on your square aluminum tube, 3" from the end. For example, the distance of the rods on my headrest was $6^{1}/_{4}$", so I made a mark at 3" and another mark at $9^{1}/_{4}$" on the square aluminum tube. Because you will be using the two tubes together, place the tubes side-by-side and make the marks on both tubes, on the seam. See Figure 18-6 for clarification. Compare the headrest posts to the marks to be sure the distances match.

FIGURE 18-6: Mark the drilling points on the square aluminum tube.

Two inches from the other end, mark a hole for the mini ball head. This hole does not have to be on the seam; in fact, it is better if it is at the center of one tube so that when you take the camera mount apart, you won't have to deal with the ball head falling off.

Now you need to mark three additional holes to fasten the two halves of the square aluminum tube together. It is sufficient to mark just one tube. The mark should be made on a side that is adjacent to the side with the headrest and ball head hole markings. Mark one hole at each end of the tube, around 1" from the end. Then mark one hole between the two metal rod markings. Mark another hole between the ball head hole and the headrest hole. Look closely at Figure 18-7—it shows all the marks you should make. If you choose to make your mount longer, you should mark additional fastening holes.

Tip   If you make a mistake in your marking, you can use Isopropyl alcohol to remove your mistake.

FIGURE 18-7: Holes for the metal rods and ball head are marked with big dots. Holes for the fastening bolts are marked in with X's.

Drilling the Holes

Before actually drilling holes, place the two square aluminum tubes together side-by-side. The side with the fastening markings should be on the outside, farthest away from the other tube. When the two tubes are aligned perfectly with each other, clamp them together with c-clamps as shown in Figure 18-8. Make sure the c-clamps don't interfere with drilling any of the fastening holes. Use enough force on the c-clamps to hold the tubes firmly, but don't use so much force that they squash the aluminum tubes.

Install the ¹/₄" drill bit in the drill press. You will be drilling the fastening holes first. The fastening bolts and nuts will have a stronger hold on the two tubes than the c-clamps. The extra strength is needed when you drill the holes for the headrest posts, so drilling these fastening holes is the logical first step. Use the hole punch at each fastening location. The indents you created with the hole punch will help the drill bits bite into the metal. Always use the hole punch before you drill.

Align each of the fastening markings under the drill bit as shown in Figure 18-9. Clamp the tubes down on the drill press to prevent them from moving. Drill each hole through both square aluminum tubes. When done, remove the mount from the drill press. You need to fasten each location with a ¹/₄"-20 bolt, washers, and nut. You end up with the hardware shown in Figure 18-10. Remove the c-clamps.

FIGURE 18-8: The c-clamps hold the two square aluminum tubes together firmly.

FIGURE 18-9: Align each fastening hole marking under the drill bit.

FIGURE 18-10: Fasten the square aluminum tubes together with bolts and nuts.

Use the drill gauge to measure the size of your headrest metal posts, as shown in Figure 18-11. The drill gauge is basically a measurement tool with different sized holes on it. The holes are marked so that you know the size of each hole. Poke the rod you want to measure through each hole until you find the one that is closest in size. The measurement beside the hole is the size of the rod. The metal rods on my headrest are just shy of $^{13}/_{32}$", so I used a $^{13}/_{32}$" drill bit for my camera mount.

Tip   You can make your own drill gauge. Take a block of wood and your drill bit set. Drill a hole on the wood block with each of the drill bits in your set. Remember to mark them, so that you know the size of each hole. Now you have a drill gauge.

You'll be drilling at the seam between the two square aluminum tubes. The best way to drill these two holes is with the camera mount securely clamped down on the drill press. Any motion could cause the mount to be misaligned.

Start with the $^1/_8$" drill bit first. The smaller bit will help you create a well to guide the larger bits. When you install the $^1/_8$" drill bit, insert the bit all the way into the chuck (see Figure 18-12). By shortening the length of the drill bit, you reduce the likelihood of deflection. With the drill bit all the way inserted into the chuck, you may not be able to drill all the way through the square aluminum tubes. But that is okay, because you can lengthen the bit after you have drilled partway through.

FIGURE **18-11**: Measure the metal rod with the drill gauge.

FIGURE **18-12**: Keep the ⅛" bit short to reduce the likelihood of deflection.

When you have drilled all the way through with the $\frac{1}{8}$" drill bit, drill through again with the $\frac{1}{4}$" drill bit. Although the well is set as a guide, trying to drill through it too fast may cause the bit to deflect. Go slow with this bit. When you're done, install the drill bit that matches the measurement to your headrest metal post as shown in Figure 18-13. Go even slower with this larger bit. It tends to grab the surrounding metal. When you have successfully drilled the two holes, the toughest part of this project is over. Use a metal file to get rid of the rough edges.

FIGURE 18-13: Use the big drill bit last, so that it stays on track.

Tip   If you weren't very successful with the hole you made, you can use a round metal file to try and finish it up (Figure 18-14). A vise is a great help.

The hole for the ball head should be the easiest one to drill, compared to the rest of the holes on the mount. You don't have to align the two tubes to drill this one. Install the $\frac{3}{8}$" drill bit on the drill press. Then align the mark directly beneath the drill bit. Clamp the tubes down. I thought it was okay to drill them without using the C-clamps, but the hole could have been rounder if I had spent a few minutes to clamp them down.

FIGURE 18-14: Metal files can help you clean up the rough edges or help you finish a misaligned hole.

Test-Fitting the Camera Mount

With all of the holes drilled, disassemble all of the fastening bolts. Now you're ready to try it with your headrest. Test-fit the camera mount on your headrest posts. It's probably not a perfect fit, because the drill bit you used is slightly bigger than the post. You'll need to find some padding to secure the camera mount to your headrest—paper, cloth, or rubber tubes will do the job just fine. Wrap the padding around the metal post to create a tight fit as shown in Figure 18-15.

FIGURE **18-15:** Wrap padding, like the paper towel in this picture, around the metal posts to create a tight fit.

Installing the Camera Mount in Your Car

When you are satisfied with the test-fit and you've found all the materials needed to make it snug, you are ready to assemble the camera mount in your car. First install the ball head mounting screw. Insert the $^3/_8$" bolt through the ball head hole and secure it with a $^3/_8$" hex nut. You can then screw the ball head into the $^3/_8$" bolt (see Figure 18-16). If the bottom of the ball head does not touch the hex nut, install additional hex nuts to reduce the thread spacing.

Tip   Do all the assembling indoors, with your headrest off your car. When everything is assembled, just pop the headrest on your car seat. This is easier than having to deal with the tight interior environment of your car.

Clamp the two square aluminum tubes together, use the padding material to keep the camera mount snug on the metal posts, and install the fastening bolts, washers, and nuts. Now the headrest camera mount is complete. Pop the headrest onto your car seat and you can head out to the track. The only thing missing is your digital camcorder, so grab it and make history!

FIGURE 18-16: Ball head attached to the nut and bolt

Building a Spycam Mount for Your Bicycle

W hether you're on a nature trail, or a scenic highway, or you just want to record your child's first bike ride, a camera mounted to the bicycle can bring great new perspective and depth to the shots you want to take. This chapter shows you what to consider when you're building a mount for a bicycle and for other types of mobile vehicles, and it provides links to web sites with different approaches to this popular contraption. You also learn how to mount a spycam on your bicycle.

Many Different "Bikes" Out There

There are many types of motorized and non-motorized vehicles out there, from two-wheeled bicycles to motorcycles to scooters to automobiles, and there are many types of mounts you can install. Each requires different approaches, depending on how rough the terrain will be, and what natural forces your camera will have to withstand to get that spectacular photo you hope to take.

Note The most important factor is to keep in focus the object you're trying to capture or to keep the camera steady if you're taking video footage. Image and video stabilization are covered in Chapter 20.

Tip Some video cameras have optical or electrical image stabilization. They make a huge difference when shooting video footage. With image stabilization turned on, the video footage is much smoother and easier to watch.

Security Is Key

As important as the capability to take a steady shot is the security of your camera in the mount. Your bike (or any other vehicle) comes in contact with many obstacles on roads and trails, such as bumps, potholes, brick walls, and so forth. You don't want your camera to come loose when you come in contact with any of these, believe me. Make sure you mount that camera of yours well, or you're going to be shelling out for a new camera or a new—expensive—lens, or both. *Velcro is not the right solution here!*

Tip   To test your stabilizer, find some books or weights that weigh about the same as your equipment. Then tie them to your homemade mount, take them out for a ride, and see if your mount can withstand the load.

Whether you're using a commercial mount or a home-built mount, the type of camera matters. It makes a difference if you're mounting a Canon EOS with an 8" lens protruding from the front, versus a $\frac{1}{2}$"-thick Sony Cybershot all-in-one camera. Obviously physics comes into play, and often the camera mount you end up installing isn't a one-size-fits-all solution.

There's another option—spycams. You can purchase these small wireless cameras on eBay (search for *spycam*) usually for around $20. The example I use in this chapter's project is shown in Figure 19-1. You can mount the spycam on the front or back of your bicycle (or any other vehicle) and, using a wireless video recorder connected to the receiver and stored in a bike bag, you can take videos that you can later extract shots from. Archos makes an excellent product for this, shown in Figure 19-2.

FIGURE 19-1: A spycam I found on eBay

FIGURE 19-2: The Archos video recorder

Buy or Build?

There's a practicality factor here when it comes to deciding whether to buy or build. Other than using your hands as a mount while you ride a bike, which is what you're trying to get away from in the first place, you obviously realize you want to stabilize your camera. However, considering your camera is likely quite an investment, relying on a mount you build may not be a very bright idea. Build-it-yourself camera mounts are more of a fun project, while professionals tend to opt for the well-researched mounts available from stores, because if the mount breaks, there's someone liable for the often expensive camera that ends up breaking in the process as well. Table 19-1 illustrates the advantages and disadvantages of buying and building your own camera mounts.

Table 19-1: Advantages and Disadvantages of Buying versus Building

	Advantages	Disadvantages
Buying	Spend less time; mount-and-go; proven to work and already fully tested for stability and holding your expensive camera	May not be exactly what you need; cost more; not built for your gear
Building	Build exactly what you want; custom built for any (or for particular) angles and perspectives you desire; could be inexpensive	Takes time and patience to build; testing can be expensive if your camera breaks on a test run

So should you buy or build? First, take a look at the projects on the various web sites presented in this chapter. If you feel they are sturdy enough (or you can make them better) and you trust your camera to those mounts, by all means go for it. However, if you have a significant investment in your camera, consider either buying a commercial mount instead or biking to wherever you want to take pictures and then getting off your bike and taking the pictures standing still (which is likely a better idea anyway).

Videotape, Film, and Motion Aren't Always Compatible

Consider the internals of your camera and how they will hold up to motion. If you are using a digital camera, you likely don't have to worry about many moving parts, and you definitely don't have to worry about film. However, if you're using a camcorder, you will likely have to worry about tape—so make sure your video camera holds up well to a lot of jarring around.

Elements other than force also have to be considered. If you are mounting your camera on a bike or any other vehicle exposed to the elements, make sure you steer clear of dust, water, road debris, rocks, and more. A rock flung up from a car could crack the lens of your camera. (Try a neutral density filter for your camera lens to help protect it by letting the filter absorb the impact rather than the glass.) Also, if you get dust inside your lens, it can be difficult and expensive to remove. Water could condemn your digital camera's electronics to an early death, and sweltering heat and direct sunlight could destroy your camera's sensors. Truth be told, just because you *have* a camera mount, doesn't mean you have to keep your camera on it all the time. You should always use he lens cap and a protective case when not using your, to prolong the life of your camera and increase your ability to get great shots from it on the nature trail for years to come.

Commercial Camera Mount Manufacturers

If you're going the commercial mount route, you can go to a camera store or you can go online and find them (some sports stores also carry them). Table 19-2 lists many manufacturers of camera mounts and their web addresses.

Table 19-2: Camera Mount Manufacturers

Manufacturer	Product	Web Site
Camera-Mount.com	Multiple	www.3rhm.com/sportbikecam.html
Desert Iron Images	CamMount	www.cammount.com/
Forman Camera Bikes	[various bikes]	www.markformanproductions.com/

Manufacturer	Product	Web Site
Jones Cameras	JonesCam Helmet Cam	`www.jonescam.tv/`
Sport Bike Cam	Sport Bike Cam	`www.sportbikecam.com/`
StickyPod	StickyPod Camera Mount	`www.stickypod.com/`
Pashnit Motorcycle Tours	*Resource Site*	`www.pashnit.com/more/ cameramount.htm`
Ultimate Camera Mounts	*Resource Site*	`www.ultracameramounts.com/`

Do-It-Yourself Projects on the Web

Since there are so many types of bicycles and projects to add brackets to them, I've listed in Table 19-3 some of the many web sites I've found for projects.

Table 19-3: Camera Mount Project Web Sites

Camera Mount Type	Web Site
Bike Camera Mount	`forums.photographyreview.com/showthread. php?t=9834`
Bottlecap Bicycle Camera Mount	`eeio.blogspot.com/2005/02/diy-bottlecap-bicycle- camera-mount.html`
Helmet Camera	`www.dirtbike.ws/node/72`
Kite Camera	`features.engadget.com/entry/4226778466722181/`
Rear-Rack Mount	`www.phred.org/%7Ejosh/bike/winder.html`
Barn Door Mount (not a bike, but a cool project)	`www.astronomyboy.com/barndoor/`

Adding a Spycam

Although mounting a camera to your bike isn't such a great idea, wireless video surveillance sure is. It can be a lot of fun to ride around getting video of the least expected, and then sharing it with your friends. All it takes is a video recorder and wireless video camera to go stealth with your cinematographer escapes!

Parts You Need

You need the following item for this project:

- Wireless "spycam" video camera and receiver or similar wired or wireless video camera and video receiver (these can often be found for around $10–$35 on eBay)

Note I chose the New Way Technology wireless video camera (about $35; previously shown in Figure 19-1). This camera is practically impossible to find for sale in stores, but you can find it easily on eBay by searching for "wireless video camera" or "wireless spycam." Make sure when you buy it on eBay that you get one that comes with the 9V battery adapter so you can use a battery pack to power both the camera and the video receiver.

- Archos MPEG-4 AV400 20GB Pocket Video Recorder (runs about $549; previously shown in Figure 19-2)

- Velcro "extreme" strip (about $7 for a whole pack; available in any fabric shop and some hardware stores)

- 9-volt battery for wireless video camera (around $4 for a long-lasting, very light lithium)

- A/C battery holder for wireless video receiver like the one shown in Figure 19-3 (about $2.99 at Radio Shack)

- Eight lithium-ion rechargeable AA batteries ($15 for two 4-packs at any convenience store; $24.99 with "quick" charger that charges the batteries in 15 minutes or less)

- Bike light mount (to hold the camera and its battery)

Converting the Light Mount and Mount the Camera

Remove the light from the bicycle light mount and put the spycam in its place. Use Velcro to keep the spycam firmly attached, yet keeping it easily removable. The battery shouldn't budge the camera, as it's pretty light and the Velcro is fairly strong. Figure 19-4 illustrates the result.

FIGURE 19-3: The battery holder

Connecting a 9V Battery to a Wireless Camera

Connect the wireless video camera to its power source—the 9-volt battery. You can always do this step later, since you're not using the battery much yet.

Make sure to *put the camera and 9V battery in your bike bag or take it with you when you leave your bike.* Don't leave the battery or the camera in direct sunlight or extreme heat for extended periods of time!

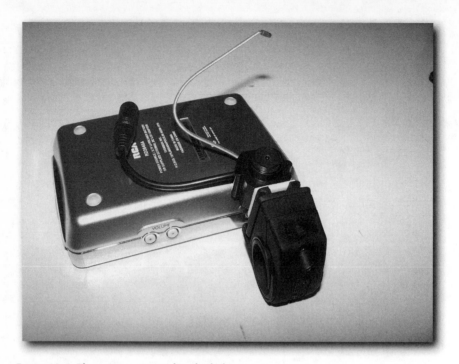

FIGURE 19-4: The camera mounted to the light mount

Storing the Video Receiver and Video Recorder

Now that the camera is set up, place the video receiver and recorder in your bike bag. Make sure the bag contains at least a little padding, as you don't want the video recorder or receiver banging against the frame of your bike.

Tip

Get a lock for your bike bag to help prevent would-be thieves from taking your stuff. Or just take the equipment with you when you're not around.

Caution

Remember to unplug it when you're done, and don't leave it in extreme heat for too long! Batteries exposed to extreme heat for too long may leak or explode, causing a safety hazard.

Plugging the Video Receiver into the Battery Pack

The video receiver will obviously need power to receive the video camera's signal. Use the battery pack's 9V adapter and plug it into the video receiver. This should give you at least 2½ hours of battery life with the receiver. If you find your 9V battery going out early on the video camera, you can use the same type of battery pack with the camera as well.

Note If you chose a different video camera/receiver combination, your mileage may vary here, so make sure you have a battery solution if you're not using what I'm suggesting for this project.

Note I am using the term *video recorder* here in place of the Archos, since you may choose a different video recorder.

Caution In hot weather, keep any video recorder with a built-in LCD screen in as cool an area as possible. These screens are not as resistant to heat extremes as larger LCD entertainment screens, and might be damaged (usually darkened) by high heat.

Cross-Reference See Chapter 4 for information about alternative power supplies.

Plugging the Video Receiver into the Video Recorder

This part's easy: Plug the composite video output of the video receiver into the video recorder. Makes sense, huh?

Recording

Everything's plugged in—so start the recorder, get on your bike, and go! When you're done taking video you can easily edit it on your computer—just follow the instructions that came with the video recorder.

There are many software solutions that let you edit video, and often those solutions come with the video recorders. If not, good choices for the PC are Windows Movie Maker 2 (free with Windows XP) Ulead VideoStudio, and Roxio Videowave, and on the Mac it's iMovie. A decent but not very flexible cross-platform editing solution is QuickTime Pro, also from Apple. But the other packages will give you much more flexibility.

Building a Camera Stabilizer

One of the most difficult issues to overcome for amateur and professional photographers alike is inadvertent movement. A flinch of the wrist can mean the difference between a masterpiece and a moment lost forever in blur. This chapter covers what you can do to get a grip on movement control, motion stabilization, and how to keep your shots steady every time (well, almost every time). But before jumping into this project, let's go over a few points.

Build or Buy?

Many digital cameras have a video mode for you to shoot movies without purchasing a separate camcorder. If you want to capture smooth motion sequences while moving the camera, you will have to use a video stabilizer.

The next time you watch a movie, pay close attention to how each scene is shot. Notice that during conversational scenes, the movie camera generally remains in one location. However, in action and panning scenes, the subject may or may not be moving—it's actually the camera that moves. The camera motion tends to be extremely smooth compared to those home movies you've shot on your vacations, where even the camera's "anti-shake" technology isn't a cure-all for your occasional jerkiness. Professionals used a motion stabilizer, more readily known as a "steady cam."

When it comes to still photography, camera stabilizers are not too expensive. Your options tend to be tripods and neck-mount stabilizers. Both can be had for under $30 from Best Buy, CompUSA, Fry's, Good Guys, and even Walmart. Figure 20-1 shows the Sima VideoProp Camcorder Support, which works great for shots where you need a steady hand but don't have time to set up a tripod. Later in the chapter, I discuss the difference between stabilizers and tripods for still photography. If you're thinking a stabilizer for photography is the same as video stabilization, take a look at the "Still Photography versus Video Stabilization" section later in this chapter.

FIGURE 20-1: The Sima VideoProp Camcorder Support

Note

Professional video stabilizers generally cost thousands of dollars. We're going to build one for about $14 in this chapter!

Tripods versus Stabilizers

Both tripods and stabilizers should be in your collection of tools for getting great photographs.

Tripods are ideal when you're taking many pictures in a single location. A tripod keeps the camera stationary for excellent portrait shots, as well as allowing it to swivel in place for excellent panoramic views.

Note Many programs are available for stitching photos together to create that panoramic view, such as Ulead's Cool 360 and IPIX Interactive Studio.

Note A common format for viewing panoramic shots is Apple's QuickTime VR (QTVR), which appeared in the 1990s as a separate component to QuickTime. All new versions of QuickTime, which is available for both Macintosh and Windows, have QuickTime VR playback capabilities built-in.

Stabilizers, on the other hand, are meant to keep the camera from shaking while you take a shot "on the go." Sometimes you don't have time to set up a tripod (for example, during sports events where you're moving around a lot), but you still need a steady hand. Stabilizers use your body as the support, keeping the camera from moving up and down or sideways while you take the shot, hopefully eliminating blur. Still photograph stabilizers are not the same as the *steady cams* used in movies—read the next section for information on the differences.

Still Photography versus Video Stabilization

While lighting may be the most important differentiator between amateur and professional photographers, motion blur affects us all. Of course, you're probably reading this chapter so you can eliminate blur in your photographs. Photographs are meant to be taken with the camera perfectly still. The approach for stabilizing the camera for still photography is different than for motion video, which minimizes bouncing of the camera to get a smooth shot where the final result is still a motion capture.

If you are looking for video camera stabilization tips and how to build your own stabilizer, there is a great web site: www.homebuiltstabilizers.com. The guidelines on this web site will help any videographer, and there are many approaches to building video camera stabilizers that suit many different needs. While this chapter focuses on digital still camera stabilizers, I will go over how to build a standard video stabilizer rig, as tripods and monopods are really the only devices you can use to stabilize photography.

Note If you shoot a video while moving the camera without a stabilizer, you get the "Blair Witch" effect. Most people get sea sick watching that kind of a movie sequence. Very rarely does it seem professional.

Tip You can buy *stabilized lenses*, but they are very expensive.

Time-Tested Approaches to Stabilization

A couple of tried and true solutions for stabilizing the camera are chains and sandbags.

In the chain approach, you limit the up-down motion of the camera by taking a metal chain and connecting it to an eye-bolt. The eye-bolt connects to your camera's mounting screw. By adjusting the chain length to your eye level and then stepping on the slack of the chain to tension it, you eliminate the upward motion of your camera. If the camera has slack, you don't have a steady shot. This solution works in the opposite way from a tripod, which instead of limiting upward motion, limits downward motion by keeping the camera pressed against a solid surface. The primary benefit of using chain is no slack. String, on the other hand, may have more tolerance, but it's a lot harder to carry around without getting tangled and knotted.

Yet another tried and true method of stabilizing a camera is by using a sandbag. This is especially helpful if you have a large lens. By placing the camera and lens on a sandbag in front of the subject, you get stability and limit all motion. This technique works great on top of cars, fences, or other irregular surfaces.

The ultimate goal of these methods is to eliminate any unwanted motion. Tripods give you the added benefit of being able to pan the camera with a moving object, keeping the moving object in focus while blurring the background.

Note Some cameras have automatic image stabilization, just like camcorders. This feature, however, is not a complete replacement for perfectly motionless snapshots.

Tip To eliminate camera shake when taking a photo, position your subject and then set the timer on your camera. This way, your camera will snap the picture, and your hand will not be touching it.

Building Your Own Steady Cam Stabilizer

Now that you have some background, it's time to build a stabilizer. This stabilizer is often called a *steady cam* because it keeps the camera stable and level even while you move. You've seen the benefit of these types of cameras in movies and in sports—they've made a huge difference in keeping live action smooth, while giving a videographer (and photographers capturing moving objects) much more freedom of movement.

Professional stabilizers tend to mount to your body. They are painful to set up because they have counterweights that must be adjusted for each camera and lens combination. Together, the camera, lens, and stabilizer become one system. When one part of the system is moved in a particular direction, the counterbalance causes the other part of the system to move in the opposite direction to eliminate vibration. Our simple stabilizer isn't as complicated or comprehensive, but with practice and proper use, it can be a great help in stabilizing your dynamic and action video sequences.

To use a camera stabilizer, you will need a way to mount the camera on the device. Most cameras have tripod mounts, which a tripod's adapter will screw into to hold the camera in place (see Figure 20-2). Figure 20-3 shows a tripod mount from the bottom of my Kodak DX6490 camera. Sometimes you will have more than just a threaded hole for the tripod mount—there may also be a second hole nearby that some tripods use for a secondary support (just like using two nails instead of one to prevent rotational movement of the camera). Generally, video cameras already have this second hole, and video tripods have the associated "stud."

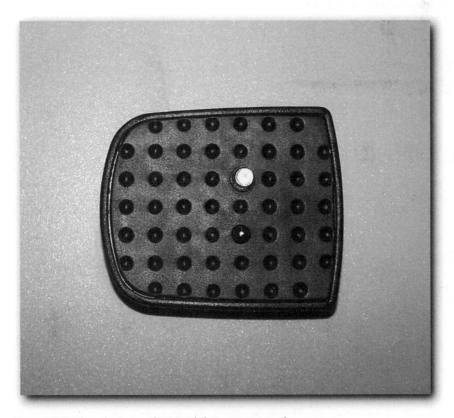

FIGURE 20-2: The adapter on the tripod that screws into the camera

FIGURE 20-3: The threaded camera
mount on the camera

Cross-Reference

Verify that your camera has a tripod mounting spot. If it doesn't have a mounting spot, see Chapter 2 for a project to add one.

Parts You Need

Special thanks to Johnny Lee (www-2.cs.cmu.edu/~johnny/steadycam) for his idea on how to put together this easy-to-build, inexpensive steady cam.

- 3 ea. $\frac{1}{2}$" diameter, 10"-length galvanized steel pipes, threaded at the ends (about $1.50 each)

- End caps, $\frac{1}{2}$"-diameter to cover up the sharp threads at the ends of the pipes and to keep things looking nice (about 80 cents each)

- T-joint that fits the pipes (about $1.50)

- 2.5 pound weight with 1" diameter hole in the middle (about $3)

- 2 ea. $1\frac{1}{2}$", $\frac{1}{4}$" machine bolts

- 1 ea. $\frac{1}{4}$" wing nut

- 3 ea. $1\frac{1}{2}$" diameter flange washers for $\frac{1}{4}$" bolts

- 3 ea. lock washers for $\frac{1}{4}$" bolts

- 2 ea. $\frac{1}{4}$" machine nuts

Tools You Need

Here are the tools you will need to complete this project:

- Drill with a $1/4$" bit
- Stationary vise (about $15 at most hardware stores)
- Wrench, screwdriver, and hammer

Assembling the Handle

This first step is pretty easy. Just attach the tee and end cap to one of the pipes to form a basic handle, as shown in Figure 20-4. You need to get these parts as tight as possible. I recommend using the vise and a wrench to accomplish this so you can get things super tight. Don't use your hands; you'll just hurt yourself and not get it tight enough.

FIGURE 20-4: The T-Joint connected to the pipe

Drilling the End Caps

Put one of the end caps in the vise, as shown in Figure 20-5.

Next, drill a $1/4$" hole in the center of the cap. It doesn't have to be perfectly in the center, but the closer the better. You really want to use the vise because you're drilling through a quarter inch of galvanized steel. It's enough to bring weak drills to a dead stop and will definitely do a number on your hand if you just try to hold it. Not to mention it can get hot.

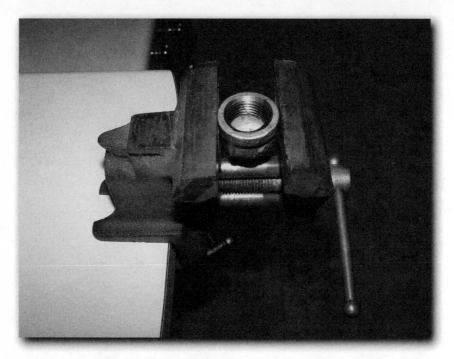

FIGURE 20-5: The vice grip holding an end cap

 Caution Protective eyeware such as safety goggles should *always* be worn when using any power tool!

A little bit of machine oil (or even vegetable oil) can make this easier, as well as preserving your drill bit. I like using a slow speed because when the bit comes out the other side it jerks from grabbing onto the metal. It's far more pleasant to have a slow jerk than to have the drill suddenly fly out of your hand. Do this in a place that's easy to clean up. You'll make lots of metal shards. I did it outside. And don't use you fingers to wipe away the shreds. They'll get in your skin. Use a brush, or blow the shards away. Do this for two end caps.

Building the Camera Mount

The mounting requires the parts shown in Figure 20-6: a bolt, two lock washers, a flange washer, nut, wing nut, and a drilled end cap. Put a lock washer on the bolt and then put it through the end cap with the bottom of the bolt coming out of the top of the outside of the end cap. Put another lock washer on and then the nut. Put the end cap in the vise and tighten with a wrench. The lock washer will keep the bolt from turning.

You'll want to make this really tight because this is where your camera attaches. You want it tight not because it'll fall off or anything, but because putting the camera on and taking it off requires lots of turning action. If it loosens, the bolt will pivot around as will your camera, making it hard to keep it still. If this happens while you're filming, you'll have to stop and find a wrench. The schematic view in Figure 20-6 shows how this goes together.

Use a hammer to dent the center of the flange washer. You can do this by putting the washer across the hole of the weight, putting the head of the bolt on the hole, and hammer the bolt. You want to have the center area of the washer higher than the rim, so when you attach the mount to the camera, the rim of the washer pushes up against the area around the bolt. This washer will distribute the force away from the single point of contact, so the wider the washer the better. If you don't use the washer, the camera will shake a lot right at this connection as well as putting a great deal of stress on this one tiny spot that could damage your camera. So if you lose this washer, I don't recommend using this steady cam without it.

Use your fingers to tighten the wing nut on the mounting. *Do not* use a wrench. You may risk stripping the threads on your camera or breaking the tripod mount. Both are equally bad.

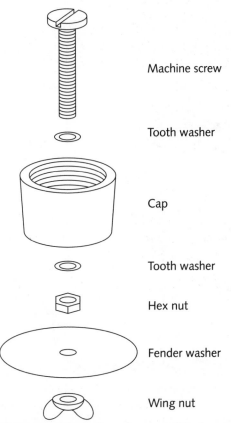

Machine screw

Tooth washer

Cap

Tooth washer

Hex nut

Fender washer

Wing nut

FIGURE 20-6: The schematic view of this step (Steadycam Assembly Instructions, Johnny Lee, 9/3/2004©)

Adding the Counterweight

You'll need the barbell weight shown in Figure 20-7 and the parts shown in Figure 20-8. The bolt goes through two washers that sandwich the weight. Then stick on the end cap, put on the lock washer, and then finally the nut. Hand-tighten the parts until they are snug. The schematic view in Figure 20-8 shows how this goes together.

The lock washer deep inside the end cap will keep a grip on the nut. So, you don't have to stick pliers down there to turn it. Just turn the cap. Stick the cap in the vise shown on the bottom left. Then you can use the screwdriver to tighten the bolt or just grab the weight and turn it. The weight should turn the bolt, and the vise will keep the cap from turning. Tighten it until the outer washer starts to bend inwards. This reduces the amount the bolt sticks out, which is good for when you want to put it down on the base. If you do use the base as a stand, you can buy rounded bolts and little rubber feet. These will make a much nicer base that won't wobble, although it's easy to knock over. You can tell I like to do this, and I can say it's easy to knock over from experience. My camera still seems to work okay, though.

FIGURE 20-7: The barbell weight

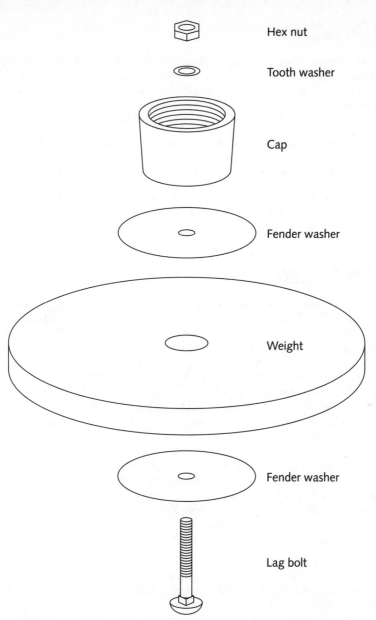

Hex nut

Tooth washer

Cap

Fender washer

Weight

Fender washer

Lag bolt

FIGURE 20-8: The schematic view of the counterweight addition (Steadycam Assembly Instructions, Johnny Lee, 9/3/2004©)

Putting It All Together

Last, take the remaining two pipes, screw them into the T joint of the handle, and attached the base and the mounting. And you're done! You can tighten these parts as much as you'd like. Either give them a good hand-tightening or the full-fledged vise and wrench tightening. The only reason not to do the vise-wrench tighten is if you want to be able to collapse this or swap components. You can vary the pipe lengths and barbell weight however you like.

I would probably refer to this combination as the sport model. Mostly because it's balance point (with camera) is near the T-joint and can be spun around by the handle pretty well. It's really agile. Longer bars and heavier weights change the handling.

When you store it without the camera, the mounting washer is left hanging on the end. I recommend taking off the wing nut, putting on the washer, and then screwing the wing nut back on. That will help keep it from getting lost.

Using Your Steady Cam

Use the side handle to stabilize side-to-side rocking. The vertical shaking is pretty much dampened by the weight. You may hold it however you'd like. How you use it is 80 percent of the smoothness. This is true even for the professional stuff with all the fancy shocks and hydraulics. Don't expect this thing to perform miracles—you have to practice using your arms and body to create a smooth motion. Watch your hands while you walk, and see how level you can keep them relative to the ground. Watching the shadow of your hands on a sunny day is an easy way to isolate their movement. Keep your legs bent and learn how to "glide". I talked with someone who has used professional steady cams and they said this was, "really, just as good." Getting good results is not so much about the equipment but how you use it. That's really true about everything.

Tip   Remember when you shoot video that most films are shot horizontally, especially with widescreen shots. Your TV has a horizontal format. When I first got a digital camera with video mode, I was used to shooting vertical pictures at the right opportunity. I immediately proceeded to shoot a vertical video when the same opportunity arose. When I got home, I realized that I had to rotate the video 90 degrees. This also threw off the aspect ratio, which really bugged the people watching my video!

Caution   Improper or irresponsible use of a steady cam can quickly result in the destruction of your equipment and injury to yourself and others. Be careful, watch where you are going, and pay attention to where you are swinging your camera.

Building a Flash Bracket

chapter

21

One of the primary skills that separate professionals from amateur photographers is their ability to control lighting. Flash brackets are used to place flashes in various optimal positions in order to get just the right amount of light. Because of this, there is no single flash bracket optimal for every condition. Some brackets may need to be mounted to the camera for macro shots, while others are mounted on poles and used with umbrellas to get the right lighting for portraits (you've probably seen this setup at weddings).

 Tip Move the flash away from the lens. This reduces the "red-eye" effect. This also helps you produce a more pleasant portrait than the "deer in the headlights" look.

Figure 21-1 shows a commercial flash bracket from one of the most popular flash bracket manufacturers.

Figure 21-2 shows the resulting flash bracket for macro shots that you will learn how to build in this chapter.

FIGURE 21-1: A commercial flash bracket

FIGURE 21-2: The finished product from this chapter

How Do Flashes Work?

It's always a good idea to know how technology works—it helps you learn how to control it and optimize conditions to get the best results. The key to flashes is power, often in the form of batteries. Flashes eat batteries quickly, so having high-capacity batteries such as Lithium-Ion rechargables makes a huge difference in power availability.

Flashes work when the batteries charge a condenser, which in turn fires the flash tube when you fire the flash. Automatic flashes sense when they believe enough light has been made available and stop the flash. The sensor for this can be in many locations, sometimes in the eye of the camera, or even external to the camera body. Having the wrong settings or a camera imaging processor that compensates poorly results in the underexposed and overexposed images we thank Photoshop for fixing. Good thing you don't have to pay to develop photos and find out after the fact, eh?

Hot Lights versus Flash Brackets

Another item to consider is whether to use flash at all. If you're working on portraits, *hot lights* may be the better alternative. One traditional problem with flash is that it needs to bring enough light to expose the entire film by staying on long enough to ensure proper exposure. However, the exposure metering computer must do a precalculation of the exposure time before the picture is actually shot and before the flash actually fires. This can lead to under-exposed and overexposed shots due to the computer's miscalculations as to how long to keep the flash discharging.

Caution

Other objects in the environment you are shooting could also cause flash firing time miscalculations. Consider a mirror that reflects more light than a flat white wall, or the flash aimed at a different angle than the exposure meter expects.

Hot Lights, on the other hand, are *always* on, so the amount of light can be tightly controlled. For the most part, this assumes the object being photographed is perfectly still. However, hot lights can be used to light up an environment with motion – shutter speed and film speed (as set in the camera's preferences) become the determining factors over light in that kind of environment.

Cross-Reference

See Chapter 23 to learn how to build your own home studio light.

Does Shutter Speed Matter with Digital Cameras?

In analog cameras, shutter speeds control the amount of light hitting the film and for how long. Digital cameras have a similar mechanism—the shutter speed controls the amount of light hitting the CCD or CMOS. However, digital camera shutter speeds are based on what the *computer* says they are. Some digital cameras don't even have shutters. Rather, the "shutter" is really just a sunblock for the imaging device (CCD or CMOS).

Building the Bracket

Now that we have the initial details out of the way, let's build the bracket! Special thanks to photographer Rick Groom (lilricky@mindspring.com, www.rgroomphotos.us) for his idea on how to put together this easy to build, inexpensive bracket.

Buy or Build?

Because so many types of flash brackets are out there, it may be best to find a bracket on eBay and just wait for the product to arrive. Building a bracket for every occasion could be cumbersome, especially if you aren't comfortable working with metal. However, if you're building only one or two flash brackets, you can get "just the right bracket" by building one yourself (and for very little money and a bit of sweat equity).

Parts You Need

Here are the parts you need to have on hand before you begin this project—most are available at hardware stores such as Loews, Home Depot, and Ace Hardware. If you want to find some good deals, check out Google's free Froogle service, which compares prices from many online stores—www.froogle.com.

- 3' of $1/8$" × 1" aluminum stock (about $3)
- 3 lock washers (about 15 cents)
- $4 1/4$" × $1/2$" bolts (about 20 cents)
- 1 Arca-style quick-release (about $35 on eBay, or check Froogle) *or* $1/4$" tripod stud (about $4 from a camera store, or check Froogle)
- 3 Giotto's M 1004 ball socket (about $10 from a camera store, or check Froogle)

Tools You Need

Here are the tools you'll use—these are also available at local hardware stores.

- A saw capable of cutting aluminum and a drill with a $7/64$" bit
- A Sharpie or pencil, for marking on the metal
- A screwdriver

Figure 21-3 shows the materials you will need. Note that the figure shows the aluminum pieces already bent—don't worry that your pieces are straight; you'll be bending them soon.

FIGURE 21-3: Needed materials

Cutting the Aluminum into Strips

Cut the aluminum into three lengths—one 4", one 5", and one 6".

Note If you aren't comfortable working with saws or metal, find someone who is. The last thing I want is for you to get hurt building this bracket. Everything else in this project you should be able to do safely.

Preparing the First Aluminum Strip

Take the 6" piece, measure in 1" from the end, and make a mark. Drill a $^7/_{64}$" hole in the middle of that square. Then measure another 1" and make a mark.

Once you have made the second mark, bend the aluminum into a U-shape, which you can see at the bottom of Figure 21-3.

After you have bent the first piece, measure one inch from the other (non-bent) side and drill another $^7/_{64}$" hole. This finishes the first piece (phew!).

Preparing the Second and Third Strips

This step is similar to the previous one. For the 4" and 5" pieces, measure 1" from each end on each piece and drill a hole between the 1" marks, just as you did with the previous piece.

After you have drilled the holes, bend the ends so the pieces are in a U-shape, as you can see in Figure 21-3.

Attaching Ball Sockets

Now that the aluminum pieces are prepared, attach the Giotto ball sockets to the bent end of each piece, as shown in Figure 21-4.

Note Multiple ball heads are very useful because of their flexibility. You can orient the bracket in many different custom positions. Often, you can even get more flexibility than many commercial brackets have.

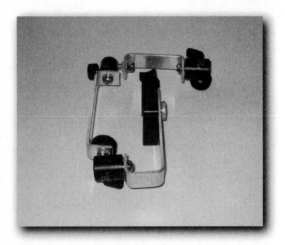

FIGURE 21-4: The connected Giotto ball sockets

Attaching Bracket to Tripod

Attach the bracket to a tripod so you can use it, as shown in Figure 21-5.

You can adjust the bracket for many different angles, as illustrated in Figure 21-6. This is accomplished by simply loosening the Giotto ball sockets and setting angles as needed.

Using the Bracket

Congratulations! You now have a flash bracket for under $100!

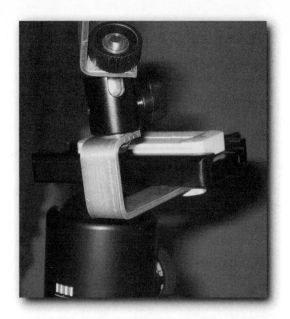

FIGURE 21-5: A close-up of the flash bracket on a tripod.

FIGURE 21-6: The bracket is easily adjustable.

Light 'em Up—Lighting Your Subjects

There are many different ways to light the subject, all of which help you get the "perfect shot." Here are some tips to help you in your lighting escapades:

- Place the flash really close to the front of the lens for macro flash.

- Place the flash above to the left or right to stimulate the sun gleaming in the subject's eyes.

- Use your flash bracket to bounce the flash from the ceiling to produce softer light. This is especially useful on electronic flashes which have no tilt and swivel head.

- If you're going to do macro photography, build a "double bracket" for two flashes. This will help tremendously when you light your subjects.

Building a Monopod

If you have ever shot sports with a tripod, you know it can be difficult; a tripod is steady and stationary, whereas most sports action is fast and dynamic. A photographer with a tripod might need to move around it quickly to get a shot, and it's easy to trip over the tripod's legs during these sudden movements.

In addition, sporting events are generally crowded. Unless the sporting event is locally organized and draws only a small crowd, a tripod is generally banned. Even if it is allowed, the extra space needed to set up a tripod might block access routes and become hazardous to spectators. In short, it can make your life as a photographer a hassle.

Some photographers stand the tripod on one leg to use it like a monopod, but sooner or later they get tired of the weight and bulk of a full-size tripod and resort to a real monopod. A monopod is easy and inexpensive to build. It is really just a camera attachment on top of a pole. A monopod is easy to carry and easy to move around. There is no excuse for a sports photographer to go without a monopod.

Parts You Need

Here are the parts you will need to complete this project:

- Round wooden pole (can be substituted as described later)
- Mini ball head (can be substituted as described later)
- $^3/_8$"-16 hanger bolt
- $^3/_8$"-16 hex nuts (2)
- $^5/_{32}$" flat-head wood screw
- Rubber foot
- Metal epoxy

All the parts in the preceding list (other than the ball head) can be had for five to ten dollars at a hardware store. Figure 22-1 shows the hanger bolt, hex nuts, rubber foot, and mini ball head. I found my Bogen-Manfrotto 482 mini ball head at the local university bookstore. You can find them at your local camera shop or you can order them online at B&H (`www.bhphoto video.com/`) or Adorama (`www.adorama.com/`). The ball head is the most expensive part, but it is not necessary, as the "Make Your Own Camera Attachment Head" sidebar later in the chapter explains.

FIGURE 22-1: From left to right: hanger bolt, hex nuts, rubber foot, and mini ball head

The Bogen-Manfrotto 482 mini ball head accepts $3/8$"-16 screw thread on the bottom. If your mini ball head uses the $1/4$"-20 thread, you should substitute those parts.

I also have an old hockey stick with a broken blade that is no longer useable for hockey and has been sitting in my closet for a while, so I used this stick in place of the round pole for this exercise. The point is that any pole you are comfortable using is fine.

Tools You Need

Here are the tools you will need to complete this project:

- Saw
- Screwdriver
- Hex wrench
- Drill
- $5/16$" drill bit
- $7/64$" flat-head drill bit
- Measuring tape

Assembly

Start by measuring and cutting the pole down to size. If you already know what monopod length you want, use the measuring tape and cut away. Otherwise, stand straight up and hold the pole so that it rests on one end. The top of the pole should be about chin level. Depending on the size of the ball head and the camera, you may want the pole a little higher or a little lower than your chin. Just keep in mind that the viewfinder of the camera should be slightly lower than your eyes. At the start, it is better to err on the long side, as you can always cut the pole shorter later.

The hanger bolt is a little bit tough to work with, since it has threads on both ends. There is really no good way to grab it for screwing into the pole. That is where the hex nut comes in. Screw the hex nut onto the hanger bolt (see Figure 22-2). Then glue the two pieces together. The hex nut will now serve as the head for applying torque. This step will make your life a lot easier if you think you will ever want to remove the hanger bolt. If you don't think you'll ever need to remove the hanger bolt, you can skip the gluing step.

While the glue is drying, start working on the rubber foot. The rubber foot may be an adhesive version. To attach the rubber foot securely, use the $7/64$" flat head drill bit to drill through it. Be sure to make a nice indent so that the screw will sit below the surface of the rubber (see Figure 22-3). In addition, drill a hole on the bottom of the pole. Attach the rubber foot to the bottom of the pole with the $5/32$" flat-head screw. Over time, the rubber foot will get worn out through use. You can replace the rubber foot easily in the same manner.

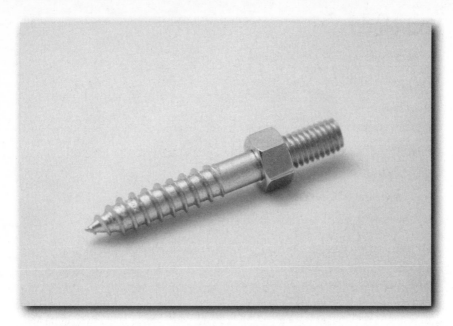

FIGURE 22-2: Screw the hex nut onto the hanger bolt. Then glue the two pieces together.

FIGURE 22-3: The rubber foot surface is higher than the flat-head screw, allowing the rubber to contact the ground.

Use the ⁵/₁₆" bit to drill a hole at the center of the other end of the pole. With the hex wrench, screw the hanger bolt into the pole, as far as the hanger bolt will go. Use the second hex nut to reducing the spacing between the ball head and the first hex nut. Attach the ball head onto the end of the hanger bolt. If any thread space remains between the second hex nut and the ball head, you might consider using additional hex nuts to reduce that space. Just be sure there are enough threads to attach the ball head securely. The completed monopod head is shown in Figure 22-4.

FIGURE 22-4: Completed monopod head

Make Your Own Camera Attachment Head

You might find that a ball head or pan head is not as valuable to you as it was to me. You can still make a monopod with your own camera attachment head. To do so, substitute the ⁵/₁₆" drill bit with a ³/₁₆" drill bit. Then substitute the mini ball head, the hanger bolt, and the hex nuts, with the following parts:

- ¼"-20 hanger bolt
- ¼"-20 wing nut
- ¼"-20 hex nut
- ¼" washer

Continued

Continued

First, glue the washer to the bottom of the wing nut with the epoxy, as shown in Figure 22-5. This contraption will serve to tighten down the camera when it is attached. The glue will keep the washer from falling off when a camera is not attached.

FIGURE 22-5: Glue the wing nut and the washer together.

Next, glue the hex nut and the hanger bolt together as mentioned in the "Assembly" section. Again, you can skip this step if you do not care about removing the hanger bolt again.

Finally, attach the hanger bolt to the monopod as instructed in the "Assembly" section. In this case, you don't want to add additional hex nuts to the hanger bolt, because you want allow the wing nut to have the freedom to move. Thread the wing nut and washer onto the hanger bolt, with the washer on top (the washer will contact the camera).

The camera attachment head is now complete (see Figure 22-6). You will be able to attach your camera's tripod socket to the hanger bolt. Once the camera is attached, screw the wing nut and washer until it contacts the bottom of the camera. Then tighten it.

FIGURE 22-6: Camera attached to the monopod head

Removal is the reverse of attachment. Loosen the wing nut and washer. Then unscrew the camera from the hanger bolt.

At this point, your completed monopod is ready to use (see Figure 22-7). To make your life easier, loosen the ball head with the knob. Stand the monopod on its foot. Use one hand to hold the camera. Hold the top of the ball head with your other hand. Screw the ball head onto the camera's tripod socket tightly.

To remove the camera, start by loosening the ball head. With one hand on the camera and the other hand on the ball head, unscrew the ball head from the camera body.

FIGURE 22-7: Camera and lens attached to the ball-head.

Making a 500-Watt Home Studio Light

Indoor lighting is quite dark compared with full sunlight, especially after diffusing and bouncing light around to soften the shadows or facial features of your subject. You may find yourself struggling with high ISO speed and noise. Shooting at a decent shutter speed at ISO 100 is quite a challenge without good strong lighting. This is why most professional studio photographers spend thousands of dollars on professional studio lighting. Just a single professional light source could cost hundreds of dollars. And the professional will generally light up a model's hair with one light source, their face with another, and so on.

Professional photographers have good justification for expensive lighting, but you can achieve similar results by exercising some creativity. Home improvement stores sell 500-watt work lights for $10 apiece. Their luminance is as strong as many professional photography light sources. For less than $100, you can build several good strong light sources at home.

Parts You Need

The following parts will go into this project:

- 500-watt halogen work light
- $2^1/_2$" double-wide corner brace
- 3" flat corner brace
- Worm gear clamps (hose clamps) (2), range: $^{11}/_{16}$"–$1^1/_4$"
- Worm gear clamps (hose clamps) (2), range: $^1/_4$"–$^5/_8$"
- $^1/_4$"-20 wing nut
- Umbrella
- Tripod

Work lights are often used at night for home improvement and automobile repair. Lowes sells a basic 500-watt version (see Figure 23-1) for about ten dollars. They also carry 150-, 250-, and 750-watt versions. If you have a work light that came with stand, you can forgo the tripod.

FIGURE 23-1: A 500-Watt work light

The corner brace, flat corner brace, worm gear clamps, and wing nut are all standard hardware used for building and for plumbing (see Figure 23-2). The $1/4$"-20 wing nut is the standard diameter and pitch for a tripod screw.

Cross-Reference   Refer to the "Reading Bolt Size" sidebar in Chapter 2 for an explanation of how to read screw specifications.

Two types of umbrellas are used in photography: reflective and translucent. Reflective umbrellas are generally coated with silver or gold fabric on the inner surface. Usually, you can find these only at a photography shop for a premium price—so in the rare instance when you see them elsewhere for a regular-umbrella price, pick up a few of them. Translucent umbrellas are also available at photography shops for a premium price, but your objective in this chapter is to build an inexpensive studio light. Your best bet is to buy color translucent umbrellas when you come across them at department stores. I've come across white, red, and yellow ones and they are perfect for the home studio light.

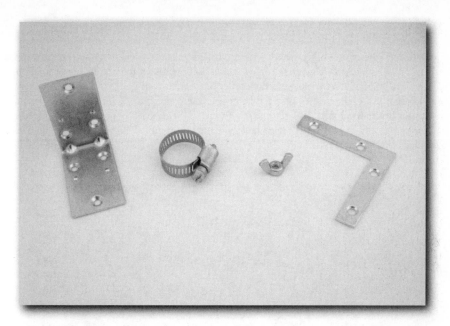

FIGURE 23-2: Hardware parts: double wide corner brace, worm gear clamp, wing nut, and flat corner brace

Tools You Need

The following tools will help you build the home studio light:

- Drill
- $1/4$" drill bit
- C-clamp
- Flat-blade screwdriver

A very basic drill is needed for this project, nothing fancy. A cordless electric drill works even better and doesn't have any wires to get in your way.

Assembly

The double-wide corner brace comes with predrilled holes. However, the holes are too small for the $1/4$"-20 standard screw on a camera tripod. You will need to enlarge one of the holes with a $1/4$" drill bit. Don't try to hold the corner brace with your hand. If the drill bit grabs hold of the corner brace, the drill could rip it from your hand and hurt you in the process. Clamp the corner brace down with a C-clamp (see Figure 23-3). The silver metal plate looks like steel and looks very tough to drill, but it is actually made out of zinc. It took me less than 10 seconds to drill through it with a drill bit.

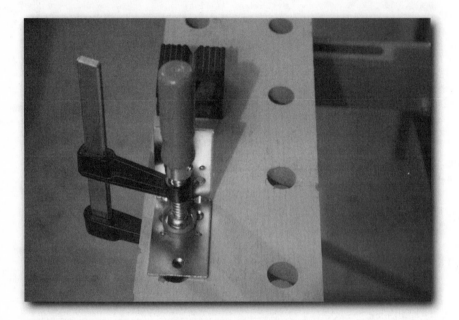

FIGURE 23-3: Clamp the corner brace down with the C-clamp.

When you finish enlarging the hole, install the corner brace onto the work light. The work light has a thumbscrew on its stand for adjusting its angle. It's the perfect location for the attachment. Unscrew the thumbscrew and thread it through one of the holes at the un-drilled end of the corner brace. Then thread the plastic spacer onto the thumbscrew as shown in Figure 23-4.

Next, thread the thumbscrew onto the work light stand. As shown in Figure 23-5, the corner brace does not interfere with the stand. The work light can still sit on the ground or the table-top when you want to use it unattached to the tripod.

FIGURE 23-4: The thumbscrew and spacer inserted through the corner brace

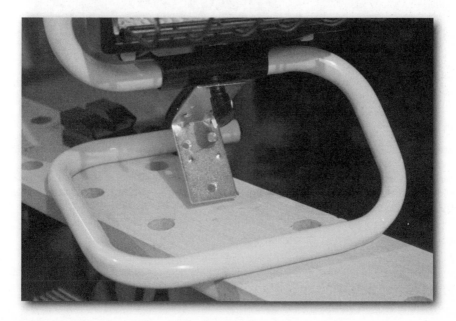

FIGURE 23-5: The corner brace installed on the work light

Now, attach the corner brace to your tripod head. The tripod screw should fit the enlarged hole on the corner brace perfectly. Fasten the corner brace to the tripod head with the ¼"-20 wing nut as shown in Figure 23-6.

FIGURE 23-6: The corner brace installed on the tripod

The work light installed on the tripod is shown in Figure 23-7. The angle of the work light relative to your subject can be adjusted with the tripod head. The height can be adjusted with the tripod legs and neck. But before we get carried away with using the work light and tripod, let's attach the umbrella.

Strap the flat corner brace onto the work light handle using the two larger worm gear clamps (¹¹⁄₁₆"–1¼"). Keep the worm gear clamps as far apart as possible but still securing the flat corner brace (see Figure 23-8). When you are satisfied with their positions, tighten them down with a flat-blade screwdriver. Tighten the two clamps in turn until the corner brace is securely fastened to the handle.

FIGURE 23-7: The angle can be adjusted using the tripod ball or pan-head.

FIGURE 23-8: Strap the flat corner brace to the handle with the worm gear clamps.

Now, strap the umbrella rod onto the flat corner brace. Remove the umbrella handle so that you can loop the smaller worm gear clamps ($^1/_4$"–$^5/_8$") around the umbrella rod. If the umbrella handle is not removable, you'll have to unscrew the worm gear clamps entirely (see Figure 23-9). Wrap them around the rod, and then re-thread the gears into the fastening mechanism.

FIGURE 23-9: An unthreaded worm gear clamp

With the worm gear clamps around the umbrella rod, insert the flat corner brace through both worm gear clamps as well. Position the two worm gear clamps as far apart as possible. Tighten down the clamps with the flat-blade screwdriver. Figure 23-10 shows what the result should look like.

If you removed the umbrella handle earlier, you can now reattach it for a finishing touch. For the convenience of taking apart the light later, you can leave the handle off.

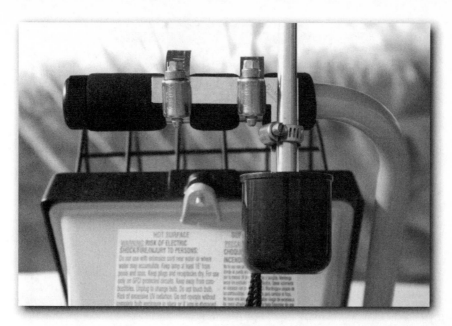

FIGURE 23-10: Secure the umbrella rod to the flat corner brace with the smaller worm gear clamps.

Mechanical Operation

The studio light you built is actually quite versatile. You can use it with the umbrella and the tripod as in a real studio (see Figure 23-11), or you can take the work light and umbrella off the tripod and place it on a nearby table. And if you disassemble everything, the work light can be used again in your home-improvement projects. Some work lights have no on/off switches. For those, you'll have to plug them in the light when you want them on and unplug them when you want them off. If that is inconvenient, you might consider getting an on/off switch for your three-prong electricity outlet.

Caution The 500-watt halogen work lights can get extremely hot. Don't touch the aluminum enclosure or the plain glass.

The angle of the light source can be adjusted with the ball head on the tripod's pan-head. The height of the light source can be adjusted with the tripod legs and neck. If you purchased a work light with a stand, you may not be able to adjust the height. The umbrella I have can be opened and closed while it's still attached to the work light. If you find an umbrella that works the same way, you won't have to remove it when you place the work light in storage.

FIGURE 23-11: The completed home-built studio light

Photography with a Home Studio Light

I mentioned earlier that two types of umbrellas are used in photography: reflective and translucent. Both types are used to soften the light on your subject. With the reflective type, the work light is facing away from the subject, but aimed toward the umbrella. A white or silver reflective umbrella is good for representing color accurately. A gold reflective umbrella increases the warmth in the color of your subject. The reflective umbrella enlarges the light source and bounces it toward the subject.

With the translucent type, the work light is aiming toward the subject, behind the translucent umbrella. The translucent umbrella enlarges and diffuses the light source. A white translucent umbrella reproduces color accurately. You can change the color of your subject with different colored umbrellas. This type of soft light is handy when the light source has to be very close to the subject or if your studio has a very low ceiling.

White Balance

Because the halogen work light wasn't made for photography, its color temperature is not calibrated, and the manufacturer does not inform the buyer of its color temperature region. It's a good thing that most of today's digital cameras have automatic white balance. In most cases, automatic white balance does a good job of reproducing accurate color. But to get accurate color consistently, you'll have to rely on custom white balance.

Tip   Black-and-white photography is not affected by color temperature. Set your camera to B&W mode to conveniently sidestep this problem. If your camera does not have a B&W mode, you can change your picture to B&W in post-processing. See the "Black and White" section at the end of Chapter 15.

Many of today's digital cameras offer a custom white balance. When you use this feature, your digital camera will be able to faithfully reproduce color accuracy under any color temperature. See your digital camera's instruction manual to see how to activate custom white balance for your camera.

Gray Card

With a studio setup at home, the lighting is controlled and the exposure is fairly constant. To work faster and more consistently, professional photographers use either a light meter or a gray card (see Figure 23-12). Both provide good, accurate exposure. A light meter is more expensive than the gray card and provides a bit more data. But a gray card is inexpensive and is sufficient for most of your home studio needs. Pick one up at a photography store for about $15. It will give you the correct exposure every time.

Continued

Continued

FIGURE 23-12: A gray card is just a rectangular cardboard that is 18 percent gray.

A long time ago, photographers determined that most scenes average to 18 percent gray. Therefore, the way your camera's metering system works is that it averages and exposes the entire scene to 18 percent gray. With lighter or darker backgrounds or subject clothing, your camera's meter can be biased to over- or underexpose. By metering an 18 percent gray card under the lighting condition of your subject, your camera's meter will be correct every single time.

When you have set up the light sources and your subject, place the gray card in front of your subject. Fill the entire viewfinder with the gray card and push the shutter button halfway to read the exposure meter. That shutter speed, aperture setting, and ISO setting combination is the correct exposure for that lighting setup. Now you can set this combination in your camera's manual exposure mode and shoot away. You won't have to change exposure settings again until you change the lighting setup.

Flash Memory Hacks

part

V

Modifying the CF Type I to PC Card Type II Adapter

After reading this title, you are probably wondering what this chapter is really about. To put it in simple terms, this chapter explains how you can read your CompactFlash (CF) memory cards on-the-go with your notebook computer. All notebook computers today have a special card slot called the *PC Card slot*. This chapter explains how your notebook computer can interface with the CompactFlash memory cards through the PC Card slot.

PC Card is a standard defined by the Personal Computer Memory Card International Association (PCMCIA). PCMCIA is an international body that establishes standards to promote mobile computer component interchangeability, where ruggedness, low power, and small size are critical. There are three PC Card types: I, II, and III. The only difference among the three types is the thickness of cards. Type I is 3.3mm thick, Type II is 5mm thick, and Type III is 10.5mm thick. Most notebooks can handle Type II cards.

Tip — PC Card is a 16-bit standard. The newer 32-bit standard is generally referred to as CardBus PC Card. PC Card was once known as PCMCIA card, but the industry now uses the term PCMCIA only for the association.

CompactFlash memory cards, on the other hand, are available in two types: I and II. The electrical interfaces of the two types are also exactly the same. Like the PC Card standard, the physical properties of the two CompactFlash types differ only in thickness of the memory card. CF Type I cards are 3.3mm thick, and CF Type II cards are 5mm thick.

To download pictures to my notebook while on a trip, I generally avoid the more cumbersome USB memory card readers. Instead, I use my trusty *CompactFlash Type I to PC Card Type II adapter* (see Figure 24-1). This adapter allows CompactFlash Type I cards to be plugged into the PC Card Type II slot on a notebook. This adapter is slim, with no wires, and it's easy to carry around.

FIGURE 24-1: A CompactFlash Type I to PC Card Type II adapter

When I first got my IBM 1GB Microdrive, I was extremely excited. This large-capacity drive allowed me to shoot several hundred high-resolution pictures on my digital camera. It has enough storage space for extended trips and high-profile photo shoots. After making some test shots on the Microdrive, I attempted to download the pictures onto my Sony VAIO notebook. However, attempting to plug the Microdrive into the CF Type I to PC Card Type II adapter proved futile, since the Microdrive has the CF Type II form factor. Figure 24-2 shows the thicknesses of the PC Card Type II card, the CF Type II card, and the CF Type I card. As you can see, the thicknesses of the PC Card Type II card and CompactFlash Type II card are exactly the same.

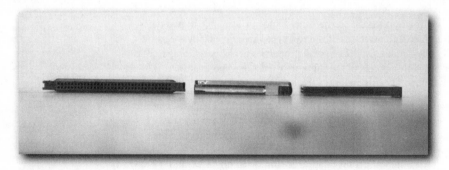

FIGURE 24-2: PC Card Type II (left), CompactFlash Type II (middle), and CompactFlash Type I (right)

CF Type II to PC Card Type II adapters exist but were hard to find several years ago. Sometimes the manufacturers of these adapters are confused about what their products actually do. I remember driving down to a Fry's Electronics and purchasing a PQI FLASHCARD Compact Flash Adapter (see Figure 24-3). The packaging claimed that it could accept a Microdrive. When I got home, I realized that the packaging had lied—it was just another CF Type I to PC Card Type II adapter.

FIGURE 24-3: The PQI FLASHCARD CompactFlash Adapter

When I started writing this book, I found that the CF Type II to PC Card Type II adapter is even rarer today. The shelves at my local CompUSA stores and Circuit City stores carried the CF Type I to PC Card Type II adapters, but not the more versatile CF Type II to PC Card Type II adapter. The CF Type II to PC Card Type II adapter is more versatile because it can accept both CF Type I and Type II memory cards.

After my disappointment at being fooled by false packaging, I decided to try hacking the PQI FLASHCARD Compact Flash Adapter to see if I could get it to accept the CF Type II Microdrive. The electrical interfaces are exactly the same. All I had to do was make some physical modifications. It worked, and I explain that hack in this chapter. Although I use the Microdrive as an example throughout this chapter, the information can be used to adapt any CompactFlash Type II card.

PC Card Interface

PC Card is a mechanical and electrical specification of mobile peripheral devices for computer notebooks. The specification is governed by the PCMCIA, which meets six times a year to improve the standard.

The PC Card interface has 68 pins and supports two different data sizes. The original PC Card standard supported 16-bit cards. The newer standard supports the 32-bit CardBus PC Card interface. The 32-bit CardBus supports burst mode, which is three times faster than the throughput of the 16-bit PC Card version.

The full PC Card standard can be ordered from PCMCIA in book format for about $300. But a very brief electrical signal definition is listed in the Frequently Asked Question on the PCMCIA web site (www.pcmcia.org/).

Parts You Need

To perform this hack, you'll need the following parts:

- CompactFlash Type I to PC Card Type II adapter
- CompactFlash Type II card

There are several different versions of the CompactFlash Type I to PC Card Type II adapter. Each manufacturer makes the adapter slightly differently. The one I used for this project is the PQI FLASHCARD Compact Flash Adapter that I got at my local Fry's Electronics. This particular adapter is easy to hack because it's two metal covers that are attached using double-sided tape. The other adapters on the market may require slightly more work but shouldn't be much more difficult to modify than the example I use here.

You'll need a CompactFlash Type II card to see if you have hacked the adapter correctly. You'll use the card for test-fitting in the modified adapter and then used to see if data can actually be read from the card. Any CF Type II card will work; including a Microdrive.

Tools You Need

The tools needed for this project are minimal and are shown in the following list:

- A pair of needle-nose pliers
- Superglue

CompactFlash Interface

CompactFlash is the mechanical and electrical specification for small, removable mass storage devices. The specification was first introduced in 1994 and has become wildly popular among digital cameras and other mobile gears.

CompactFlash cards have a 50-pin interface. The interface provides complete PC Card-ATA functionality and compatibility. Although the PC Card interface has 68 pins, a CompactFlash card can be slipped into a passive (pass-through) PC Card to CompactFlash adapter and works fully with a PC Card-compatible device.

The full CompactFlash specification with mechanical dimensions and electrical interface pin-out is available for free download on the CompactFlash Association web site (www.CompactFlash.org/).

The needle-nose pliers will help you disassemble the adapter. Without them, you might have a hard time removing the metal covers on the adapter. The superglue will come in handy when you are ready to reassemble the required parts. You can pick up both of these tools from a home improvement store. In fact, both tools are so common, you can probably find them at your local 99 cent store for less than a dollar each.

Making the Modification

The PQI FLASHCARD Compact Flash Adapter is a piece of black plastic sandwiched by two metal covers, with the circuit board in the middle of the adapter. To begin making the modification, pull off the top metal piece. Use a pair of needle-nose pliers for more leverage. It is held to the plastic by some sort of double-sided tape. Be careful so that you do not damage the plastic piece underneath or bend any pins on the circuit board. Figure 24-4 shows the top metal cover removed.

Note The instructions provided here are for the PQI FLASHCARD CompactFlash Adapter. Other adapters may be manufactured slightly differently. For example, one of my PC Card adapters has metal covers that wrap around the entire plastic piece.

Next, turn the adapter over and carefully pull off the bottom metal piece (see Figure 24-5), without breaking the black plastic. The plastic piece and the circuit board are vital parts of this adapter. Obviously, the circuit board is used to interface the CF Type I and CF Type II cards to the PC Card port. The black plastic is used as a guide for the easy insertion and removal of the adapter card.

FIGURE 24-4: The top metal cover removed

FIGURE 24-5: The bottom metal cover removed

After pulling off both metal covers, you are very close to having it work with your Microdrive. However, the Microdrive still cannot be inserted into the adapter. Two tabs are blocking the Microdrive from being inserted. The two tabs are on each side of the plastic guide. You'll have to break off these tabs. I was able to break them off with my thumb. But it's probably even easier with a pair of needle-nose pliers. Figure 24-6 shows one of the tabs broken off the plastic guide. With the tabs out of the way, the Microdrive can be inserted into the adapter as shown in Figure 24-7.

Note   As mentioned before, the electrical interfaces of CF Type I and CF Type II cards are identical. Therefore, any CompactFlash card can be easily slipped into this modified adapter and still work with your notebook computer, as long as the original adapter meets the full PCMCIA electrical interface specifications. However, using the Microdrive and your notebook with this kind of hack may void the warranty on your equipment.

FIGURE 24-6: The plastic tab broken off

FIGURE 24-7: The Microdrive inserted into the hacked adapter

Although I can't guarantee that this hacked adapter will work with all of your equipment and that it won't void your warranties, I have used this hack successfully with my Sony VAIO notebook and my IBM 1GB Microdrive (see Figure 24-8). Based on the electrical interface specifications for CompactFlash and PC Card, it should work with all gears that conform fully to the specifications. This hacked adapter can still be used with a regular CompactFlash Type I card, allowing you to carry only one type of adapter instead of two.

Without the metal covers, the hacked adapter is rather fragile. The circuit board is also not glued to the black plastic guide. You can glue the circuit board and the black plastic guide together for easier insertion into your notebook computer. A small drop of superglue at each corner will suffice. If you have a spare clear plastic PC Card case, you should store the hacked adapter in it. The case will keep the circuit board from harm and the pins from being bent (see Figure 24-9). You can even carry one Microdrive or one solid-state memory card with the adapter in the case.

FIGURE 24-8: The Microdrive and hacked adapter inserted into the PCMCIA slot of a notebook computer

FIGURE 24-9: The hacked adapter should be protected in a strong plastic case.

Using the Adapter

After making the modification to your adapter, slip the Microdrive into the adapter. Then slide the adapter into your notebook. Because you have removed some material from the adapter, it is now thinner than the original adapter. You may need to wiggle it a little bit for it to insert snuggly into the PC Card slot. Once the Microdrive and the adapter are properly inserted into your notebook computer, turn the computer on. After the computer boots, the CompactFlash card should show up as a distinct drive in your computer system. You will be able to drag-and-drop files as you would normally with your computer.

To remove the drive from your computer, follow the instructions that came with your computer system. Normally, this would mean "ejecting" the drive first through software, before physically removing the card. But to be safe, you can always power down the computer before removing the memory card.

Removing the 4GB Microdrive from the Creative Nomad MuVo² MP3 Player

A year prior to the completion of this book, Creative Labs released a small MP3 player called the Nomad MuVo² (see Figure 25-1). The MuVo² has 4GB of capacity and is only slightly larger than a Type II CompactFlash card. Some people speculated that its core uses a real CompactFlash memory card that can be used in digital cameras. If so, it was tremendously beneficial to take apart the MuVo² and recover the flash card. For one thing, a stand-alone 4GB CompactFlash Microdrive was selling at more than twice the cost of a MuVo².

It turned out that those people were right. The MuVo² contained a genuine CF+ Type II compatible Microdrive, which can be used in a digital camera. News spread like wildfire as everyone attempted to purchase this player. MuVo² was in great demand and that caused a shortage in supply. People who managed to get them were rewarded with working Microdrives.

Today, music-player manufacturers use "locked" Microdrives to prevent consumers from stealing them out of the player for digital-camera use. These "locked" drives are not CF+ Type II-compatible. They operate in True IDE mode, like real hard disks. Therefore, they cannot be used with your digital camera. Perhaps one day a digital camera manufacturer will design a digital camera to use True IDE Microdrives. But for now, you can still take the drive out of the MuVo², use the Microdrive with your CompactFlash reader, and install a different sized CF card in your MuVo².

FIGURE 25-1: Creative Nomad MuVo^2

Soldered the Microdrive

A few months after the discovery of the Microdrive in the MuVo^2, the number of Microdrives sold on eBay peaked. To make a handsome profit, rogue dealers pirated most of them out of the MuVo^2. Soon after, it was rumored that many consumers had seen a picture of the MuVo^2 with its Microdrive soldered onboard. The story was that Creative Labs soldered the drive to prevent its removal. Ebay MuVo^2 rogues quickly took up the chance to advertise that they are the only ones with unsoldered MuVo^2's. The story reached far and wide and created a scare among consumers looking to purchase a MuVo^2 for the Microdrive. Though many have heard the soldered Microdrive story, none have ever seen an MuVo^2 with a soldered Microdrive in person. It turned out to be an elaborate hoax and an overblown rumor spread by a rogue dealer as an attempt to control the MuVo^2 market.

MuVo Models

Creative Labs makes and distributes a number of MP3 players under the Nomad MuVo and MuVo² designation. Currently the MuVo² and the MuVo² FM contain the Microdrive. The MuVo² X-Trainer has the same enclosure and may contain a 512MB CompactFlash card (I have not verified it). The instructions in this chapter will work with these MuVo² models. The other MuVo models, with their smaller form factor, contain solid-state flash memory soldered onboard but do not contain Microdrives.

The Creative Labs Zen Micro also contains a 5GB Microdrive, but its form factor is different; thus, the instructions here cannot be followed exactly. If you are careful, you will be able to take the Zen Micro apart for the Microdrive.

Creative Labs makes a number of different MP3 players. And they are constantly adding new players to their lineup. I am confident that they will add more Microdrive models in the future.

Downloading the Firmware

Before disassembling your MuVo², download the latest firmware from the Creative Labs web site. You will need to reload the firmware to enable the MuVo² again after taking it apart. As of this writing, there are three models of the MuVo²: 512MB, 1.5GB, and 4GB. Make sure you download the firmware that is right for your model. The firmware I am using, as of this writing, is version 1.11.01 for the 4GB model. By the time you read this chapter, they may already have a more recent one in place.

Which Firmware Version Should I Use?

The obvious answer is "the latest." However, the question is almost moot, because you probably don't have a choice. Manufacturers have been pretty diligent about releasing new firmware and eliminating older firmware from their web sites. They do this to reduce the number of technical support calls, such as when the user installs the wrong firmware or when the older firmware causes new problems. Unless you have a friend that is collecting firmware for your specific brand and model of MP3 player, you will probably find only the latest firmware online.

Tools You Need

You need a precision screw driver set that contains the screwdrivers in the following list. You can buy a set from Home Depot or other home improvement stores.

- #0 Phillips precision screw driver
- #00 Phillips precision screw driver
- #000 Phillips precision screw driver

Disassembling the MuVo^2

Of the MP3 players discussed in this book, the MuVo^2 is the easiest to take apart and reassemble. Everything is fastened together with standard Phillips screws. And nothing is secured with one-use clips or plastic tabs.

Taking the Case Apart

The MuVo^2 enclosure is made of white plastic. Its surface is covered in silver paint. When you look at the bottom of the MP3 player, you'll see two silver screws. But don't be hasty. If you only unscrew these two screws before trying to pull the enclosure apart, you will damage the shell. There are two hidden screws in the battery compartment (see Figure 25-2). One is further hidden under the warranty sticker, which says if you tamper with the sticker, your warranty is void. Don't worry about the sticker for now. Remove the battery pack and get it out of your way. Then you can make the decision on whether to void the warranty.

Tip To make it easier on yourself, you can carefully remove the battery cover before dealing with the screws. Creative Labs had designed the battery cover to be installed and removed when inserted from an angle.

Once you decide to void your MuVo^2's warranty, remove the sticker. There is no clean way to remove it. It is made tamper-proof, so that the sticker will not stay intact when you try to remove it. Don't bother trying to remove it in one piece. You can even poke right through it with your screwdriver. The #0 Phillips precision screwdriver is a perfect fit for these screws. Unscrew all four screws. Then lift the back cover up.

After removing the back cover, you'll see the circuit board sitting nicely in the enclosure. Every free space on the circuit board is covered with surface mount components (see Figure 25-3). The designer of the board layout is very good.

FIGURE 25-2: There are two screw holes in the battery compartment.

FIGURE 25-3: Screws, battery, battery cover, MuVo² internal circuit board, and back cover

Nothing is holding down the circuit board at this point. The four screws that were holding it down were removed when you unscrewed the cover. By holding the circuit board at the three connectors on top of the MuVo², you can pull the circuit board up and flip it out of the way as shown in Figure 25-4. It's still attached to the Microdrive below with a ribbon cable, so you can't remove it completely, yet.

FIGURE 25-4: Flip the circuit board up and out of the way.

Removing the Microdrive

Once you flip the circuit board out of the way, you'll discover additional screws. They are black this time. You need a #00 Phillips precision screwdriver for these. When I first took my MuVo² apart, I saw only two black screws. Then I noticed a tiny silver one by the ribbon cable. There is actually a fourth one under the black tape (see Figure 25-5). So, as when you removed the back cover, don't be too hasty. Locate all four screws first.

FIGURE 25-5: A black screw is hidden under black tape.

Peel back the black tape carefully. You'll want to reuse this tape. I suspect its purpose is to isolate the screw from the circuit board. When you've located the three black screws and the one silver screw, you can start the unscrewing process. You can use the #00 Phillips precision screwdriver on the black screws, but the silver screw is tiny. You will need to have a #000 Phillips precision screwdriver on hand to deal with the silver screw.

With all four screws removed, you can now flip the metal plate up in the same manner as the circuit board (Figure 25-6). The Microdrive is attached to the circuit board via ribbon cable. But don't try to unplug the ribbon cable just yet. Being hasty in this project just doesn't pay off.

Remove the circuit board and Microdrive from the enclosure. Look at the other side of the Microdrive. You'll see why I asked you not to remove the Microdrive. The ribbon cable is taped to the Microdrive with a transparent orange tape. Peel the orange tape back as carefully as possible. Reusing it will give you a good secure connection when you reassemble your MuVo². Once you've peeled back the orange tape, hold the edge of the ribbon cable connector firmly between your thumb and index finger. Pull the ribbon cable away from the Microdrive. Exert force back and forth between the two sides in a firm but controlled manner. Pulling too hard on one side but not the other will result in bent pins. The detached Microdrive is shown in Figure 25-7.

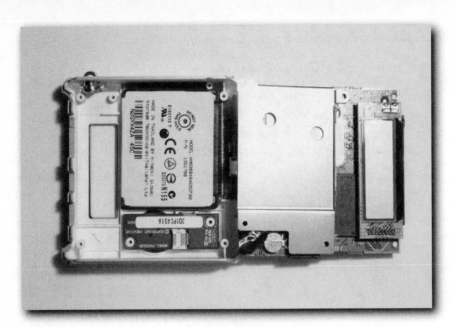

FIGURE 25-6: Flip the metal plate up to reveal the Microdrive.

FIGURE 25-7: The Microdrive detached from the ribbon cable connector

My MuVo² came with a Hitachi 4GB Microdrive. Yours probably includes the same drive. But it is possible that Creative Labs will manufacture future MuVo²s with a different brand and model Microdrive. In fact, MuVo² FMs are already shipping with 5GB Microdrives. With 8GB and 10GB Microdrives being released to the consumer market by the time this book goes to press, it's likely you'll find new models with bigger drives. Don't be surprised if your drive is different from mine.

Putting the MuVo² Back Together

Putting the MuVo² back together is the reverse of taking it apart. The Creative Labs engineers have done a wonderful job of designing a device that can be disassembled and reassembled easily, without causing any damage to its components. When you install the Microdrive, make sure it is facing down toward the enclosure. The only other thing you have to watch out for is that the main circuit board is seated properly. It has a positional contact that interfaces with the button and control circuit, located on another board (see Figure 25-8). Once you've seated both circuit boards, push the main circuit board down until the connectors snap together.

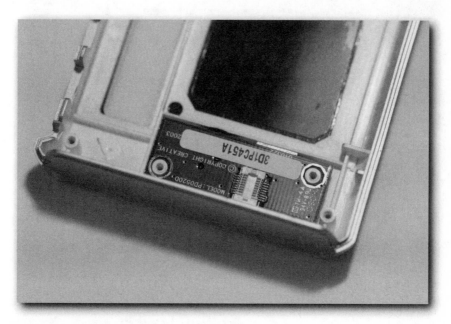

Figure 25-8: The button and control circuit board

Substituting CF Cards

When you put your MuVo² back together, you might be tempted to substitute a smaller or bigger drive. The good news is that you can. Every CompactFlash memory card and Microdrive has a chance of working inside the MuVo² enclosure. The bad new is that whether a card works or not is a hit-and-miss proposition. The results are mixed. Some CF cards work, some don't. Even the same brand and same model cards may work in some cases but not in others. The only way to know if your card will work is to try it. You might do some research online to see what brand and models of cards have worked for other people. Just realize that although following their lead gives you a better chance to have a working card, it is not a guarantee.

Tip If a card does not work with MuVo², the MP3 player will display "Media Error" during its recovery (see Figure 25-9). See the next section for a thorough coverage of the recovery process.

FIGURE 25-9: The "Media Error" screen

Booting Up

After you have installed the MuVo² battery pack, the MP3 player will boot up automatically. If you installed a new drive or have erased the original Microdrive, MuVo² will enter Recovery Mode (see Figure 25-10). When the phrase "Recovery Mode" is displayed, you can see the recovery options (Figure 25-12) by pressing the MENU button.

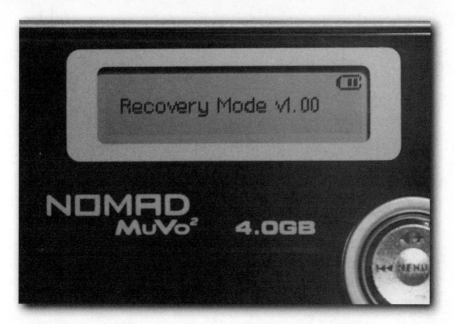

FIGURE 25-10: After booting up, the MuVo² will enter the Recovery Mode

Tip

If you see "Recovery Mode" but pressing the MENU button doesn't get you anywhere, it means that the button and control circuit board are not snapped together with the main circuit board. You'll have to open it up again to reseat the circuit boards.

The recovery option screen, shown in Figure 25-11, has six options. Use the previous track and next track buttons to move between the options. The description for the current selection will be displayed below the numbers. The options are as follows:

1. Run PC ScanDisk

2. Clean Up

3. Format All

4. Reload Firmware

5. Connect to PC

6. Reboot

FIGURE 25-11: The recovery options

The first step to recovering your MuVo[2] is to format the drive, so select option 3: Format All. Move the selection to the check mark with the previous or the next button. Push the MENU button to confirm. The MuVo[2] will display the "Formatting . . ." message shown in Figure 25-12. When it's done formatting, the MuVo[2] displays the amount of space available for about two seconds. Don't worry if you miss that message. It is not too important.

Next, you have to reload the firmware. You need a PC to accomplish this task. Make sure you already have the firmware downloaded at this point. If you ran the firmware without connecting the MuVo[2] to the USB port, the firmware will show the message shown in Figure 25-13. Before actually reloading the firmware, charge your MuVo[2]'s battery. The firmware upgrading software will not let you continue if it determines that the battery level of the MuVo[2] is too low.

In recovery mode, select option 4: Reload Firmware. MuVo[2] will ask you to connect it to the USB port of your computer. After connecting it, run the firmware upgrade program. The program will detect your MuVo[2] and display the current and upgrade firmware versions as shown in Figure 25-14. Click the Upgrade button to start the upgrade. If the battery level of your MuVo[2] is too low at this point, the upgrade program will tell you so and terminate the process.

FIGURE 25-12: The formatting screen

FIGURE 25-13: The MuVo² is not connected screen

FIGURE 25-14: The firmware upgrade program
detected the MuVo².

If your MuVo[2] has enough battery power, the firmware upgrade program will complete the rest of the process automatically. The progress bar moves from left to right, as shown in Figure 25-15. When the bar reaches the right side, the firmware upgrade program reboots the MuVo[2] (see Figure 25-16). When the firmware upgrade program detects the MuVo[2] on the USB port again, it displays the screen shown in Figure 25-17. At this point, your MuVo[2] player is working normally. You can start using it as your MP3 player or as your file transporter once again.

FIGURE 25-15: Upgrade-in-progress screen

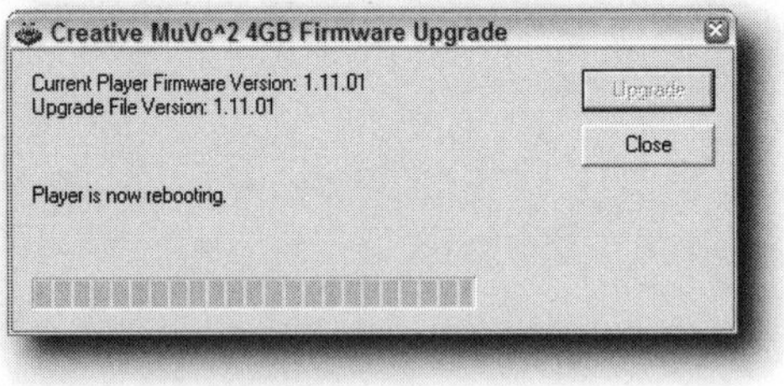

FIGURE 25-16: Player-reboot screen

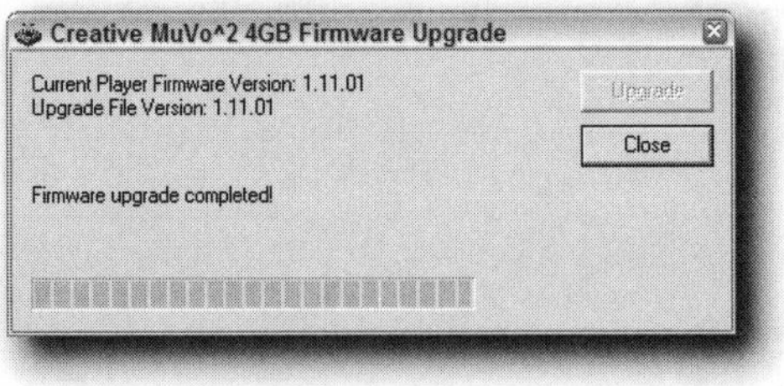

FIGURE 25-17: Firmware upgrade-completed screen

Using the Microdrive

We've spent a lot of time and effort taking apart the MuVo². But what can you do with the Microdrive once you remove it?

If you have the first generation MuVo², you have a real gem on your hands. The Microdrive from the first generation MuVo² is a CF+ Type II card. This type of card is compatible with all digital cameras and devices that have the CompactFlash Type II slot. Just plug the Microdrive into your digital camera and format it. If your digital camera doesn't display an error message or hang, then it'll work just fine.

On the other hand, if you have the second generation MuVo², like me and many other users, you have a Microdrive that operates in True IDE mode. In this mode, the Microdrive will only work in devices that can interface to a True IDE CF card, such as other MP3 players. I've found that my MuVo² Microdrive works with some of my card readers. Older card readers may have a problem accessing these newer, larger storage standards.

Theoretically, digital camera manufacturers can design their digital camera to be compatible with True IDE mode. If MP3 players and CF card readers can access cards, then a digital camera can be designed to as well. As of this writing, there is no digital camera on the market that will interface to True IDE devices. But I'll keep my fingers crossed for the day that they will work with digital cameras.

Removing the Microdrive from the Rio Carbon 5GB MP3 Player

Ever since the community uncovered the secret to hacking the Creative Technology MuVo² (see Chapter 25), everyone is experimenting with MP3 players in the 4–5GB storage range. As of this writing, most of these players use the new Hitachi Microdrives. The Rio Carbon is one of these candidates. Of all MP3 players on the market, the Rio Carbon is the most flexible to hack. It's even possible to swap Microdrives from other MP3 players into the Rio Carbon shell. Since the original movement, the desire to remove the Microdrives for digital cameras has died off a little bit, mainly because the price of stand-alone Microdrives has dropped close to the price of these players and the new Microdrives operate in True IDE mode, which will not work in today's digital cameras. However, dissecting the Rio Carbon is still a useful exercise for a number of reasons, not least of which is that it's fun (hey, that's why you're reading a book on hacking, right?) and because the concept can be used on similar devices. Also, it's possible that future digital cameras will be able to store photographs on True IDE Microdrives.

Overview of the Rio Carbon

The Rio Carbon is an ultra-thin MP3 player of minimalist design (with very few control buttons) that is small enough to fit in your palm (see Figure 26-1). In addition to being an MP3 player, it doubles as a removeable mass storage device because with it you can carry data back and forth between two computers. In fact, I am currently carrying the content of this entire book in my Rio Carbon so I can edit it anywhere I go.

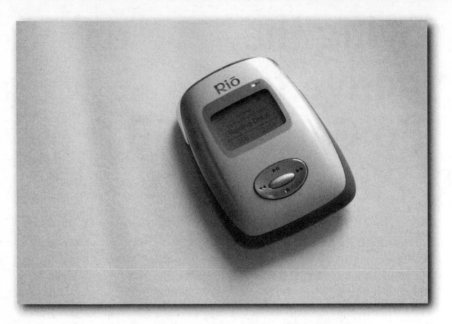

FIGURE 26-1: Rio Carbon is an ultra-thin MP3 player with a 5GB Microdrive.

The Rio Carbon also has an internal non-removeable rechargeable lithium ion battery. It is charged through the USB port and therefore can be charged any time it is connected to a computer. No external wall-socket power supply is needed, though one is supplied. The external power supply powers the Rio Carbon through the USB port and provides unlimited playback time.

This chapter focuses on the internal 5GB Microdrive. The 5GB Microdrive is a CompactFlash (CF) Type II card that can be used in a digital camera. What makes this hack so attractive is that the cost of the Rio Carbon is currently less than the cost of a stand-alone 5GB Microdrive. In addition, as I describe later in this chapter, it is possible to put in a smaller Microdrive to keep the Rio Carbon alive while you use the bigger Microdrive for shooting pictures.

Disassembling the Device

Before starting, make sure you read this entire chapter to familiarize yourself with the process.

Disassembling your gear is a risky process. Copy anything of value off your Rio Carbon MP3 Player before you take your Rio Carbon apart. You can do this easily by plugging the Rio Carbon into the USB port of your Windows XP computer, where the Rio Carbon will show up as a "Removable Disk" in Windows Explorer. See your Rio Carbon manual for instructions.

The audio files that came with your Rio Carbon are not recoverable through the firmware install. Therefore, if you want to keep them, make sure you back them up before disassembling it.

Tools You Need

The tools you need for this project are quite minimal. Just a set of tiny, precision screwdrivers will do fine.

The precision screwdriver set, sometimes called the jeweler's screwdriver set, should have at least two flat-head screwdrivers, one of which should be twice as big as the other.

Taking the Case Apart

The Rio Carbon is a slick device with a classic front plastic face and a sturdy metal backing. A piece of rubber runs around the sides for easy, non-slip gripping. Control components surround top, also encased in metal. There are no screws, making it looking clean and simple, but the lack of screws makes it a little harder to open. The secret to getting inside the Rio Carbon is the back cover.

The easiest way to get the back cover off without breaking any components is to start from the bottom. Insert a small flat-blade screwdriver between the metal cover and the rubber. Work your way around the bottom to spread out the pressure. Eventually, you will work the cover loose and see the two metal tabs that are holding the case together (see Figure 26-2).

FIGURE 26-2: These metal tabs hold the Rio Carbon case together. You'll have to work them loose on the bottom and on the sides.

Caution Be careful as you work the bottom loose because the rechargeable battery pack is on the bottom of the case and two wires are located very near the right tab (looking at the back of the Rio Carbon). Work the corner first so that you can get a sneak peak inside the case.

The fun is not over when you get the bottom is loose. Two additional metal tabs are on each side of case, and they are deep down inside and are harder to reach (see Figure 26-6). The best way to disarm them is to use the largest flat-head screwdriver out of the small screwdriver set to hold the side open. Then reach in with a smaller flat-head screwdriver to disable the tab. Use the case to apply leverage when you loosen it.

When the cover is loose on both sides, you'll see two small tabs on top holding the metal cover on. Use your hands to lift the metal cover out and then up. The metal cover should snap off without any damage.

Removing the Drive

Internally, the Rio Carbon is divided into three major portions: control components on the left, Microdrive in the middle, and rechargeable lithium ion battery on the right, as shown in Figure 26-3. The circuit board is below these three components and is held down by three screws. Fortunately, you don't need to deal with the circuit board for this hack.

Figure 26-3: The inside of the Rio Carbon

Carefully lift the Microdrive up, but do not tug on the ribbon cable (see Figure 26-4). Consumer electronics nowadays are built using surface mount technology (SMT) components that are extremely small. Any damage to these components will render the device useless and virtually impossible to fix at home. Lifting up the battery slightly may help you to gain access to the Microdrive, but do not force the battery —it is soldered onto the circuit board via four wires.

FIGURE 26-4: The Microdrive is attached to the circuit board with a short SMT ribbon cable.

Hold the Microdrive, shown in Figure 26-5, firmly in one hand and with your other hand, carefully detach the ribbon cable. The trick is to use the tips of your thumb and index finger to hold both side of the ribbon cable connector. Then slowly wiggle the connector away from the Microdrive. Be careful not to bend the pins or break the connector.

Note I made the mistake of detaching the ribbon cable from the circuit board first. With SMT ribbon cables, the connector on the circuit board has a clip that holds the ribbon cable down tightly on the contacts. With other devices, you can flip the clip up to release the cable and down to tighten the connection. On the Rio Carbon, the clip is an independent plastic piece installed with SMT equipment. It took me a long time to secure the ribbon cable and the clip back onto the circuit board by hand.

FIGURE 26-5: The Seagate 5GB ST1 Microdrive

A piece of copper foil and rubber are taped to the Microdrive. Peel them away slowly and carefully. (I suggest you keep the copper foil and rubber, inside your Rio Carbon, in good condition in case you ever want to put the Rio Carbon back together.) I suspect that the copper foil is there to control the characteristics of the electromagnetic field the Rio Carbon generates.

Putting the Device Back Together

Putting the Rio Carbon back together is much easier than taking it apart. All you have to do is tape the copper foil back onto the Microdrive and reattach it to the ribbon cable. Once the Microdrive is installed, you can snap the metal cover back onto the case. But before you do that, bend the metal tabs back in place for a firm hold (see Figure 26-6).

Tip If you put the Rio Carbon back together and it looks dead, don't panic. Insert a small pin into the tiny hole on top to trigger "Emergency Reset." The hole is located between the volume knob and the headphone jack. When I was hacking my Rio Carbon, I thought I killed it. But after a day of attempting to revive it, I discovered the emergency reset hole.

After putting the Rio Carbon back together, you will find that it no longer boots up properly. Instead of the familiar music screen, it displays a single word that reads, "UPGRADER." This simply means that the Microdrive has to be reformatted and its firmware reloaded. I describe that process in the next section.

FIGURE 26-6: The tabs on the inside of the metal cover hold the Rio Carbon case together.

Installing Firmware

Whether you want to put your Rio Carbon back together or you just want to upgrade the firmware to the latest version, you can download the firmware from the Rio web site located at www.rioaudio.com/. At the time of this writing, four versions are available: 1.02, 1.16, 1.22, and 1.32. I tend to install the latest version, because it has the most advanced features and generally fixed previous versions' bugs. Follow the instructions that come with the downloaded firmware to install it.

Installing a Different Microdrive

In case you want to use the 5GB Microdrive for your digital camera, but also want a working Rio Carbon, you can install a different Microdrive. However, the Rio Carbon operates the Microdrives in CompactFlash True IDE Mode. Because the drive has to be operating in True IDE Mode, the following CF storage devices cannot be used:

- Any solid-state CompactFlash memory
- Creative Labs 340MB Microdrive
- IBM 340MB Microdrive
- IBM 1GB Microdrive
- Magicstor 2.2GB Microdrive

Currently, only a handful of drives can be used in the Rio Carbon, but there may be more in the future. The drives that can currently be used are:

- Any Hitachi Microdrive
- Seagate 5GB ST1 Drive (included in my Rio Carbon)

Install either of these drives by following the instructions mentioned in "Putting the Device Back Together" earlier in this chapter. Then install the firmware as mentioned in the previous section and your Rio Carbon will be ready to be used once again.

Using the 5GB Microdrive in Your Digital Camera

Insert the drive into your digital camera. Most likely, your digital camera will not recognize the Microdrive at first. Try formatting the drive while it's in your digital camera. If the formatting is successful, it should be ready to use. Otherwise, your digital camera is probably not compatible with this drive.

Why It Might Not Work with Your Digital Camera

Most digital cameras today use one form or another of the File Allocation Table (FAT) file system: either FAT16 or FAT32. The original FAT file system was invented for Disk Operating System (DOS) for Personal Computers (PC). Older operating systems with FAT16 supported drives up to 2GB. Newer operating systems allowed FAT16 to support drives up to 4GB. For drives bigger than 4GB, FAT32 must be used.

My Rio Carbon came with a Seagate 5GB ST1 Microdrive. Because it is too big for FAT16, it was preformatted to FAT32. Older digital cameras, such as my Canon EOS D30, can only use FAT16, so this drive cannot be used with those digital cameras. Newer cameras, such as the Canon EOS Digital Rebel, use FAT32 and are capable of reading and writing to this drive.

Removing the 4GB Microdrive from the Apple iPod mini

Apple iPod mini (see Figure 27-1) is the least cost effect MP3 player to get a Microdrive out of. At the time of this writing, both MuVo2 and Rio Carbon come with 5GB Microdrives and are much cheaper than the iPod mini. Nevertheless, you might have an iPod mini that you no longer use, your iPod mini might be broken, or you simply might want to do it because you can. These are all valid reasons, and this chapter shows you how to get inside your iPod mini.

There are several different models of iPod as of this writing: the very original iPod, iPod photo, iPod U2 Special Edition, iPod mini, and iPod shuffle. I am sure more models are on their way. Currently, of all the different iPod models, iPod mini is the only that uses a Microdrive in the form of a CompactFlash Type II card. All the other iPod models use hard disk drives sized for notebook computers. These drives are 2.5" wide; much too big for digital cameras. Therefore, this chapter is geared solely toward the iPod mini and its internal Microdrive.

FIGURE 27-1: The iPod mini is an elegant MP3 player with a Microdrive inside.

Disassembling the iPod mini

The following section shows you how to disassemble the iPod mini.

Tools You Need

The iPod mini has small and delicate parts. To disassemble it, you will need a precision screwdriver set.

The precision screwdriver set can be found at a home improvement store. I have even found a set at the local ninety-nine cent store for $1. It should contain at least one flat-head screwdriver and one Philips-head screwdriver.

Getting Inside the Enclosure

The design of the iPod mini is quite elegant, with straight edges and round corners. The shell of the iPod mini is made of aluminum, and it has a very nice, smooth finish. There are no industrial bolts or nuts visible on the outer shell. The device looks like high-tech, precision-engineered, alien ware. However, the lack of industrial hints also means that there is no easy access to the iPod mini.

Tip

Before starting the disassembly process, turn off your iPod mini. Then turn on the Hold switch to prevent the iPod mini from turning on accidentally.

White plastic pieces cover the top and bottom of the iPod mini enclosure. They are the only source of entry, so you will have to remove both pieces. The method of removal is the same for both the top and bottom pieces, so you can start on either side. With your fingernail, exert some force between the white plastic and the aluminum enclosure. Pull the aluminum away from the white plastic slightly. When you have created a slit, insert the small flat-head screwdriver. Then work around the plastic and pry it upward. The plastic pieces are attached with adhesive, but they're not too hard to remove. Just go slowly and be careful so that the plastic covers and adhesive can be reused without any damage. After you've removed the plastic from one side, start on the other side.

Caution

Be especially careful when you work on the top of the iPod mini. The hold switch is fitted over a smaller electronic switch below (see Figure 27-2). It is small and fragile and snaps off easily. When you start to pry the white plastic up, do it slowly all the way around. Make sure you pry straight up and not slanted to the side.

FIGURE 27-2: When you remove the plastic top, be very careful to pry it straight up. Note the small hold switch.

After you remove the bottom plastic cover, a metal bracket is revealed (see Figure 27-3). With rounded ends, four curved arms, and a bubble at the end of each arm, the metal bracket looks like a sculpture from a contemporary art gallery. But don't let its design fool you; the metal bracket is actually quite functional. The four curved arms are actually springs that provide tension to keep the bracket in place. Looking closely, you can see that the arms are clipped into recesses in the aluminum shell. The bubbles at the end of each arm are used to draw the arms out of the recession. With the right tool (a tweezers-like tool for two bubbles at each side of the bracket), you can remove the bracket fairly easy. With two such tools, you hardly have to do any work. All you have to do is put your tweezers into the two bubble holes, squeeze, and pop the bracket out.

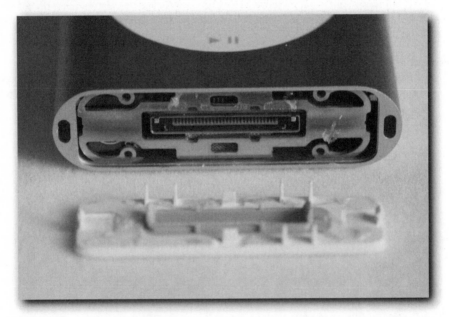

FIGURE 27-3: After you pull off the bottom plastic piece, a metal bracket is revealed.

On the other hand, if, like me, you don't have the right tool, you'll have to try something else. You can insert a strong screwdriver into the hole and move each arm out of the recess. But if your screwdriver is weak, you'll bend it (don't ask how I know). Without a strong screwdriver, a better choice is to fit a flathead precision screwdriver between the end of the arm and the recess, then use the leverage to move the arm out. Do this one at a time for each of the spring arms.

Tip

I found it easiest to move the two arms closer to the front or the back of the iPod mini, rather than having the two arms at each side.

With the metal bracket out of the way, the circuit board and a ribbon cable are revealed (see Figure 27-4). The ribbon cable is the communication interface to the front click wheel and buttons. In order to remove the circuit board, you must disconnect the ribbon cable from it. Do so carefully, with a flathead screwdriver. Pry it outward.

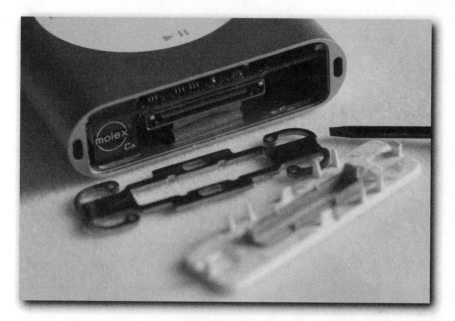

FIGURE 27-4: Removing the metal bracket reveals the circuit board and the ribbon connector.

Caution

Surface mount components, such as the ribbon cable and connection (see Figure 27-5), are very small. They are very difficult to repair or replace and may be impossible to fix at home. Disconnect with care.

With the ribbon cable disconnected, you are almost ready to slide the circuit board out of the aluminum shell. Look at the top of the iPod mini closely. You'll see two very tiny Phillips screws (see Figure 27-6). Unscrew these with your precision screwdriver and put them in a safe place. If you ever drop them on your carpet, it will be like looking for a needle in a haystack.

FIGURE 27-5: Carefully disconnect the ribbon connector from the circuit board.

FIGURE 27-6: The screws on top of the iPod mini are tiny. You need a small Phillips-head screwdriver to remove them.

Now you are ready to slide the circuit board out. From the bottom of the iPod mini, push the circuit board upward. A flathead screwdriver can help with the leverage, but don't be tempted to pull on the metal bracket on top when it pops out. It is not very sturdy and seems to be soldered onto the circuit board. Pulling on it a few times could weaken its joint. Push the circuit board out a little more with a flathead screwdriver. Be careful to push only the edge of the circuit board—don't touch any components on the circuit board.

As soon as the battery connector is out of the enclosure, on the back (see Figure 27-7), stop pushing and disconnect it. I have many times seen sparks arc between components on the circuit board and the metal click wheel bracket inside the enclosure. The sparks occur when I slide the circuit board in and out of the enclosure. After awhile, I wised up and started disconnecting the battery.

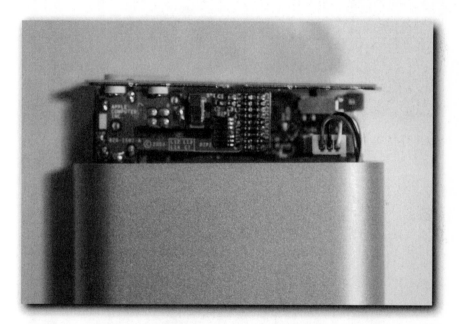

FIGURE 27-7: Unplug the battery connector as soon as it emerges from the aluminum enclosure.

The front of the iPod mini has the LCD screen and the circuit board (see Figure 27-8). The back holds the battery and Microdrive (see Figure 27-9).

FIGURE 27-8: iPod mini front view

FIGURE 27-9: iPod mini rear view

Removing the Microdrive

The Microdrive is attached to the circuit board via a surface mount ribbon cable. No other mechanism is securing it to the circuit board. It is held in place solely by friction and the constraint of space in the enclosure.

The Microdrive is wrapped in tape and rubber bumpers (see Figure 27-10). In order to unplug the Microdrive from the ribbon cable, you have to unwrap it. I see no way to salvage the green tape, but the rubber bumpers can be reused.

FIGURE 27-10: The Microdrive is wrapped in tape and surrounded by rubber bumpers.

With the tape and rubber out of the way, a Hitachi 4GB Microdrive is revealed. Move the battery pack out of the way. It is attached to the circuit board with a tiny piece of adhesive at one corner. Pop the Microdrive up slightly to give yourself better access to the ribbon cable (see Figure 27-11).

Insert a flathead screwdriver between the Microdrive and the ribbon cable connector. Pry one end of the connector loose, then the other end (see Figure 27-12). Keep working back and forth in this fashion until the Microdrive is disconnected. Be careful not to bend any pins.

FIGURE 27-11: The Microdrive is attached to the circuit board via a short surface mount ribbon cable. Move the battery out of the way and pop the Microdrive up for easy access to the ribbon cable connector.

FIGURE 27-12: A flathead screwdriver can help you disconnect the Microdrive.

The Hitachi 4GB Microdrive (see Figure 27-13) is now ready to be used in your digital camera, computer, card reader, or other device. You may need a CompactFlash to PCMCIA card to use it in your notebook. And you may need to modify the card for use with the Microdrive.

Cross-Reference See Chapter 24 for information about modifying CompactFlash cards.

FIGURE 27-13: Hitachi 4GB Microdrive disconnected

Putting the iPod mini Back Together

At some point, you probably want to listen to music or play games on your iPod mini again. You can put it back together at any time. Now that you know how to take it apart, putting it back together will be fairly straightforward. Just remember not to plug the battery back in until the circuit board is almost all the way in the enclosure.

If you are replacing the Microdrive after using it elsewhere, when you first power up your iPod mini it displays the Apple logo and then a folder with an exclamation point (see Figure 27-14). Next the iPod mini turns off. At this point, you need to reset the iPod mini and reload the firmware.

FIGURE 27-14: Folder with an exclamation mark

Resetting the iPod mini

To reset the iPod mini, switch the Hold switch to *on* and then *off*. Then hold down the Menu and Select buttons at the same time. When you see the Apple logo (see Figure 27-15), your iPod mini has reset.

FIGURE 27-15: The Apple logo

After the Apple logo, you may see the folder with the exclamation mark again. Don't despair—you'll have to put the iPod mini into disk mode to update the firmware.

Updating the Firmware

To update the firmware on your iPod mini, you need to install the iPod mini Updater program. It is already installed if you installed iTunes on your computer. If not, you can download the latest version from Apple's web site: www.apple.com/.

Load the Updater program on your computer. With your computer and software ready to go, put the iPod mini into disk mode. You can do this by bringing up the Apple logo on the iPod mini (either by turning it on or by resetting it). While the Apple logo is being displayed, hold down the Play and Select buttons until you see "Disk Mode" on the screen (see Figure 27-16).

FIGURE 27-16: iPod mini in Disk Mode

Plug the iPod mini into the USB or FireWire port on your computer. After a little while, the Updater program will recognize the iPod mini and give you two options: Update or Restore. Pick the Restore option, and the firmware will be installed in your iPod mini.

FireWire vs. USB

I have a Toshiba Windows XP notebook and I naturally used the USB port on it with the iPod mini (my notebook computer did not have a FireWire port). When I was trying to reinstall the firmware on my iPod mini, I kept getting the message "Disk write error" (see Figure 27-17). It took me three days to figure out what was wrong.

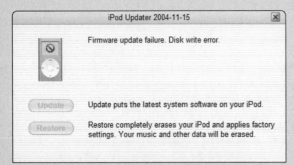

| iPod Updater 2004-11-15 | ☒ |

Firmware update failure. Disk write error.

Update   Update puts the latest system software on your iPod.

Restore   Restore completely erases your iPod and applies factory settings. Your music and other data will be erased.

FIGURE 27-17: When the Updater program cannot successfully complete, it displays this message.

I happen to have a FireWire PCMCIA card, so I tried to connect the iPod mini to my notebook with it instead. To my surprise, the Updater installed the firmware with no trouble. It turns out that there is an incompatibility between the iPod mini and the USB port on my notebook computer. If you ever experience this problem, you might consider trying a different port, a different computer, or a different connection type.

The Update button will be clickable only when the Software Version line indicates that an update is required. It will be grayed out if the software on your iPod mini is already up to date.

Keep in mind that when you "Restore" your iPod mini, all data will be lost. If you have important data on the Microdrive, you should back it up prior to this operation.

Avoid Problems, Use the Latest iPod Updater

Observe the Name, Serial Number, Software Version, and Capacity in the iPod Updater window (see Figure 27-18). They should all be filled in, and none of them should show "N/A". If the software shows "N/A" in the Serial Number and Software Version entries, it is unable to read from your iPod mini and your restore operation will not work during the firmware re-flash.

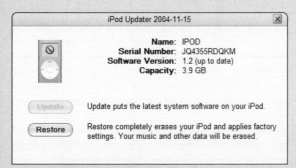

FIGURE 27-18: The iPod Updater window

This problem occurred to me when I tried to use iPod Updater 2004-04-28 on my iPod mini. The restore operation was successful, but during the firmware re-flash, the iPod mini displayed the exclamation mark with folder logo again. I solved the problem by using the iPod Updater 2004-11-15.

Once the recovery operation is complete (see Figure 27-19), disconnect the iPod mini from your computer. A power supply and power outlet logo is displayed on the LCD screen (see Figure 27-20). This logo is the iPod mini's way of telling you to plug it into the external power supply to allow firmware re-flash. Plug the iPod mini into the power supply with the FireWire cable, and then plug the power supply into the power outlet. The iPod mini will attempt to re-flash its firmware while it displays the Apple logo with a progress bar. When the re-flash completes, your iPod mini is ready to use again.

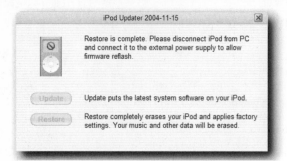

FIGURE 27-19: When the iPod Updater successfully restores the iPod mini, it displays this message.

FIGURE 27-20: The power supply and power outlet logo

Soldering Basics

Soldering is a technique for joining two electrical contacts. When you join multiple contacts, you end up forming a circuit. Electrical contacts can be as simple as wires, capacitor leads, or switches. Some of the projects in this book require that you solder wires, chips, or electronic components to accomplish the goal. Soldering is not very difficult and is a tremendously useful skill. This appendix will walk you through choosing the right tools, preparing the soldering iron, and performing a successful solder.

Soldering Tools

Soldering requires three basic items: soldering iron, solder, and sponge. In the past, the soldering iron had to be assembled from multiple parts, which included the tip, the heating element, and the grip. You also needed to find a soldering iron stand and a sponge tray. Today, the soldering iron is sold in pre-assembled packages (see Figure A-1). These packages may even include the soldering iron stand and the sponge. Radio Shack generally has several different packages in stock. Usually the packages differ in the heating element wattage and the tip type.

Soldering irons are available in different wattages. They generally range from 15 watts to 60 watts for home use. The soldering iron wattage translates directly to heat. Soldering irons with higher wattage generate more heat at the tip than lower wattage soldering irons. Temperature-controlled soldering stations are also available. These stations cost a great deal more than a soldering iron, but temperature can be varied over a continuous range. Selecting the right soldering iron is the key to success.

The right soldering iron supplies just enough wattage to heat the parts being soldered and to flow the solder without supplying too much heat to damage the electronic parts. Some electronic parts are extremely sensitive to heat and can only withstand heat for a short period of time. In many instances, these electronic parts can only withstand heat long enough for you to solder it to the circuit board.

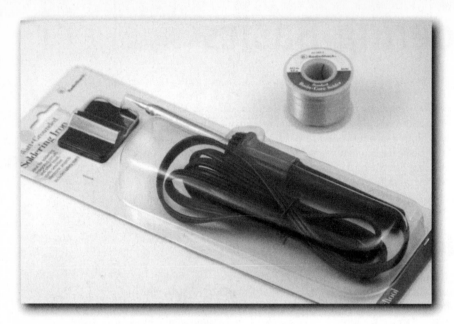

FIGURE A-1: Soldering iron package and solder

As a rule of thumb, a 15 watt soldering iron is ideal for small wires, surface mount components, and small-printed circuit boards. 25 and 30 watt soldering irons, commonly found for home use, are suitable for use on household wires, standard electronic components, and circuit boards. Forty watts and higher soldering irons are suited for soldering battery cells, sheet metals, and chassis. The smaller soldering irons will serve best for the projects in this book.

The soldering tip that came with your soldering iron is probably a standard pointy type (see Figure A-2). Other tips are available, such as a flat blade type to spread heat over more surface area. But the pointy type is sufficient for the purpose of the projects in this book.

For electronic projects, you'll need a roll of 60/40 resin-core solder. Radio Shack and other electronic shops carry these solder types. The diameter of the solder should match your soldering iron. For a 15 watt soldering iron, use a 0.32" solder. You can move up to the bigger 0.50" solder for a 25–30 watt soldering iron. And there are bigger solders for the bigger soldering irons. The smaller diameter solder and smaller soldering iron are more suitable for sensitive electrical components.

Any household sponge will help with your soldering task. Because you will contaminate the sponge with solder and resin, dedicate a sponge for your soldering tasks. I have even gotten away with a folded wet paper towel. Paper towels rip, so they don't serve as well as sponges. But in a pinch, you can give them a try.

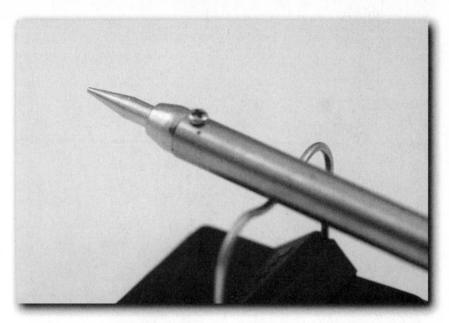

FIGURE A-2: A brand new soldering tip

Preparing the Soldering Iron

Before a fresh new tip's first soldering job, it is worthwhile to tin it. The heating element heats the soldering tip to a very high temperature (several hundred degrees Fahrenheit), which causes the surface to oxidize and burn. Tinning gives the tip surface a uniform shiny coating that is easy to clean, allowing the tip to last longer. The uniformity also allows you to heat up the electronic components quicker and more consistently.

Caution The soldering iron tip's heating element is extremely hot. If you accidentally touch it, you can be seriously burned. Resting the soldering iron against objects, other than the soldering stand, may cause damage to the object and even start a fire. Keep the soldering iron away from its own power cord, or it may result in a serious shock hazard. When you are done using the soldering iron, remember always to unplug it to reduce the likelihood of an accident.

Tinning the tip involves heating the soldering iron up to temperature, coating the tip with solder, and wiping off the excess solder on a sponge. While you are waiting for the soldering iron to reach operating temperature, wet the sponge. The sponge should be soaked in water. Squeeze excess water needs out of the sponge, but only enough so that it exhibits dripping from one of the corners. As soon as the soldering tip is hot enough to melt the solder, coat the tip (see Figure A-3). You may want to replace the tip one day, so keep the solder away from where the tip attaches to the heating element. Coating the entire tapered surface of the tip is sufficient (see Figure A-4). When you are satisfied with the coat, wipe the tip on the wet sponge and remove the excess solder.

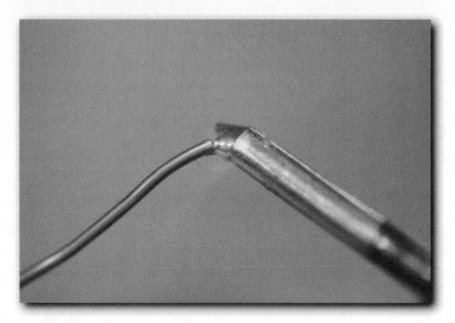

FIGURE A-3: Coat the soldering tip with a layer of melted solder.

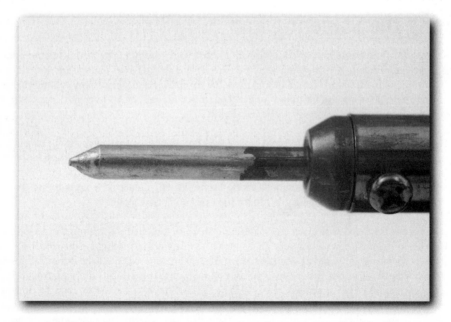

FIGURE A-4: The tip is coated, but the tip-to-heating-element joint is free of solder.

Once you have successfully tinned the tip, the heated soldering iron can sit on the soldering stand for hours (if you are working on a long project). While it's sitting, the tin coating will oxidize. So when you are ready to use the iron, wipe the tip on the wet sponge to remove the oxidation. Remember to unplug the soldering iron from the power outlet when you are no longer using it.

How to Solder

Most beginners, myself included, start learning by melting the solder on the soldering iron first, then trying to transfer the melted solder to the electronic parts to be soldered. Or we heat the electronic parts to be soldered, and then melt the solder on the soldering tip, hoping it would flow onto the parts. It frustrates us that the melted solder tends to stick to the soldering tip and refuses to flow onto the actual parts that we want to solder. In both cases, we are typically unsatisfied with the final soldering result, which takes a long time to produce in the first place. So far, I have described the wrong way to solder in detail, so that you won't be tempted to try it. Read the rest of the appendix to understand the right way to solder.

Unintuitive to most beginners, the basic concept of soldering is to heat up the parts to be soldered with the soldering iron, and then apply the solder directly to the heated parts. When the electronic parts are heated fully, their contacts will melt the solder and flow it evenly. The result is a properly formed connection. This basic concept is the most efficient and fastest method to apply solder. If you start with this basic concept, you can learn to solder successfully from day one.

When you heat the electrical parts, make sure you heat both parts at the same time. Both parts need to be fully heated in order to flow the solder. Figure A-5 shows a correctly heated connection; both circuit board and component lead are heated correctly and the solder flows evenly onto both parts. Figure A-6 shows an incorrectly heated resistor lead. The circuit board was fully heated, but the resistor lead was not fully heated. Solder flowed onto the circuit board but failed to flow onto the resistor lead.

Once you've applied solder to the two parts, do not move the parts relative to each other until the solder has cooled down to a solid. The solder provides the best electrical connection when it has a chance to cool down fully. Sometimes the electrical connection fails if the parts moved prior to the solder cooling completely.

FIGURE A-5: Two correctly soldered connections

FIGURE A-6: The resistor lead was not fully heated. Solder failed to flow onto the resistor lead.

Soldering Tips for Different Components

Before soldering wires, tin the wires by heating them and flowing solder onto them. Tinning a wire end helps you manage the multiple conductive wire strands as one. It also increases the durability of the wire ends. When you flow solder onto the wire end, make sure the wire is tinned all the way to the insulator. I have found that wires become brittle at the un-tinned and un-insulated portion over time. On circuit boards, use solder sparingly. Too much solder may cause excess flow to nearby contacts, causing short circuits. Although removing the excess solder and cutting traces are possible resolutions, they can be a real pain to perform. You will need additional tools to remove solder and cut traces.

Use the tapered surface of the tip on both electronic parts to solder. The tapered surface provides maximum contact area, which allows maximum temperature transfer. Using only the pointy tip can cause uneven heat distribution on the parts and slow down your soldering. Uneven heat distribution on heat-sensitive parts is the major cause of component failure. The process of transferring heat, applying solder, and removing the heat source should be done quickly, so that you won't fry heat-sensitive parts.

Circuit Symbols

S everal chapters in this book contain electrical hacks that require you to look at circuit diagrams that use common circuit symbols. Figure B-1 shows some commonly used circuit symbols and their meanings for your reference.

Battery

Capacitor

Resistor

Diode

Ground

Relay

Normally closed switch

FIGURE **B-1: Commonly used circuit symbols**

Glass Cutting Basics

Glass cutting is mysterious to most of us. The thought of cutting glass ourselves seems impossible and best left to the masters. We view glass cutting at hardware stores as if it is magic performed in front of our naked eyes. Perhaps our reluctance to cut glass comes from the conditioning we received when we were young—that glass is dangerous and we should avoid it at all costs. There is really nothing magical about cutting glass. Glass cutting is really a rather simple task and quite easy to learn.

Cutting glass is not like cutting paper. There are neither scissor-like nor saw-like tools to help you cut glass. If you try any of those tools on a glass pane, you'll just shatter it. Glass cutting really includes two parts: scoring and breaking. It only takes a few minutes to perform each part. Once you learn how to cut glass, you'll find that you spend more time taking measurements than actually cutting the glass.

Tools You Need

You need a few tools before you can start cutting glass. All of them are easy to find at the local hardware store. The following is the tool list.

- Glass cutter
- Cutting oil
- Carborundum file
- Non-slip ruler
- Safety glasses
- Gloves

The first thing you need to get is a glass-cutting tool. This tool should be called a glass-scoring tool, instead. As I said before, there is no such thing as cutting glass. You have to score it and then break it in two. So despite all the glass cutters and glass-cutting tools you'll find at the hardware store, they are all glass-scoring tools. There are many different kinds of glass-scoring tools, but all you need is a basic hand tool (see Figure C-1 for an example). The glass-scoring tool costs only a few dollars.

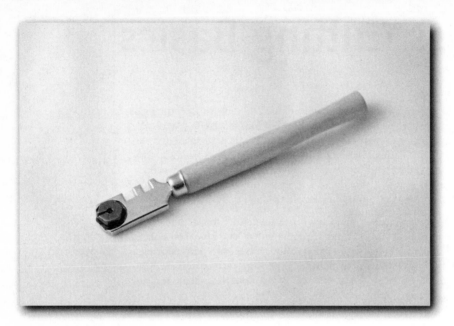

FIGURE C-1: A glass cutting tool

To score glass, you'll need a lubricant. The lubricant will clean off glass slivers from the glass-scoring wheel, allowing the wheel to spin freely. In addition, the lubricant will take up space in the score-line, delaying the score-line from sealing. Any kind of oil can serve as lubricant. You can also find prepared lubricants, which are generally a half-and-half mix between kerosene and light oil.

When you break glass, even with a clean score line, you are bound to have jagged edges. Get a carborundum file (sometimes called a glass file) from the hardware store. The carborundum file will help you smooth the sharp edges.

The ruler allows you to make straight score lines. Plastic and wood rulers are basically useless on the slippery glass surface. Look for rulers with rubber or non-slip bottoms. Most of these are metal rulers, but you may find plastic or wooden ones as well.

As when performing other home-improvement tasks, never attempt to cut glass without safety glasses. During the breaking portion, glass shrapnel will be flying all over the place. Just a tiny glass particle getting into your eye can do some serious damage. Don't take any chances—always wear safety glasses.

I will make the same recommendation with gloves. You will be working in close relationship with glass. Glass is sharp (like your mama told you). A pair of gloves cost only a few dollars, prevent your hands from getting cut, and prevent the glass from slipping.

Preparing to Cut

When you cut glass, tiny particles and slivers will be flying all over the place. Consider finding a location not commonly frequented by bare-footed folks. A garage or backyard may do if you notify everyone around and clean up afterward. Wherever the location, you will need to set up a work surface. The work surface must be absolutely flat. Any unevenness in your work surface can cause you to score crooked lines and may even cause your glass pane to crack. Keep your work surface clean. Any glass particles cause the surface to be uneven. A small bench brush does the job. If you want to cut glass often, you can cover your surface with commercial carpeting. The carpeting lets you cut large sheets of glass. Otherwise, a few layers of newspaper are sufficient.

Holding Your Cutter

Hold your cutter firmly in a manner that is comfortable to you (see Figure C-2). Just keep in mind that however you hold it, you must be able to exert 5 to 15 pounds of force on the glass pane. You can score toward yourself, away from yourself, or sideways. But with practice, you'll find a way to use the hand tool that works best for you.

FIGURE C-2: One way to hold your cutter

Scoring Glass

Prepare the lubricant. You can place the lubricant in a jar. Use a small piece of paper towel to pad the bottom of your jar to prevent dulling the glass scoring tool. Before each score, make sure you dip your glass scoring tool in your jar of lubricant.

When you are ready to score the glass, look for the shiny side or the smooth side of the glass. If both sides are equally shiny or smooth, scoring either side is the same. Lay your non-slip ruler on the line that you'd like to score. Use your scoring hand tool to make one score from start to finish without stopping along the way. The scoring wheel should be perpendicular to the glass surface. Only make one score line, so make sure you exert enough pressure the first and only time. Maintain even pressure along the score line. The score line should look like a strand of hair (see Figure C-3).

FIGURE C-3: The score line is as thin as a strand of hair. It is barely visible in this 1:1 macro shot.

Tip

While maintaining pressure along the score line, you will hear a gentle whispering sound. It sounds kind of like you're drawing a line on paper with a ballpoint pen. After you're done, you'll see a fine strand. If you don't see or hear the score, then you did not exert enough pressure. On the other hand, if you hear the sound and see a heavy fuzzy line, you have exerted too much pressure.

Breaking Glass

There are lots of ways to break glass. Once you've made a nice clean line, the breaking part should be relatively straightforward. You probably already have a method in mind.

Caution

Wear eye protection. If you score well, the glass will break cleanly. But it takes only one glass particle to damage your vision. Don't take that chance.

One way to break glass is to place the scored line over the edge of your work surface (see Figure C-4). With the score line on top, hold the side on the surface firmly with one hand. The other hand holds the edge of the overhanging glass. Apply downward pressure on the overhanging piece until the score line snaps.

FIGURE C-4: Glass pane over the table edge

You can also place the entire glass pane on your work surface. With the score line on top, slip a pencil, pen, or other cylinder-shaped object under the score line (see Figure C-5). Exert pressure on both sides of the score line with your hands. The glass will snap in two along the score line when you have exerted enough pressure.

With a small glass pane, you can hold it in your hands, with the score line outward. Apply bending pressure to the glass pane. The glass pane will snap into two along the score line. But if the glass pane is too small, it will be too hard to snap by hand. You can find some pliers or vise-grips to hold and break the glass (see Figure C-6). If your tools are metal, use some paper towel between your tools and the glass for a nice soft padding.

FIGURE C-5: Glass pane over a rod

FIGURE C-6: Glass pane in plastic grips

A more advanced breaking method is to tap the score line with the ball end of the scoring tool. Place your glass pane flat on your work surface. With the score line on the bottom, firmly tap along the score line. The glass will break apart along the score line in sections; you'll have to tap along the line until the glass separates.

Photographer's Glossary

angle of incidence   The angle at which light rays strike a surface.

angle of reflection   The angle at which light rays reflect from a surface. The angle of reflection equals the angle of incidence. The angle of reflection applies only to a specular reflection where the surface is uniform. In a diffused reflection, light is reflected in all different angles.

aperture   The lens opening that lets in light. The diameter of this opening, in addition to the focal length, determines the f-stop number. The f-stop number is sometimes referred to as the aperture number, or aperture for short. The f-number is the focal length divided by the aperture diameter. Both units are in millimeters and the resulting f-number is unit-less.

aspherical lens   A lens that is not spherical in shape. The technology to create non-spherical lenses was developed to reduce image distortion that is a common characteristic of a spherical lens. Aspherical lenses are generally molded out of plastic or the plastic is coated onto the surface of a glass lens.

chromatic aberration   Occurs when light rays travels through glass (or a lens). Each light wave frequency bends (refracts) at a different angle while traveling through the lens. Short wavelengths (toward the blue) are refracted more than long wavelengths (toward the red). Thus, different color wavelengths are exposed on different portions of the photosensitive material (film or sensor). Achromatic lenses solve this problem by combining lenses with different refractive indexes.

color fringing   One of the effects of lateral chromatic aberration. It appears as magenta and green bands at contrast boundaries. Color fringing is always more apparent on the edge of the image than the center because of the lens curvature. It becomes worse at the image corners.

depth-of-field (DOF)   The distance range at which the subject is acceptably sharp is defined as DOF. DOF can be changed by changing the size of the aperture. A larger aperture (smaller f-number) causes a narrow DOF range. A smaller aperture (larger f-number) creates a wide DOF range.

dispersion   The variation in a lens-element's ability to bend light.

exposure latitude   The range of exposure at which the photosensitive material (film or sensor) will produce an acceptable image. Most slide films have small exposure latitude (in the 1-stop range). Most print films have large exposure latitude (in the 5-stop range) because exposure can be compensated in the printing stage.

focal length   With a pinhole camera, the focal length is the distance between the pinhole (serving as the aperture) and the film sensor plane. An equivalent lens (glass element with the same focal length as the pinhole) capturing an object will produce an object image that is the same size as the object image produced by the pinhole.

ISO   In photography, ISO refers to the light gathering capability of the photosensitive material (film or sensor) used to capture the image. Because the International Organization of Standardization defined this standard, the term "ISO speed" has become synonymous with film speed. The sensitivity of the material increases as the ISO number increases. Every doubling of the ISO number is a one-stop increase in exposure. Every halving of the ISO speed is a one-stop decrease in exposure.

reflection   When light rays strike a surface, they are bounced away from the surface. The act of being redirected from the original path is called reflection. There are two types of reflection: specular and diffused. A specular reflection occurs when light is reflected from a smooth uniform surface, such as a mirror. In a specular reflection, the entire light wave continues to travel in the same direction after being reflected. A diffused reflection occurs when light is reflected from a rough, non-uniform surface. In a diffused reflection, the light wave is scattered in different directions because of the irregular surface.

refraction   The property that light exhibits when traveling from one transparent medium into another transparent medium, such as from air into water. When light travels from one medium into another, part of the light ray is reflected away from the second medium. Another portion of the light ray enters the second medium and is bent at the boundary. This bent ray in the second medium is called the refracted ray. The angle of the bend depends on the difference between the two mediums, the wavelength of the light ray, and the angle of incidence.

Index

Continued

Continued

Continued

Continued

IF YOU ENJOYED THIS EXTREMETECH BOOK YOU'LL LOVE...

EXTREMETECH Magazine

The most hardcore technology magazine out there, for the do-it-yourselfers who jump at the chance to be involved with the latest and greatest technology products.

How to take it to the Extreme.

If you enjoyed this book, there are many others like it for you. From *Podcasting* to *Hacking Firefox*, ExtremeTech books can fulfill your urge to hack, tweak and modify, providing the tech tips and tricks readers need to get the most out of their hi-tech lives.

WITHDRAWN

EXTREMETECH™   Available wherever books are sold.

WILEY

Now you know.